WITNESS TO
NUREMBERG

WITNESS TO
NUREMBERG

RICHARD W. SONNENFELDT

Arcade Publishing
New York

FIRST ENGLISH-LANGUAGE EDITION 2006

First published in 2002 in Germany as *Mehr als ein Leben* by Fischer Taschenbuch Verlag

Library of Congress Cataloging-in-Publication Data

Sonnenfeldt, Richard W.
  [Mehr als ein Leben. English]
  Witness to Nuremberg / Richard W. Sonnenfeldt. —1st English-language ed.
    p. cm.
  ISBN-13: 978-1-55970-816-6 (alk. paper)
  ISBN-10: 1-55970-816-6 (alk. paper)
  1. Sonnenfeldt, Richard. 2. Nuremberg War Crime Trials, Nuremberg, Germany,
1946–1949. 3. World War, 1939–1945—Personal narratives, American. 4.
Translators—United States—Biography. 5. German Americans—Biography. I.
Title.

  D804.G3S58813 2006
  341.6'90268—dc22   2006018636
  [B]

Published in the United States by Arcade Publishing, Inc., New York
Distributed by Hachette Book Group USA

Visit our Web site at www.arcadepub.com

10 9 8 7 6 5 4 3 2 1

Designed by API

EB

PRINTED IN THE UNITED STATES OF AMERICA

Contents

WITNESS TO
NUREMBERG

Introduction

"Sonnenfeldt! Private sonnenfeldt!"

The war in Europe had ended two months ago and my unit, the 106th Armored Reconnaissance Group that had led Patton's Third Army through France, had gone back to America to be demobilized. I had joined the group in December 1944, during the Battle of the Bulge, and ridden reconnaissance during the conquest of Germany, all the way to Austria. But I had not served long enough to return to America with the unit, and I became a grease monkey, driver, and occasional interpreter in the motor pool of Second Corps, Seventh U.S. Army in Salzburg, Austria.

I looked up from under the armored car that I was lubricating.

"On the double, Private!" yelled the sergeant. "The general needs an interpreter!"

As I scrambled for the washroom, up dashed a colonel in a pressed garrison uniform, something I had not seen since leaving the States a year ago. "We are in a hurry, Private," he said. "Get going."

So with grease smudged all over my hands and face, in my soiled fatigue uniform, I followed him to the command car. There sat General William "Wild Bill" Donovan, the head of the Office of Strategic Services—the OSS forerunner of the CIA. A Medal of Honor winner, Donovan had acquired his nickname in World War I as commander of a unit of the famous "Fighting 79th" division. I had always imagined Wild Bill as a John Wayne–like figure, with rows of ribbons on his chest and pistols at the ready.

Instead I saw a somewhat pudgy, gray-haired man with the cloth stars of a major general sewn on his Eisenhower jacket.

"We're interviewing witnesses to prepare for the upcoming war crimes trials," General Donovan said to me. "How are you as an interpreter?" He spoke a little German and had me translate a few sentences from a document. That satisfied him. Then I interpreted while he interviewed a member of the German underground whose name I was told to forget. I was surprised how smoothly it went. When we had finished, he said, "Your English is better than we've heard from any other interpreter. Hinkel here will take care of you."

"So," said Colonel Hinkel, walking with me back toward the motor pool. "How would you like to work for the OSS?"

I asked, "Where are you based?"

"In Paris. Our other translators have such thick accents we can hardly understand them. I think you will work out better."

"That sounds good to me," I responded. "How do I get there?"

"Let's go," he said, "we are flying back to Paris."

Colonel Hinkel waited impatiently while I rushed to throw my belongings into a duffel bag, with hardly time to change into a clean uniform and to wash my hands and face.

"Where in hell do you think you are going now?" shouted my lieutenant as we got into the car to drive to the Salzburg airport.

"With the general!" I shouted back, and Colonel Hinkel yelled, "Lieutenant, we are OSS. We'll send you transfer orders for him when we get to Paris."

Little did I realize that it would take months for my paperwork to catch up so I could again be paid. Even less did I understand at that moment that my life had just taken another twist, perhaps as momentous as fleeing Germany for England at fifteen to escape the Nazis, or being deported on a prison ship to Australia at seventeen. Now just twenty-two, by a combination of natural gifts, hard work to acquire an American accent, and a series of chance events, I had been spotted as a bilingual soldier in the exact right place and moment. I was being plucked from utter anonymity as a motor pool private to be thrust onto the main stage of postwar history: the trials of the Nazis.

I climbed aboard a C-47 transport with Colonel Hinkel. We flew over much of southern Germany, where I had fought as an armored reconnaissance scout, then across the Rhine and on to the old Le Bourget airport in Paris. It was my first flight ever, and I thought of my childhood in Germany, the coming of the Nazis, my life in England, and my solo odyssey to Australia and India to get to America via South Africa and South America at the height of the U-boat war.

It was only seven years since I had fled from Germany.

I

Nuremberg, 1945–46

*F*ROM PARIS'S LE BOURGET AIRPORT we were driven to rue Presbourg, a street that circles the Arc de Triomphe. We stopped at a stately mansion, No. 7, which was to be my workplace for the next month.

There I started translating stacks of captured German documents. I soon learned to spot and excerpt incriminating passages, to find witnesses for the impending war crimes trials. Within days I began to accompany officers to interview suspects, potential defendants. It was clear that there was going to be a big trial of the Nazis, but the defendants had not yet been named, the organization of the trial had not been determined, and its location had not been selected. Hitler and his principal henchmen, Himmler, Goebbels, and Bormann, were dead by their own hand. Only Göring, once Hitler's designated successor, was alive. While the Control Council of the Big Four — the United States, the USSR, Great Britain, and France — were deciding what kind of a trial they wanted, we were looking for prospective defendants without knowing how many there would be and what they would be indicted for.

I have often been asked: "Didn't you hate the Nazis?" Of course we hated them as a group, but we had to determine what each individual to whom we talked had actually done. We were investigators.

In August 1945, Nuremberg was officially named as the site for the trial and our OSS unit became the Interrogation Division of the Office of the U.S. Chief of Counsel (OUSCC), reporting directly to the commanding general of the U.S. Army in Europe. Later we became part of the American prosecution for the upcoming war crimes trials. At the beginning, I was the only interpreter.

Leaving at the crack of dawn and returning after sunset, we flew almost daily to Germany and Austria, to Warsaw and Prague, to interview prospective defendants and witnesses, including senior Nazi officers now in captivity and victims who had survived Nazi crimes. Slowly it began to dawn on me that what I had seen at Dachau, during my brief visit there as a soldier in the last days of the war, was just an example of the enormity of a carefully organized Nazi killing machine.

Between trips I enjoyed Paris, a city less ravaged physically by war than tainted by French memories of defeat and collaboration, but now trying to get back to its normal self. There were few American soldiers there then, and I have fond memories of Pigalle, the Gaîté Parisienne, the steps of the Madeleine, and the Bois de Boulogne on a Sunday morning. French whores abounded, but I became quite good at finding more respectable French men and women whose company made it a delight to return to the City of Light from trips to the lands of darkness. Though the customary fare of French cafés was still in short supply, I felt like a boulevardier as I sat admiring the parade of French women walking in their finery and glancing ever so discreetly at the patrons of the sidewalk establishments.

One visit to Austria took us to the concentration camp at Mauthausen. We were seeking witnesses to prove that Ernst Kaltenbrunner, the senior surviving SS officer who was likely to be a defendant at Nuremberg, had personally observed the butchery going on at Mauthausen during repeated visits. Though "only" a few hundred thousand had been killed at Mauthausen, as compared to millions at Auschwitz, this concentration camp was not just an ordinary death factory. Mauthausen was infamous for the extreme cruelties and satanic tortures invented and practiced by Franz Ziereis, its commandant. Ziereis himself had died before we arrived, wounded mortally while trying to escape. But we did talk to Ziereis's wife and teenage son.

Although I have forgotten the son's name, my conversation with him is burned in my memory. He was a fresh-faced towhead, who could have been an American kid by his looks, but not by his words or experiences. I asked him, "How did you get along with your dad?"

"My father was okay," he said. "The only thing I have against him is that he gave me a rifle as a present on my tenth birthday, then had six prisoners lined up, and I had to shoot until they were dead. That took a long time and it was very hard and I did not like it."

I later found out that the gun was of very small caliber and that Commandant Ziereis had invented this particular pastime because he knew it took dozens of shots to kill prisoners this way.

Usually, as we traveled, it was a nuisance for me to be a private among colonels. At night I would be separated from them, as they would go to their posh quarters while I used crummy enlisted men's accommodations. To relieve this awkwardness, Colonel Curtis Williams, my operations officer, arranged for European headquarters of the U.S. armed forces to cut special orders for me with a "presidential priority," signed "by Command of General Eisenhower." With that I could join my superiors in their quarters or travel alone, often to the chagrin of indignant high-ranking officers whom I preempted from seats on planes or jeeps at motor pools by showing my orders. By invitation, I, a mere private, was soon on a first-name basis with colonels with whom I worked closely, but I knew that I could be court-martialed if overheard offending army etiquette so flagrantly. One day at a remote airstrip, I called crew-cut Colonel

Williams by his nickname, Curly. When he spotted a nearby peaky-faced female officer raising her eyebrow, he grinned and said, "Private Sonnenfeldt, I don't see Curly. Go and find him right away. What are you standing around for? We need him now! Hurry up!"

"Yes, sir!" I said, and saluted him snappily.

Because Germany had surrendered unconditionally, the so-called Allied Control Council, staffed by the Big Four victorious powers, now exercised all governmental functions for defeated Germany, and it was they who decided that trials of the major surviving Nazis were to be held in Nuremberg. The city was chosen over Munich because Nuremberg's Palace of Justice could be restored in time for the trials, while its cavernous, virtually undamaged jail could house the Nazis awaiting trial, along with witnesses. Nuremberg was also the city where Hitler had evoked Nazi mass hysteria and venomous xenophobia and where Göring, as president of the Reichstag, the German parliament, had proclaimed the infamous Nuremberg Laws, which terminated the civil rights of German Jews and demolished their ability to earn a livelihood. Nuremberg had also been the base of Julius Streicher, that vile pornographer and perverted defamer of Jews, and his anti-Semitic hate paper, *Der Stürmer.*

The Soviets had wanted the trials to take place in Berlin, a Soviet-controlled enclave, but they had only two major Nazi prisoners, while we held all the rest, because the Nazis had deliberately fled to the West to surrender. In one acrimonious session, which also resolved other disagreements, Justice Robert H. Jackson, representing the United States, is reported to have said to the Soviets, in exasperation, "Okay, you try your Nazis and we will try ours!" That settled Nuremberg as the site of the trials.

In late July 1945, the American prosecution team and I flew from Paris to Nuremberg. For what seemed like an eternity we could not land in our six-passenger C-45 twin-engine plane, because a warning light indicated that our wheels had not come down. We circled above Hitler's stadium, where he had mesmerized legions of male storm troopers and uniformed Nazi women. It struck me as ironic that we might have to crash-land in the erstwhile coliseum of Nazism!

The pilot shook the plane violently from side to side, pulled up, and dove, but the light indicating "wheels down" had still not come on.

During the long circling and jockeying I imagined seeing the old newsreels once more and hearing Hitler's rasping voice, with that Austrian accent, rising in pitch until he was answered with rhythmic shouts by thousands of voices. The stadium itself was undamaged except that American soldiers had blown up the towering review stand, where Hitler had stood before a giant swastika now knocked off its perch. Though Hitler's tirades still rang in my ears, it was hard to imagine now, when I saw the emptiness of the huge stadium below, how it had been filled by an ocean of brown- and black-shirted troopers and women in black skirts and white shirts, all yelling in a loud chorus "Heil Hitler" with outstretched arms.

The great field was deserted. It was emptier than the ruins of Rome, empty as Germany itself — because Hitler left no legacy. This ultimate egoist left only his deathbed accusation that the German race had failed him by allowing itself to be defeated. Instead of taking responsibility for launching and losing a horrendous, doomed, mad war of aggression, Hitler blamed the very people who had followed him enthusiastically for years and had later died for him as the consequence of his lunacy. Those of his followers who remained alive might well wonder why they had ever believed him.

As the plane made its low circles over the field, I got a view of Nuremberg, a city utterly destroyed. I could pick out the massive Palace of Justice as the only large building with even a partial roof. All the rest of the city was an ocean of destruction, as far as the eye could see. When we looked toward the horizon, we saw a red-brown desert of grotesque brick ruins with huge patches of black from fires. When we looked straight down, we saw houses

9

whose floors hung at crazy angles, with bathtubs dangling from pipes, and piles of rubble with only grotesquely damaged chimneys and small remnants of walls left standing.

A ground controller verified with his binoculars that the wheels of our plane were finally down, and we were cleared to land. While I had sweated about the possibility of a crash landing, only a defective warning light had fooled the pilot! From the airport we drove in motorcycle-escorted jeeps, equipped with machine guns on tripods on their hoods, into the ruined city. Huge piles of rubble had narrowed its streets into twisting lanes. Our convoy snaked through an endless maze of destruction, past cellars and underground shelters still reeking with the stench of rotting corpses two months after war's end. The pungent odor of long-burned-out fires and cordite hung in the hot summer air. Even in daytime, mangy, bony cats chased rats among the crumbling ruins.

Most German men of military age who had survived were now prisoners of war. Occasionally we saw an old man or a one-legged or one-armed veteran piling bricks from the rubble into stacks. Along the lanes roamed haggard and ragged German women of all ages, hungry, gray with unwashed hair, who were trying to survive among the ruins. When I tossed a cigarette butt from the jeep, three women raced for it like gulls swooping down on breadcrumbs.

Finally we reached the massive Palace of Justice. Jeeps with machine guns, armored cars, and tanks were parked at strategic approaches. American soldiers in combat uniforms were everywhere, though they were far outnumbered by German prisoners of war passing debris hand to hand, clearing the building for renovation. By the shreds of their uniforms, I recognized many as ex–Waffen SS, Heinrich Himmler's shock troops. Two months after their defeat, they were now safe and plump, supplied with cigarettes and U.S. Army rations, with coffee to drink and soap to use for washing. Meanwhile, their civilian compatriots grubbed for turnips and potatoes, slurped ersatz coffee, made do with ersatz everything else, and scrambled to collect cigarette butts tossed from a jeep.

Military police colonel, later general, Robert Gill was the station commanding officer. Cavalry colonel Burton Andrus, a spit-and-polish West Pointer who sported riding breeches, a shiny helmet liner, highly polished boots, and bejeweled pistols on his belt, was commandant of the jail. Both were to become good friends. I presented my orders with my "presidential priority" to be assigned quarters and to receive the passes I needed for access to the jail and the interrogation rooms where the Nazis would be brought for questioning. Seeing that I had been selected to interpret the pretrial interrogations of the most senior Nazis, these officers might have suspected that I was an incognito VIP disguised as an army private. My special status was always respected, and my relationship with them and their staffs was collegial rather than that of a private to regimental commanders. I made sure never to fail to salute them when we met.

I was given an office adjoining that of my boss, Colonel John Amen, the chief interrogator of the American prosecution, not far from that of Justice Robert H. Jackson, the chief U.S. prosecutor. I even had an anteroom with a receptionist! How amazing that I, a twenty-two-year-old private, younger even than the young army secretaries, was being treated as a full-fledged member of the staff!

Mornings, to reach my office, I had to pass by the outside guardhouse, show my credentials, and then start the long walk up the dimly lit stairs. Once, I noticed a block-long line of civilians in front of the entrance reserved for them. When I asked what was going on, I was told that they were applying to be cleaners. Why, I wondered, were they so eager for such a menial job? "It isn't the job or the pay. It is the cigarette butt concession," the interpreter standing next to the guard sergeant told me. Yes, of the hundred or more Allied staff in the building then, most were smokers; many, like me, left a dozen or more long cigarette butts daily in their ashtrays. Collecting the butts after working hours, stripping the remaining tobacco out, and rolling it into the finest blends in new paper made for a great business in the ruined city! There was also real coffee available for us, and, a few times, my cup that had been half full of coffee when I left for an interrogation was empty when I returned.

The Grand Hotel in Nuremberg was being rebuilt as a social center and as quarters for visiting journalists and dignitaries. As its restoration progressed, the hotel opened a nightclub and a lively bar to which I was admitted. One of the highlights of my young life occurred when ravishing Marguerite Higgins asked me to dance with her. She was a well-known war correspondent, who died just a few years later from a blood disease contracted while covering the Vietnam War. But then she made me feel like a prince!

I was also friendly with other famous correspondents, who were interested in using my help to obtain the views of German generals concerning their American counterparts. Not unexpectedly, German generals acclaimed General George Patton as the best American tank commander, while Ike Eisenhower was rated tops among all generals. Surprisingly, perhaps, British field marshal Sir Bernard Montgomery was regarded as a plodding martinet. The German general best-known among the allies, Erwin Rommel, the Desert Fox, was not rated highly by other top German generals who had commanded armies ten times the size of Rommel's Afrika Korps.

While the Grand Hotel was a social center, villas in the outlying undamaged sections of Nuremberg had been commandeered to house senior prosecutors and tribunal staff, including me. Often the German owners were allowed to stay — in the basement or garage — to work as cleaners and valets for the tenants. Most owners, who had been affluent merchants or professionals before the war, were now eager to watch over their properties. For their efforts they got soap, coffee, cigarettes, chocolate bars — all far more priceless commodities than money in Nuremberg in July of 1945. My "landlord" owned a bookstore, now destroyed, and spent much time explaining to me that he had never been an active Nazi. When he realized that I had grown up as a young Jew in Germany, he began to avoid the subject and find other ways to ingratiate himself; he realized he was straining my credulity. Yes, like most Germans that I talked to, he finally admitted that he had become a member of the Nazi party because he had to, for business reasons. In postwar Germany, it was interesting how so many Nazis had disappeared along with the Jews!

Most of my waking hours were spent at the Palace of Justice. I acquired the title of chief interpreter, actually Chief of the Interpretation Section of the Interrogation Division of the Office of U.S. Chief of Counsel. I received this title for having been first on the scene, but I kept it because interrogations interpreted by me were never held up by language disputes. Early on, I earned an important recommendation from an older native German who had become an American prosecutor. I had dictated an English rendition of a lively session totally in German between that prosecutor and a future defendant. The prosecutor found no errors or omissions in the stenographer's English-language record of my translation, and certified me as reliably bilingual.

My title, Chief of the Interpretation Section, was not a military rank, but it required all the other interpreters and the stenographers and typists of the Interrogation Division — over fifty in all, eventually — to report to me. I made all of the assignments. Naturally, everyone wanted to meet the senior Nazis, so I rotated the interpreters for the various interrogators and the witnesses as much as possible. While I worked mostly with Colonel Amen, who concentrated on the most senior Nazis — Göring, Hess, Ribbentrop, and Keitel — I worked with all of the defendants at least once. Meeting these top survivors of the world's most evil empire was such a coveted experience that captains, and even a major, were happy to take orders from me.

Shortly after my arrival at Nuremberg, Hermann Göring was to be interrogated by Colonel Amen. Before his suicide, Hitler had named Göring his official successor. He has been described as a jolly and venal fat man with the instincts of a barracuda, the heft of an elephant, and the greed and cunning of a jackal. He was a man with brains and no conscience. So, as Amen's interpreter, I was to meet Göring, who had the imposing title of Reichsmarschall, a "six-star" rank created especially and only for him. Göring was more familiarly known as *Der Dicke* (Fatso).

When Göring surrendered to the American army, he acted as though he was a celebrity, like Napoleon on his way to Elba. He had brought with him a large staff and a dozen suitcases. Prior to being lodged in the jail in Nuremberg, he had been held in two locations where he had charmed or intimidated interpreters. I had transcripts of his interrogations by Military Intelligence in Mondorf, where he had been very arrogant when confronted with questions based on newspaper reports and common knowledge of his activities. He had confused his questioners, who did not have the captured documents we were now studying, with haughty, irrelevant replies. Now Göring, in Nuremberg as a material witness and a likely defendant, was incarcerated in the maximum security, starkly uncomfortable Nuremberg jail.

By now I knew from captured documents that Göring was a decorated flying ace of World War I. He had succeeded Manfred von Richthofen, the famed Red Baron, as squadron commander. His father had been governor of Germany's colony Southwest Africa. His mother had made the long trip to Germany so that he could be born there, and left him in charge of a nurse. As an adult, he had good connections with the old imperial officers and also with right-wing industrialists. Between the world wars, he had been the first commander of the SA (the Nazi militia) and the organizer of the Gestapo as a national force of terror and head of the newly established Luftwaffe — which had been forbidden by the Treaty of Versailles. As the head of the Gestapo, he had arrested politicians who opposed the Nazis, and as president of the Reichstag he had proclaimed the Nuremberg Laws, which terminated the civil rights of German Jews. He had been the man of iron in the bloodless capture of Austria when Hitler almost lost his nerve, and he was the bomber of Rotterdam. He was also the man who had ordered my father to be put into a concentration camp and later ordered him to be released because he had earned the Iron Cross in World War I! Now Göring was the most senior surviving Nazi. His actions as the number two Nazi indicated that he was deeply involved in Hitler's conspiratorial drive to war.

I wondered how he would react to me when we put him under oath for pretrial investigations. Although I had already interpreted interrogations of other once-exalted Nazis, some of them fluent in English, I felt apprehensive about the impending encounter with Göring. He had been such a legend while I was a youngster in Germany, so feared while I was a frightened refugee in England when the RAF was desperately fighting off his Luftwaffe. At Nuremberg, as I anticipated meeting Göring, I felt the Jewish refugee I had once been tugging at my sleeve.

Our interrogation room, Number One, like a half dozen others on the second floor in the Palace of Justice, was near an enclosed stairway that led to the jail. The room itself was bare, without a carpet on the polished terrazzo floor. Colonel Amen, the interrogator, sat at a plain wooden table with his back to the window. The witness would sit across from him, with the light from the window in his face. I sat at the narrow end of the table with Colonel Amen to my left, the witness chair to my right, and a stenographer slightly behind me. An armed guard would stand in the corner at the opposite end of the table.

Now with the door ajar, we heard shuffling footsteps. And there, accompanied by a white-helmeted guard, was Göring, in his faded gray uniform, with discolored rectangles on the collar and the lapels where his marshal's insignia had been. With felt boots provided by his jailer to protect his feet from the cold stone floors, he was being weaned from drugs — about forty pills a day of a derivative of morphine — and his face was puffy and gray. Breathing heavily, he was apparently exhausted from dragging himself up the stairs from his prison cell. But as he entered,

I noticed that his eyes were alert, his eyebrows were slightly raised, and he moved deliberately, somehow managing to keep an aura of authority. I looked at his hands, now stripped of the huge rings he had once worn. With no jeweled field marshal's baton to clasp, his fingers were trembling, ever so slightly. He undoubtedly realized that this was going to be different from previous sessions, which had been quasi-social occasions. He knew that we were here to get him to incriminate himself and that he was here to defend himself.

Not a word of greeting was exchanged. Colonel Amen motioned him to sit down, and then the guard walked behind him to his right. For Colonel Amen, I translated: "State your name."

"Reichsmarschall Hermann Göring," he said.

"Record that as Hermann Göring," said Colonel Amen to the stenographer.

Now Colonel Amen addressed me: "State your name." I did. And then, "Hold up your right hand. Do you swear that you will accurately, completely, and truthfully translate my questions from English into German, and the answers of the witness from German into English?"

I said, "I do."

That was the first time I was formally sworn in as an interpreter. From now on, my swearing-in would be repeated for every pretrial interrogation. I resolved to be extra careful. Next the court stenographer was sworn to record accurately in English everything that was said. And so we began.

I translated, "Do you, Hermann Göring, swear that you will tell the truth, the whole truth, and nothing but the truth?"

"First, I want to know, am I before the judge?" countered Göring.

As I translated, I tried to assume alternately the voice and mien of Amen, the bloodhound New York prosecutor of Murder Incorporated, and of Göring, now a caged and clever rogue trying to confound his captors.

"I ask the questions here and you answer them," said Amen to Göring. I translated Amen's rejoinder into German, but Göring tried to correct my translation. Amen whispered to me: "Don't let him interrupt you."

Suddenly, I thought of Churchill's remark of Germans being either at your throat or at your feet. I asked Amen for permission to teach this witness how to conduct himself with me.

"Go to it," said Amen.

I also remembered the captured German general whom I had forced to walk in front of the truck carrying his men after he complained that he did not want to ride to prison camp in the back of the truck with subordinates. Simultaneously I remembered an old joke about Göring. I said, "Herr Gering" — a deliberate mispronunciation of his name I had heard as a child. The word *gering* means "little nothing" in German. I said: "Herr Gering. When I translate the colonel's questions into German and your answers into English, you keep quiet until I am finished. You don't interrupt. When the stenographer has recorded my translation, you may tell me whether you have a problem, and then I will decide whether it is necessary to consider your comments. Or, if you would like to be interrogated without an interpreter, just say so, and I will merely listen and correct you."

His eyes flickered, and he gave me a long look. He said, "My name is Göring, not Gering."

He knew that it was to his advantage to have an interpreter. While his English was good enough to catch the gist of questions asked in English, it was not good enough for him to assert himself, which was what he really wanted to do. Why else would he talk to the Americans at all when he could be silent? Besides, hearing questions first in English and then in German gave him an advantage. The delay made it much more difficult for Colonel Amen to surprise him, and, since everything had to be said and repeated in two languages, we could ask only half as many questions in a given session.

I said, "I am the chief interpreter here, and if you will never again interrupt me, I will never again mispronounce your name, Herr Göring." Colonel Amen watched our facial expressions and waited patiently during this interchange. I turned to him and said, "Prisoner Göring will now answer your questions."

From then on Göring demanded that I be his interpreter. Göring was the Chief Defendant, Amen was the Chief Interrogator, and I was the Chief Interpreter. All in apple-pie German order! Later it became known that I was Göring's favorite interpreter, and I never knew whether to be proud of that fact or resent it. And so we began interrogating him.

In August 1945 the Control Council established the legal charter for the Nuremberg trials. The courtroom procedure was to follow essentially common-law rules, with prosecution and defense in adversarial positions, presided over by the eight judges, two each from the United States, the USSR, Great Britain, and France. Interrogations under oath would constitute "discovery," evidence to be used in the trial. A key component of the law promulgated by the Council was the inclusion of a charge of long-standing conspiracy to wage aggressive war, to violate treaties, and to exterminate prisoners. Arguments of the type "tu quoque" (citing crimes committed by the prosecuting nations) would not be allowed as a defense for Nazi crimes. Nor would illegal orders from a superior be a defense for criminal actions. I recognized that these rules made it a slam-dunk against those defendants who had been with Hitler while he plotted war and extermination and against those military men who carried out his criminal orders. Our interrogation now had the clear goal of documenting the actions of potential defendants.

Justice Jackson, General Donovan, and Colonel Amen all chose me as their interpreter because Göring cooperated with me, and I spent more than a hundred hours with him.

At various times General Donovan, who enjoyed special status as presidential advisor, and once Justice Jackson, the chief U.S. prosecutor, interrogated Göring, after reviewing the extensive transcripts that Colonel Amen was producing. These interrogators each had different agendas for questioning. Amen, an experienced trial litigator, was building evidence for nailing Göring in the courtroom by questioning him about criminal documents bearing his signature. Amen only asked Göring questions to which he knew the answer from captured documents. Göring invariably denied knowledge of their existence until we showed him his own orders with his signature. Amen would thus destroy Göring's credibility in court by using transcripts of interrogations under oath in which he denied actions that could be proved. He would be unmasked as a common liar! Fifty-five years later, in 2001, the History Channel aired a TV documentary, *We Can Make Them Talk*, in which I was a principal commentator. I showed that no torture was ever used at Nuremberg to extract incriminating statements from the Nazis.

General Donovan wanted Göring to turn state's evidence with a total indictment of Hitler's regime in open court. Donovan was convinced that a confession by Göring would be more impressive to Germans than documents. But Donovan never got Göring to confess to the evils of Nazism.

Göring's relationship with me became evident when General Donovan pushed Göring to acknowledge issuing orders to lynch American aviators who had parachuted from crippled planes. I translated one of Göring's answers as "I don't admit that I said that." General Donovan turned to me and said, "Dick, you did not translate that right. Göring said, 'I don't agree to that.' He did not say, 'I don't admit that I said that.'"

As I, the private, started to argue with Donovan, the general, Göring crossed his arms and, with a big grin on his face, said: "I ssaitt, 'I du not attmitt to zat.'" A power play for his protégé, if ever I saw one! And a testimony to General Donovan, who allowed accuracy to triumph over rank!

Justice Jackson wanted to convict Göring as a war criminal to create world law and punish crimes hitherto shielded by national sovereignty, but he was able to spend less than an hour with Göring in interrogation. Göring characterized the trial as theater staged by the victors to punish the vanquished, and he saw himself as the man exposing that farce — a martyr who was going to be hanged for serving his people. He decided that continuing to profess loyalty to his dead Führer would establish his martyrdom.

As I interpreted these various conversations, I understood the full extent of the ghastly crimes that had been committed against millions of innocent humans by powerful men without morals or conscience. I became a passionate believer that Göring and his cohorts had to be convicted and punished in an international legal proceeding that must not ever be mistaken by fair-minded people as mere revenge by victors or vengeful survivors over the vanquished. I also saw the Nuremberg trial as a never-to-recur opportunity to write the history of Nazi Germany by extracting it under oath from those who made it the crime of the century.

As more prisoners and witnesses were scooped into Nuremberg's jail to be questioned, we soon needed more interpreters. There must have been hundreds of bilingual soldiers with the U.S. Army and Air Force in Europe, but, strangely, it was left to the State Department in Washington to find potential interpreters for the Interrogation Division and for the upcoming trials.

When the potential interpreters arrived in Nuremberg, these candidates sat in the anteroom of my office or paced back and forth expectantly while waiting to be interviewed by me. They were incredibly eager for this once-in-a-lifetime assignment that involved meeting those Nazi monsters that had terrorized the civilized world. I had to check each one's German and English before hiring or rejecting them.

Whoever sent them to Nuremberg from the United States did not do a good job. There was much guttural English with heavy German accents and transliteration of German syntax and much German with Hungarian and Polish accents. Early on, a pushy, rotund little man literally danced into my office with hand outstretched, saying, "Misster Tzonnefelt, I amm sooo glat to mit you. I speeka de seven linguiches and Englisch dee besst." "Englisch dee besst" became our pet phrase.

The absurdity of recruiting interpreters this way was captured in a memorandum from Major Silliman, an officer of my division:

"The present procedure is for civilians to be sent to Miss Galvin [Colonel Amen's secretary], who sends them to Lt. Col. Hinkel [Colonel Amen's deputy], who refers them to Col. Williams [division operations officer], who refers them to Sonnenfeldt [chief interpreter], who, because of their lack of qualifications, usually declares them surplus and returns them to Miss Galvin. It is recommended that the administrative section rather than our office act as receptionists and send us only qualified personnel."

I finally selected a dozen who spoke fluent German, though they managed only accented and grammatically mangled English. I reasoned that interrogators and stenographers could get used to imperfect English, or ask for repeats, but I wanted no mistakes in German. When interrogations were based on captured documents, especially papers of which we had multiple copies, interrogators often needed only to identify signatures or prove that a witness or defendant had been a recipient of incriminating documents. For such simple matters, interrogators got used to their interpreters' thick German accents.

Some of those who failed as interpreters but were nonetheless proficient in both languages became translators of German documents into English. Translators, unlike interpreters, could take their time and use dictionaries to look up words that baffled them. Theirs was, of course, a very important function, given that captured Nazi documents were the basis for almost all interrogations and later for direct and cross-examinations in court. Documents did not require accents and fluency in spoken language. Unfortunately, these translations were often not double-checked and often created serious errors in court.

An assignment as interpreter was definitely considered

superior to one as translator. I discovered recently how deep those feelings ran, upon reading a piece of recorded and published "oral testimony" from one whom I had rejected as an interpreter:

"There was a guy named Sonnenfeld [Author's note: I forgive him for omitting the "t" at the end of my name]. He was probably the single most important person at the Nuremberg trial. He was so powerful that he could take anybody that the State Department had sent there and send them right back to Washington as unqualified. He was in charge of personnel at the Nuremberg trials and his name was constantly on the intercom."

I was not in charge of "personnel," only in charge of selecting interpreters for the interrogation section. Besides, there was no intercom system at Nuremberg. In the intervening years, I have also seen many claims about meetings with Nazi defendants at Nuremberg. Access to the Nazi prisoners, before they were named as defendants, was rigidly controlled, and all access to them, except by their own lawyers and prison personnel, was restricted after they were indicted. Being at Nuremberg was an emotional outlet to those whose lives revolved around their hatred of the Nazis, and they lusted for a confrontation with the Nazi monsters. Unable to meet the prisoners, some people, frustrated, simply invented conversations with the Nazis at Nuremberg. All official interrogations were recorded and can be verified in the U.S. National Archives.

Of course, I felt great satisfaction to be at Nuremberg, but my mind was more on doing my job than avenging a personal past in Nazi Germany, which, after all, had dulled almost into insignificance compared to what I experienced afterward! As to punishing the defendants for what they had done to humanity — that was the assigned task of the tribunal.

Despite the overall seriousness and responsibility of these proceedings, interpreting and interrogating was not all work. Once I was called to an interrogation room where Colonel Howard Brundage, a distinguished American jurist with a southern accent, was attempting to interrogate Julius Streicher, whose coarse

German was thick with Franconian intonations. Colonel Brundage was at the end of his rope. His interpreter was a German-Jewish émigré who had a thick Swabian accent in English. Streicher, of course, was that repulsive hatemonger and pornographer who caricatured and defamed Jews by ascribing his own perversions plus fraudulent horrifying slander to them in his newspaper, *Der Stürmer.*

The interrogation stalled at the very beginning as Colonel Brundage attempted to administer an oath. Streicher and the interpreter became locked in a long, heated exchange. "What's he saying?" Brundage finally broke in.

"Kernel," explained the interpreter, "he vants tu noh, em I beforr de chuch?"

"Chuch, there is no church here," drawled Brundage. "What in God's name are you talking about?"

When I was called in, Streicher asked in German whether he was facing a trial judge. I asked the interpreter why he kept saying "church."

"Chuch! Chuch!" he replied. "He vants tu noh is he beforrh de chuch adwocatt!"

The stenographers, all qualified as American court reporters, made verbatim transcripts of interrogations in English. Their job was relatively easy, because they could relax with a cigarette while the German-language conversation was going on. They were automatons and so was I, at first, when I repeated the interrogator's questions in German and the prisoner's answers back in English. My friends claimed that my job had permeated my behavior to such an extent that when they told me something in English at the Grand Hotel Bar in the evening, I would automatically repeat it in German!

High-quality interpreting, though, was not entirely automatic, and we tried to ensure strict accuracy while preventing defendants from using the situation to their advantage. We were aware that the back-and-forth translation gave witnesses extra time to plan answers. Soon, interrogators gained confidence in me, and would show me an English translation of an incriminating German document or a proposed line of inquiry and whisper to me, "Just ask him the right questions." Multiple questions by me surprised and startled the defendants. I used my notes to write an accurate translation into English, which was officially recorded. Sometimes witnesses asked to amend their answers as they listened to my translation. I often called the witnesses back late in the day, showing them a German version of their interrogation, asking for their authentication. I also often talked with them off the record.

There were some embarrassing moments in the interrogations. On occasion, future defendants were accused of acts they could not possibly have committed, or there were other times when interrogators failed to nail down charges for crimes the defendant had actually committed. These errors occurred when American questioners incorrectly assumed that the Nazi government had operated like our own.

Justice Jackson once interrogated Joachim von Ribbentrop, a platitudinous, babbling onetime champagne salesman and social climber who had become Hitler's foreign minister. Ribbentrop had offered to "take responsibility" for all that had been done in his name. When Jackson asked him to identify something specific he took responsibility for, Ribbentrop drew a blank. He rejected Jackson's suggestions of aggressive war, persecution of the Jews, breaking of treaties, et cetera. Jackson then accused Ribbentrop of denying passports to Jews who wanted to flee Germany. Jackson was equating Hitler's foreign minister with our secretary of state. However, in Germany, the police under Himmler, not the Foreign Office under Ribbentrop, issued passports. To break up a meaningless exchange that was degenerating into a shouting match, I passed a note to Justice Jackson explaining that passports had not been a responsibility of this yammering ex–foreign minister.

The harder Jackson pounced on other points, which were

well taken, the more convoluted were Ribbentrop's denials. He was an incredibly voluble windbag who never once said anything that made any sense. Was he demented? How could this ashen-faced, worried-looking, hand-wringing wreck of a man, who once had greeted the king of England with the Hitler salute, ever have risen to become foreign minister of Germany? Of course, under Hitler, Germany had no foreign policy, except to deceive and bully its neighbors and make vacuous plans for economic self-sufficiency in an increasingly interdependent world.

Once I asked Ribbentrop's principal deputy, Baron Ernst von Weizsäcker, the father of Richard von Weizsäcker, German president from 1984 to 1994, "How did you react to the minister's mouthings when he was in office? Is he demented now because he is fearing for his life?"

Weizsäcker said, "Hitler never noticed Ribbentrop's babbling, because Hitler always did all the talking."

Eventually Ribbentrop's blather irritated Sir Geoffrey Lawrence, chief judge of the International Military Tribunal. No matter how sternly Lawrence demanded brevity, Ribbentrop prattled on. He stopped jabbering only shortly before the hangman slipped the noose over his neck.

When we began our interrogations, all the defendants blamed Hitler, Himmler, and Goebbels, who had confessed their criminality either in their recorded speeches or by committing suicide. Of those we were interrogating at Nuremberg, we knew very little at first.

The interrogations were being conducted to obtain sworn evidence that could lead to indictments and convictions for criminal acts. In the best American tradition, however, we presumed a man innocent until proven guilty, and my job was to help find the proof. I made sure never to be Nazi-like by letting indiscriminate hate dictate my actions or color my work. But I couldn't help despising almost all of the defendants. Not one of them ever offered a defense or even an intelligent explanation of the so-called

25

doctrine of National Socialism. It had been a bag of hate providing equal opportunity to be anti-Semitic, to covet and steal one's neighbor's possessions, to loot from conquered countries, or to attain promotion by fawning to one's superiors.

As the trial approached, the lawyers slaved away at briefs, preparing for examinations of witnesses. Besides securing convictions of the Nazi leadership, they were hoping to make epic contributions to the development of international law in the process. Many lawyers' careers were enhanced by their Nuremberg experience.

Unlike the legal staff, I did not have to wrestle with juridical theories or prepare for a role in the upcoming battle in the courtroom. Instead, I had ample opportunity to observe the future defendants and to divine the motives and credibility of witnesses who were to testify for the defense or the prosecution. Before the trial finally got under way on November 20, 1945, I had probably spent more time with these defendants than anyone else. I had worked for months, usually six and more hours a day, face to face with these Nazis, in private conversations. After the trials, I kept careful notes.

The mediocrity, the lack of distinction of intellect, knowledge, or insight, of virtually all defendants was appalling. At first I was surprised to find such lack of education and absence of character. Shielded by their ignorance of history, familiar only with past German triumphs and tales of Teutonic knights, ignorant of the rest of the world, unsuccessful in ordinary life, driven by ambition without integrity, servile to their superiors and arrogant with all others, how had these sycophants risen to such exalted positions? To serve a dictator, one must be gullible and ambitious and have no scruples. One must not mind being insulted by a Führer or else have an intellect so deficient as not to notice insults. Who else would fawningly and forever feed the vanity of a man who never listened but only spouted inane theories of conquest, racism, and economic nonsense, no matter how hypnotic his delivery? The length of service of these men and their closeness to Hitler was a perfect measure of their lack of personal stature and morality.

Dictators have no peers; only sycophants to do their bidding. That is how it was in Nazi Germany. And so it is wherever autocrats rule in government or in business. Dictators and braggarts cause their own demise, because when they finally are in extremis, they have only their lackeys to call on, while their adversaries attract the best of men. An exception to the mediocrity of these defendants was Hjalmar Schacht, that financial magician, an arrogant mustachioed Houdini in striped trousers. Another exception was Albert Speer, that brainy and clear-minded careerist architect, who ran German war production with slave labor. And there was Göring, in a class by himself.

Though nearly sixty years have passed since I wrote those notes, my memories of these people are as sharp and detailed today as they were then.

I learned that besides Hitler, only Göring was charismatic and powerful enough to have had a German constituency of his own. Perhaps his followers were besotted by his geniality and attracted by the jolly mirth of a fat man, convenient covers for his cunning and satanic initiatives. In the early days of Hitler's regime he was the man of action. I learned that his evil genius had made the Gestapo into a state-sanctioned instrument of terror, and that he had been inventive in bending the power of the state to his own acquisitive ends. He also had used his official power to persecute personal enemies while promoting favorites. He had laughingly perverted truth, lacing his venality with isolated good deeds to impress his humanitarian half-brother or to indulge some weird streak of sentimentality — which fooled people into thinking he knew right from wrong. Göring used to lounge about in his hunting lodge with rouge on his cheeks, huge ornate rings on his pudgy fingers, and a flowing toga enfolding his ample girth. I did wonder why his actress wife, Emmy Sonnemann, who had a daughter by him, remained vocally and demonstratively loyal to him to the end. She criticized her husband only when

Hitler ordered Göring to be executed for trying to exercise his powers as designated deputy when he believed Hitler was irredeemably trapped in his Berlin bunker.

Göring was extraordinarily versatile. When he nominated Erhard Milch as commanding general of the Luftwaffe under him, jealous rivals complained that Milch had a Jewish father, a Nazi liability if ever there was one. As chief of the Gestapo, Göring arranged for proof that Milch's real father was a full-blooded Aryan who had had an extramarital relationship with Milch's gentile mother. To memorialize this feat, Göring proclaimed: "I decide who is a Jew and who is not a Jew." When I reminded him of that episode, he slapped his thigh with mirth at his own great wit. No one ever encapsulated the difference between the rule of law and the rule of man so pithily.

Göring was also versatile when it came to first courting, then emasculating the powerful German army generals of the old school who would not accept Hitler's leadership. In 1993, when Hitler became chancellor and Göring became Reich minister without portfolio, traditionalist high-ranking officers of the army maintained their loyalty to Hindenburg, the revered Generalfeldmarschall of World War I and president of Germany. Looking down on Hitler, they considered him, an ex–lance corporal, a mere enlisted man, to be an ignorant, uneducated, and dangerous adventurer. Still, they recognized that Hitler's loyal SA militia, the nearly one million jackbooted storm troopers, were dangerous adversaries to their small army, which was restricted to one hundred thousand by the Treaty of Versailles.

In 1934, Hitler tried to buy the loyalty of the generals by directing the assassination of Ernst Röhm, head of his own SA. Hitler claimed that Röhm and his lieutenants were planning a seizure of power. Göring and Himmler, who then still reported to Göring, were astute enough to be Hitler's executioners in that vile plot. Göring was in charge of the assassinations in Berlin — reported to be about one thousand. The murder of Röhm and his top lieutenants appeased the army's top generals but did not buy their enthusiasm for Hitler's leadership. When I asked Göring how he felt about the murder of his friend Röhm, he responded chillingly, "He was in our way."

When Hitler proposed that two battalions of their army re-occupy the demilitarized Rhineland, the generals opposed it vocally as too risky, because of the vast superiority of French and British forces then arrayed against them.

Speer was with Hitler at the time and reported in an interrogation how worried everyone was about a military counteraction. "We could not have done anything if England and France had made the slightest protest and backed it up by military action," he said. Instead, they twiddled their thumbs and Germans deified Hitler, now convinced he was a military genius, determined to get rid of the conservative generals.

In a spectacular series of maneuvers, Göring plotted to seize leadership of the armed forces and other uniformed services of Germany and nearly succeeded. After the murder of Röhm, well over a million SA storm troopers were put under Göring's control. As Himmler's senior, he would also effectively control the Gestapo, the police, and the SS. Göring began maneuvering to be named minister of war, head of the traditional armed forces. Two senior conservative army leaders stood in his way.

First, Göring went after top-ranking, sixty-year-old General Werner von Blomberg, minister of war. Göring had discovered that Blomberg was marrying a notorious prostitute, and made sure Hitler was invited to the wedding. Afterwards he told Hitler of his shocking "discovery" about the bride. As atonement for this embarrassment of the Führer, Göring made Blomberg resign to avoid a public scandal.

Göring's next target was General Werner von Fritsch, the supreme commander of the army, the highest-ranking officer under Blomberg. Fritsch would normally have been Blomberg's successor as minister of war. The Gestapo targeted a notorious and sleazy homosexual who was made to claim he had sex with Fritsch in a Berlin railroad station lavatory. Göring had Hitler stand behind a curtain in the Reich Chancellery while this plant "confessed" the affair to a Gestapo thug. That eliminated Fritsch, despite the fact that a court of investigation headed by Göring later found the charges false.

But Hitler was not outfoxed by his lieutenant. He abolished the war ministry and named himself supreme commander of the armed forces. All soldiers, from Göring and the generals on down, had to swear fealty to Hitler personally as their supreme military commander.

Remaining loyal to his Führer who had outsmarted him, Göring settled for Hitler's offer to name him Germany's highest-ranking officer; later Hitler also named Göring his official successor as head of state. With his old imperial army training, which demanded loyalty, Göring then served Hitler until defeat was certain for the Führer, marooned in his Berlin bunker.

At Nuremberg, Göring continued to display his versatility. He tried to deny complicity in planning an aggressive war, and he denied participating in or commanding war crimes, genocide, and crimes against peace. Yet he continued to brag extensively about his role, as the number two Nazi, in subjugating Germany by demolishing democracy (not a crime being tried by the tribunal). When asked whether the German people had wanted war, he explained breezily how easy it was to dupe them:

"Why, of course, the people don't want war. Why would some poor slob on a farm want to risk his life in a war when the best he can get out of it is to come back to his farm in one piece? Naturally, the common people don't want war, neither in Russia nor in England, nor in America, nor in Germany. That is understood. But, after all, it is the leaders of the country who determine the policy and it is always a simple matter to drag the people along, whether it is a democracy or a fascist dictatorship or a parliament or a Communist dictatorship. The people can always be brought to the bidding of the leaders. That is easy. All you have to do is tell them they are being attacked and denounce the pacifists for lack of patriotism and for exposing the country to danger. It works the same way in any country."

At Nuremberg, Göring declared repeatedly, with inclusive sweeps of his once-bejeweled hands, that he would take responsibility for all that was done in his name, while at the same time he denied knowledge of virtually everything that had been done in his name. Unlike Ribbentrop, he did not babble, he just repeated this one explanation: "You don't think, do you, that I could ever know all of the nonsense that went on in my many offices? I had so much to do. But if you have papers that I signed or that I saw, then I accept responsibility for what my subordinates did."

Göring did claim that he was deceived and misinformed by overzealous colleagues like Heinrich Himmler, who had committed suicide, and Martin Bormann, who had disappeared. When asked directly about some atrocity, Göring always answered, "It is possible that I heard something about that, but I had so many official roles, and I spent so much time giving the Führer my advice; I was so busy and important. How can you expect me to remember such details now?"

Throughout the interrogations, Göring insisted that Hitler knew little of concentration camps and even less of exterminations, mass starvation, and all the other "regrettable" abuses that had been perpetrated in secrecy by that conveniently dead fiend Heinrich Himmler. And if Hitler did not know about extermination camps, how could Göring have known? Too bad that Himmler was dead! Describing the evil Himmler, Göring once commented to Amen, "My dear Colonel, you would have enjoyed questioning that man." As though talking about the Holocaust were some kind of fun.

As slippery as he was, occasionally I could catch him. Göring had sometimes been used by Albert, his younger half-brother, an improbable humanitarian who claimed he had befriended many that had been persecuted by the Nazis. Ensign Bill Jackson, the son of Justice Jackson, and I suspected Göring's brother of having

31

taken money for his help in freeing concentration camp inmates. He was a diffident witness who constantly volunteered information for which we had not asked. But several, including the famous composer Franz Lehar, attested to Albert's munificent humanity, corroborating his story. At his brother's urging, Göring repeatedly arranged the release of concentration camp prisoners who should never have been imprisoned. Perhaps brother Albert thought that reporting reprieves arranged by brother Hermann would create mitigating circumstances for him, but it did not work out that way.*

"You testified that you had nothing to do with putting people in prison or concentration camps," I said to Göring one day.

"Yes, I told you that many times," he replied.

"How then could you get prisoners released when you had no power to have them incarcerated?" I asked.

He grinned. "*Ach so,*" he said.

Touché! I thought.

Göring told prison psychologist Dr. Gustave Gilbert, that he expected to have marble monuments erected for him as a German hero thirty years hence. When I heard this, I mentioned it to him and he said, "It won't matter that my body isn't there. Napoleon's body is not in his grave either." No doubt about it, Göring had charisma, a naturally powerful bearing, and limitless ambition.

I do not think Göring ever gave up his grasp for immortality. Once I was sitting with him in an interrogation room with only an armed guard present, to have him sign a statement, when we heard that familiar rolling rumble that signaled the dynamiting of another wall to facilitate reconstruction of the huge Palace of Justice. I saw a crack opening and widening in the wall to Göring's right. He saw it, too, and I caught a look of undisguised triumph on his face. I sensed he was composing a news broad-

---

*In the year 2000 the History Channel aired a documentary of the life of Albert in which I was a principal narrator.

cast: "Reichsmarschall Hermann Göring was killed today as he was being grilled by a vengeful Jewish-American accuser, when the Palace of Justice collapsed as American engineers mishandled explosives charges. Göring will long be remembered as . . ." Soon, however, the rumble stopped — and so did that smile on Göring's face.

Even though Hitler had ordered Göring's execution as practically his last act before committing suicide, Göring boasted at Nuremberg about his loyalty to the Führer and about his own acts as Hitler's official successor, in a show of bravado that he calculated would make him a German hero.

Although Göring acted sometimes independently of Hitler, most Nazis — Hans Frank for instance — never did. Frank (no relation to the Jewish family of Anne Frank) completely subjugated German law to Hitler's will. Before becoming the cruel and murderous governor of occupied Poland, Frank was the Nazis' chief legal officer. In 1934 he said, "Previously, when we had to make a legal decision, we had to ask, what does the law say we should do? Now, we only ask, what would the Führer want us to do, and we decide accordingly."

This warped definition of law by Frank as "whatever Hitler wishes" allowed for terrible perversions. At Hitler's wish, Nazi regulations required all Germans to ostracize Jews or forbade them to ask questions about the disappearance of their neighbors or to listen to foreign broadcasts. Hitler's government removed sitting judges and prosecutors and appointed Nazi toadies in their places. Anyone who tried to defend opponents of the Nazis was prosecuted and persecuted. After the Nazi conquest of Germany, anyone opposed to Hitler had no political party, no church, no court, no institution that could help him. Any dissident had to confront the vast power of the state as a lone and helpless individual. Men like Frank enforced the Nazi creed. Frank later repented his wickedness and embraced Catholicism in the Nuremberg jail, where he prayed for a reconciliation of Jews and Germans.

One could not have found two more different men than Göring and Rudolf Hess, that loony Nazi party deputy to whom Hitler dictated *Mein Kampf*. He lost his sanity in May 1941, when he stole a Luftwaffe plane on a self-appointed mission to persuade Great Britain to make peace. He was imprisoned there for the duration of the war. Hess arrived at Nuremberg with packets of food scraps saved from his imprisonment in Britain. The scraps were to prove that his British jailers had tried to poison him. But in the Nuremberg jail, he lost his memory: he claimed to be an amnesiac.

Colonel Amen, eager to prove that Hess was faking, brought in a battery of psychiatrists and psychologists to help expose what he thought was a ploy to evade prosecution. During one of those sessions when the medical men tried to probe his memory, Hess used the German word *Kladde*, students' slang for a hard cover for papers.

"Kladde?" I asked. "What is that?"

"I don't know how I came to use that word," said Hess.

But I was stopped from following up Hess's slip, because the learned men who did not speak German did not realize that this teenage slang could hardly be the vocabulary word of an amnesiac.

Next, Amen decided to confront Hess with Göring to see whether Big Hermann could jog his memory. Göring surely tried. "Rudolf," he said, assuming his grand pose of old, "don't you remember me, the Reichsmarschall, president of the Reichstag? Don't you remember me as the supreme commander of the Luftwaffe, the designated successor to the Führer, how we marched together in Munich in 1923 when we were shot at by the police?" Nothing helped. Hess looked uncomprehendingly at Göring, who was visibly deflated that his exalted past persona had not penetrated the amnesia of Hess. I never saw Göring more crushed!

We brought in the private secretaries who had served Hess for years. The two women departed, weeping, when Hess showed no sign of recognition, theatrically cupping his ears to catch their names. The last to confront Hess at Nuremberg was a tragic figure of German history, Professor General Karl Haushofer, the geopolitician who had preached the theory of Lebensraum and was then astonished that Hitler understood the need for "living space" as authority to rape the territory of others. Hess had spent many of his student days as a houseguest of the Haushofers, and their son Albrecht had been a friend. Frau Haushofer was a woman of Jewish ancestry, whom Hess shielded. Father and son had been horrified when Hitler proclaimed that no excuse was needed for aggression because victors didn't need to answer any questions, and both had ended up in a Nazi concentration camp. The son was executed when he joined the conspirators to assassinate the Führer.

The elder Haushofer, newly released from imprisonment in the concentration camp at Dachau, assumed Hess had flown to England to seek peace, when his objective had only been to free Germany to conduct a one-front war with the Soviet Union, the dream of German militarists. The old man broke down in tears when his onetime protégé, Rudolph, did not recognize him. In a quaking voice, Haushofer tried over and over to remind Hess of incidents and conversations, all to no avail. We will never know whether this meeting caused or contributed to the suicide of Haushofer, the tragic sorcerer, together with his wife, soon afterwards.

Hess himself had no apparent reaction to the meeting; nothing shook him out of his professed amnesia. But when the tribunal ordered Hess examined by a team of psychiatrists after his indictment as a war criminal, to determine whether he was mentally fit to stand trial, he announced in open court: "From now on my memory will once again be available to the outside world!"

Hitler's chief of staff, Generalfeldmarschall Wilhelm Keitel, was nicknamed "Lakeitel," a play on the German word for lackey, and that is what he was. Early on, I had a staring contest with him, until he lowered his bright blue eyes. I had translated the interrogator's question "Are you telling the truth?" as "Why are you lying like a coward?" More than losing his insignia and his marshal's baton, this challenge, coming from a mere private, shattered the composure of this Herr Generalfeldmarschall, whose moustache was now quivering. I remembered the pronouncement of his father-in-law, General Blomberg, the deposed minister of war, whose aide he had been: "Keitel is just *ein Briefträger*" — a mailman. That, about the most senior of German army generals!

Keitel eventually did admit some culpability. In his final statement to the court Keitel said, "I am guilty of not derailing such criminal acts." He was speaking of Hitler's orders that resulted in the deaths of millions of Russian prisoners of war in the territories occupied by the German armed forces.

Colonel General Alfred Jodl, Keitel's deputy, and reputed to be much smarter than his superior, had the bearing of a robot and the looks of a tom turkey, as someone else has described him. Jodl translated Hitler's wishes into precise military orders whose wording was beyond Keitel's ability. Many of these orders were violations of the Geneva Convention, which Germany had signed, and violations of the German Army articles of war. Jodl understood that knowingly issuing or transmitting illegal orders that killed millions of Russians would not be a defense for him, but he persisted in presenting himself as the loyal subordinate.

Yet there must have been a heart in that soldier's chest, because his wife, Luise, tried harder than any other wife to see him when he was a defendant in the courtroom. She had to be removed from the visitor's gallery after she waved to him. She also petitioned Churchill, Eisenhower, and Truman to pardon her husband, to no avail.

Unlike Frank, Keitel, and Jodl, all Hitler yes-men, some of the German generals did have opinions of their own and took stands against Hitler. For example, Erwin Rommel, famous not only in Germany but among the Allies as the Desert Fox for his exploits in North Africa, eventually came to regard Hitler as the scourge of Germany and joined the conspiracy to remove him. When the plot failed and Hitler survived, Hitler did not dare to have Rommel, the war hero, named a conspirator and garroted with piano wire, as were the other conspirators. Instead, he delegated Keitel to tell Rommel that if Rommel took his own life at once, he would be given a state funeral as a hero who had been killed by enemy airplanes. Rommel killed himself, and was given a state funeral. The German people never knew of Rommel's attempt to join the conspirators to remove Hitler for the good of Germany, until the Nuremberg trials revealed it.

Rommel's son, Manfred, later the lord mayor of Stuttgart, put it this way: "The Nazis made it impossible for Germans merely to be *anständig*" (decent).

Junior attorneys interrogated the other defendants, and I found most of their sessions, which I interpreted, boring because they fell into a predictable pattern. Until confronted with documents that bore their signature or with sworn witness statements, these future defendants either denied their actions or claimed loss of memory, which they repeated on the witness stand in court. At various times, interrogators pursued subjects outside the scope of the trial. Thus with Speer much time was wasted on how German industry operated under Allied bombs and on his activities as Hitler's architect, which were not criminal under the charter of the tribunal.

After I had been Chief of the Interpretation Section for several months, Colonel "Curly" Williams arranged my "discharge from the army for the convenience of the government." I became a "civilian on service with the U.S. armed forces" with the pay of a lieutenant colonel and "the privileges pertaining" to my new status, a villa in the American compound and the use of an army staff car. Not bad for a twenty-three-year-old private first class, an immigrant who had never graduated from high school.

Late one afternoon I found myself driving alone in a 1942 Ford two-door sedan, painted olive drab, from Nuremberg to Munich to pick up one of Hitler's secretaries, Johanna Wolff, an unremarkable middle-aged woman with baggy clothes, no makeup, and the general dowdiness that passed for modesty among middle-class Germans. It was already dark, but I decided to drive back to

Nuremberg with her. Die-hard German saboteurs were reported to be stringing steel wires across this autobahn to decapitate American soldiers riding in jeeps. I drove at high speed, ready to snap the wire, if there was one. The autobahn was very slippery, and at one point the car suddenly made a 360-degree turn before heading once more in the right direction. Fortunately for us, the autobahn was deserted, because Germans had no gasoline for the few cars they had salvaged. I had only the skid to report when we arrived back in Nuremberg, where I delivered Wolff to the safe house.

Although Wolff had not said much prior to the skid, the near accident loosened her up, as though we now had something in common. She had traveled extensively with Hitler before the war started, she told me, but later, in his military headquarters, other secretaries were brought in.

Her claim to fame was that she could type as fast as Hitler could talk. He had become frustrated with dictating his speeches to stenographers whose notes he could not read. With her he could watch his words emerge from her typewriter. She described how he stood beside or behind her and worked himself up into a frenzy as he rasped about Germany's enemies, the foes of his Nazi Party, and especially the Jews. His voice would get louder and hoarser, his sweat-soaked hair would droop over his brow, and his fist would punch the air. He would exhaust himself with passion, pause to catch his breath, and then start all over again.

She said, "Can you believe it, it was just me and the Führer!" No one else was ever allowed to be there when she typed his tirades, nor was anyone ever allowed to see them in advance of his delivering them. It was clear that she would have reverently gone back to typing for him. She referred to him as "mein Führer" throughout our conversation, and her voice and demeanor radiated awe when she spoke about him. I felt as though Hitler were there with her now. I shuddered. Would I have fallen under his spell?

I asked her whether she would write her memoirs. I got a blank look. "What would I write about?" she said.

One day I talked to Erich Kempka, Hitler's longtime chauffeur, who had miraculously escaped from the Berlin bunker after Hitler's death. Kempka had wrapped the dead bodies of Adolf Hitler and Eva Braun in army blankets and doused them in gasoline before setting fire to them. Kempka then dodged bullets and shells as he fled from the bunker and zigzagged down Unter den Linden on his way to the West. His companions were Martin Bormann (an absentee defendant at Nuremberg, presumed dead) and Heinrich Müller, the shadowy chief of the Gestapo under Himmler.

At the end, when Hitler recognized inevitable defeat, he dictated his last testament. In it he required all of Germany to die with him because he felt betrayed by this nation that had allowed itself to be defeated in war. Adolf Hitler felt no remorse about what he had brought upon his country, let alone the rest of the world. He blamed defeat on the failures and weaknesses of his fanatically loyal followers. The true nature of his tyranny was unmasked in Hitler's last words: demagoguery, reinforced by conceit, ignorance, and his ability to mesmerize sycophants, all based on limitless, unfathomable, sick egotism!

Kempka recognized the tyranny of Hitler's last demand and told me why he had refused to obey it. "That was not right," Kempka said. "I did not deserve to die." Apparently Kempka believed everything else Hitler had done was right, but took exception to dying with his Führer.

Kempka also denied any knowledge of duplicity by Gestapo chief Heinrich Müller, with whom he fled from Hitler's bunker. A story was circulating that Müller, accompanied by Kempka, had walked straight into the arms of the Soviets, who welcomed him. I had found it incredible that Gestapo chief Heinrich Müller could have been a Soviet agent. But we also discovered that a Himmler delegate in Paris had hosted a whole band of Soviet spies who called themselves *Die Rote Kapelle* (the Red Orchestra), working from inside the Gestapo.

Though not relevant to the upcoming trial, other stories of incredible duplicity at the highest levels of the Gestapo and the SS and evidence of Himmler's treachery and personal cowardice underlined to me over and over the utter lack of conscience and moral values of so many highly placed Nazis. I could now equate cruelty, corruption, and criminality with prominence of position in the SS, an alleged knighthood based on the Teutonic example. I had yet to meet or hear about a high Nazi with honorable motives or a respectable character. Germany had truly fallen into the hands of its worst elements!

General Franz Halder served as a witness at Nuremberg against the Nazis. Halder, as army chief of staff, was the military genius who blueprinted the blitzkrieg that carried the German army through Western Europe and later within sight of Moscow. Halder was not indicted, because Hitler had cashiered him for pulling back the exhausted German columns from the outskirts of Moscow in November 1941, with the intention of regrouping and smashing the Russians the following spring. Hitler thought a strategy of "no retreat ever" would bring him victory and ordered his generals to organize mass killings in Soviet Russia. Halder was one of the few who disagreed with Hitler and survived.

Halder was lodged at Nuremberg in a safe house set aside for witnesses not accused of war crimes. Also living there were General Erwin Lahousen, the second most important man in Germany's espionage service, who was to become the first prosecution witness; two of Ernst Kaltenbrunner's mistresses; Hitler's official photographer, Heinrich Hoffmann; Hitler's prewar court jester, Putzi Hanfstaengl; and others.

Halder liked to talk to me. One day he told me he had once dined with Hitler and Göring at the Führer's headquarters in East Prussia and Göring had bragged — in the company of a dozen people — "The Reichstag? You all know that I was the one who torched it!" Göring was probably tipsy at the time, but sober enough to flush bright red after his boast. When I later showed Halder's statement to Göring, he said, "Oh, that was just one of my jokes."

"Reichsmarschall," I said, "tell me about another joke you told Hitler."

For once — just for a moment — Göring was speechless.

Another time I went to the safe house because Halder still wanted to justify himself as a better general than Hitler and wanted me as his audience. To help Halder recreate the battle of Moscow, I had the owner of my living quarters search high and low and buy hundreds of toy soldiers and toy tanks, which had miraculously survived the war in their original packages. Kneeling by my side on the carpet of the safe house, with chairs and tables pushed out of the way, Halder reenacted for me the 1941 battle for Russia. The irony of our image struck me: What other Jewish private in the U.S. army has ever had Hitler's top general crawl on a carpet with him for a lesson in blitzkrieg strategy?

I was working with Halder in an interrogation room on the morning when the army newspaper, the *Stars and Stripes*, announced in huge front-page headlines that an atom bomb had been dropped on Japan. The brief story stated that this atom bomb was the equivalent of thousands of ordinary bombs. I spread the newspaper for Halder and asked, *"Herr General, was sagen Sie nun?"* (What do you have to say about that, General?)

He pondered. *"Clausewitz ist tot"* (Clausewitz is dead), he responded.

What did he mean? Clausewitz was a German military philosopher, a general who had said, "War is only the extension of diplomacy by other means." Not anymore, we thought then. Atomic war is not an extension of anything; it is the end of everything. Halder saw that rational nations could never go to war with atomic bombs to pursue nationalistic ends.

At that moment, with General Halder next to me, I lost my fear that Germany would ever try a conquest of other nations again, or that any sane leaders would launch an atomic war. Of course, we could not even imagine Korea, Vietnam, and all the other nonatomic wars yet to come, nor could we foresee that the possession of mutually destructive weapons may have kept the cold war cold. We only knew that Germany was finished as a progenitor of nationalistic wars trying to conquer her neighbors with access to nuclear weapons. I saw in one astonishing flash that Germany could prosper in the future only by becoming a member of a community of nations. All the green linen-covered books of German martial heroism I had read so avidly under the covers as a child now belonged on the trash heap of history. Neither Germany nor other nations would ever again be inspired by saber-swinging generals on horseback making war on their neighbors if both sides possessed atomic weapons!

I interpreted several interrogations of Speer, who impressed everyone with his civilized manners. He had been appointed minister of munitions long after the war started and therefore could not be prosecuted as a conspirator to plan it. Every one of his questioners was fascinated with his ability to increase German war production even as the country was being bombed into ruins. He also reported that he became so disenchanted with Hitler and with dictatorship that he planned to assassinate him but was unable to carry it out. As it turned out, his prosecutors glossed over Speer's use of tens of thousands of slave laborers, many from concentration camps, who died from overwork and undernourishment.

At two o'clock in the afternoon on Friday, October 19, 1945, my phone rang, and Colonel Williams bade me to come to his office immediately. Now what? As I entered, several other members of the interrogation staff were in his office, all looking solemn. A stenographer recorded my oath, which is still one of my treasured possessions. It had never occurred to me that I would be part of the indictments of the Nazis.

"Harry" Neave was really Airey Neave, a British major, an

ex–prisoner of war who had escaped Nazi incarceration. After the Nuremberg trials he became a leading member of the House of Commons, only to be murdered by the IRA outside Parliament. But on that day in 1945, he represented the International Military Tribunal, while I stood as the official interpreter and representative of the prosecution.

And so we started on our tour of the Nuremberg jail, Neave and I.

I had been down there before. On each side of a central passageway there were long rows of cells, each with an observation window in the door and a guard stationed outside who could see the prisoner's cot, with his chair and a small table, but not the toilet. Aware of this blind spot, one of the defendants, Robert Ley, would hang himself over the toilet within the week.

A solemn-faced and silent Colonel Burton Andrus, the commandant of the Nuremberg prison, kept his hand on his bejeweled pistol as he and two Russian officers marched several steps behind us. (Even at that moment I wondered why the Soviets never let anyone do anything alone!) We went from cell to cell. A guard opened doors one at a time, and one prisoner after the other was brought out to a small table. We read the indictment to each.

Göring was first. His pale blue eyes mysteriously aloof, he greeted us with a request for counsel before I could read the charges to him. Looking at me, he said, "Now I need a good interpreter even more than a lawyer." I understood immediately that he thought he could make a better case for himself than any defense counsel! Schacht managed to look contemptuous and said that the indictment did not pertain to him. Keitel, bluff and ruddy-faced as ever, stood stiffly erect, but I could see the pounding of the artery in his throat. For each defendant I repeated, in essence: "You are charged with Crimes against Peace, War Crimes, Conspiracy to Commit Aggression, Crimes against Humanity, Genocide." That indictment, the pages yellowed and its staples rusted, lies before me now, and that day will forever be fresh in my memory. Speer took his copy of the document and went back to his cell silently.

As we went through the awful recital of crimes over and over, for each of the twenty-one inmates, hour after hour, I envisioned anew the stacks of pitiful corpses and gagged once again on the smell of assembly-line extermination these men and their cohorts had unleashed. Their clean hands reached out for the bundles of stapled documents that catalogued their past. Elsewhere they might easily have been taken for a group of very ordinary men, picked at random from a crowd. We saw no evil stares, no animal lips baring murderous fangs. The physical normality, the man-in-the-street appearance of these men was more frightening than signs of insanity would have been. To me, it drove home the fact that another evil dictator, someday, someplace, might again inspire ambitious, amoral yes-men to kill or order subordinates to kill humans because of race, creed, or color — or for the sheer joy of it!

After the indictments were served, we of the interrogation division could no longer take statements from the accused unless they volunteered to be interrogated. In the month remaining before the trial was to begin, we tried to find additional witnesses to bolster the prosecution's case. After months of unremitting pressure and hard work, I arranged to have orders cut for myself, with no expiration date and with my enduring presidential priority, to proceed to St. Valentin, a place I invented to cover travel in Bavaria, Austria, and northern Italy. I invented St. Valentin because I wanted no one to find my destination on a map and question my route. I wanted to be totally free to go wherever I wanted. (Was I astonished many years later when I discovered that there was a real St. Valentin, rather near Berchtesgaden!) Because I had an OSS car, I was rarely challenged, and even then my "presidential" travel orders got me waved through all checkpoints.

During this trip I located Himmler's wife and daughter, Göring's wife, and two of Kaltenbrunner's mistresses. Though I talked to all of them, none of these women revealed anything relating to misdeeds by their husbands or lovers. Frau Himmler said that her husband had told her repeatedly that his work was so demanding he did not want to talk about it at home. Himmler's pimply teenage daughter was incredulous when reading about her father's career, which was now being serialized in newly appearing German-language papers. When I tried to interview her, she ran crying from the room. I was surprised that Himmler's daughter had feelings! From Frau Himmler, I got her husband's SS uniform collar insignia, which I still have, and two pages of his diary, in which he made hard-to-decipher notes in that old-fashioned stilted German Suetterlin script. Frau Himmler was the plainest of women, and I surmised that she must have been glad to find a husband, even one as singularly unattractive as her Heinrich.

During the interval between the serving of the indictments and the start of the trial, the staff of the interrogation division finally had time for celebratory parties. Colonel Amen invited me repeatedly to his quarters, and his capacity for scotch whiskey was truly impressive. I remember the advice of a savvy woman major who suggested I eat two tablespoonfuls of butter or drink a pint of milk to line my stomach before the evening's festivities began. Whether due to this immunization or not, my capacity for hard drinking improved spectacularly.

I often saw the American lawyers working late hours preparing their briefs for the approaching trial. Justice Jackson was impassioned by his mission to outlaw nationalistic aggression and genocide. Colonel Amen was preparing for his own courtroom appearance, where he would examine witnesses and cross-examine defendants using materials we had developed in the interrogation. I admired General Telford Taylor, the principal deputy prosecutor, who was dedicated to the proposition that military personnel must be punished for following orders they knew to be illegal. Robert (R. M. W.) Kempner, a pre-Hitler Prussian police official and voluntary émigré, was here to incarcerate onetime superiors who had become Nazi tools. Tom Dodd, second man to Justice

Jackson, later to be senator from Connecticut, was here as a civilian expert in the law of conspiracy. All of them were at Nuremberg to practice their profession — and many to advance their careers. That did not apply to me. I had no profession, not even a college education.

After my solo trip to "St. Valentin," I had time to read stacks of captured documents. Without minimizing how dangerous Hitler had been or how costly had been the ultimate victory over him, I was startled to see in those documents how limited the Nazis' knowledge of the world they had set out to dominate was. Though they correctly assessed French weakness, they misread the English character and overestimated the limited reach of British power. The Nazis had no idea of American determination and industrial might. They vastly underestimated Soviet staying power and ludicrously overestimated the effect of the Japanese attack on Pearl Harbor on America's ability to conduct a winning war in the Pacific and in Europe. Would they have tried to take on the world, I wondered, had they known more?

All of Hitler's early successes were achieved without war, for which Hitler earned acclaim from ordinary Germans who saw him tear up the hated Treaty of Versailles and restore German national self-respect. With an ever more inflated ego, veneration at home, and accommodation from abroad, Hitler cultivated his foes' quaint notion that he would reciprocate their devotion to peace. And he became convinced of his own military genius.

But despite journalists' vivid imagination, beguiled by Nazi propaganda, he never had a master plan; Hitler was an opportunist, with a fantastic gift for exploiting the weaknesses of his opponents. After marching into Czechoslovakia in late 1938, without war, and while Chamberlain talked about "peace in our time," Hitler told his most intimate ministers and generals the following in a secret conference recorded by his adjutant:

"Autarchy [economic self-sufficiency] is impossible. I shall attack France and England when it is most favorable. And I must name my own person as irreplaceable and infallible. I am convinced of the strength of my intellect and my power of decision. I am going to gamble; I now have to choose between victory and destruction. I choose victory — I hope that some swine does not come along with a peace offer I have to consider."

Hitler believed he must choose between "victory and destruction" to the last minute of his life. A Nuremberg psychiatrist, Douglas Kelley, explained to me how the alternative of either being almighty or being nothing dominated Hitler's entire adult life.

Opponents at home and abroad should have realized who the man was and rejected him and squashed him when it would have still been easy to do so, before 1936. Hitler's example convinced me it is advisable to fight tyrants before they become monsters.

I also realized that exterminating Jews was not essential to Hitler's territorial conquests. Dictators need enemies so that their people venerate them as saviors. Inside Germany, only Jews were left for the dual role of enemies and scapegoats. Hitler needed enemies more than a few additional supporters to get Germans to unite behind him.

Only by the grace of fate could I now, at Nuremberg, look upon Hitler's perversions with leisure and contempt. Had I not escaped in time, I would have been one of his victims.

German people had put maximum value on their material well-being and their national pride, becoming accessories and tools of an evil empire.

We Americans at Nuremberg, long before scholar Daniel Goldhagen raised the subject, kept debating among ourselves why most Germans had followed Hitler. As I read the piles of Nazi documents, I asked myself, "What did the great mass of German people actually know about the crimes of Hitler's gang, and when did they know? And what could they have done to thwart the criminal behavior of their government?"

Once President Hindenburg conferred total power on Hitler "to protect German democracy" in January of 1933, there was no force in Germany to remove Hitler or to moderate his actions. His true venom emerged as his power became absolute, and after that, only his own perception of what he could get away with restrained him. The Holocaust was years in the making. It took almost nine years after the Nazis came to power for Göring to issue the order for the Final Solution to the Jewish Question, three years before the Nazis' defeat.

I never forgot Halder's answer to me when I asked him, "What were you fighting for?"

"We had sworn an oath to obey the Führer," he replied. "We had no choice."

He confirmed what I knew already. We Americans, after being attacked by the Japanese and having received a declaration of war from Hitler, had fought to defend our land and our belief in human rights, not to glorify an all-powerful leader or subjugate others. Our president was the servant of our country, not the other way around. When Roosevelt died, we were shocked and sad, but our values were intact. When Hitler was gone and, with him, any chance of victory, Germans had nothing left to fight for. The object of their oath was gone and nothing took its place. There were no humanistic ideals, no defense of the rights of man, no definition of nobility or honor, only blind obedience. It was as though Goethe, Beethoven, Brahms, Schiller, Luther, and the great German philosophers had never existed. The only goals of Nazis had been to make slaves of their neighbors and to advance in their own hierarchy. When their enemies defeated them, Germans were made to confront the stupidity of Nazi delusions and the perversity of their crimes, survey their utterly destroyed cities, and long for their imprisoned men to come home.

Hitler had so thoroughly destroyed all traditional values and decency in Germany that the generation that swore loyalty to him had virtually no moral values or ideals to fall back on. There were habits of daily living, of course: industriousness and cleanliness. Germans who had gladly hidden behind Hitler while he was successful, but could not emerge from his shadow when he was failing, now found themselves under a merciless light that bared the material and spiritual vacuum of Nazi evil. Nowhere was that light more revealing than in Nuremberg, first in the interrogation rooms and later in the courtroom. Not one of the defendants ever cited a single salutary aspect of Nazism or demonstrated a shred of surviving faith in its dogmas. Not even Göring, who professed loyalty to Hitler and extolled Nazism to enhance his own reputation as a hero, ever cited ideals, only the lust for power.

I was deeply grateful to be a citizen of a country with ideals and values that enshrined human rights; they were not always perfectly practiced, but I could devote my life to attaining them, and I had already braved death to assure their survival. Not once did it seem to occur to the Nazis at Nuremberg that their enemies had fought for their own cherished values as much as against Nazi evils.

The lessons of history are always forgotten unless permanent institutions are created to prevent a repetition. Those who hope that, if we simply remember the horrors of Hitler or grieve over his victims, another outrage will not happen again, somewhere, sometime, have to accept the fact that tyrants can still seize power as Hitler once did. I appreciated anew how critical it is for Congress and the Supreme Court to do their work in checking a president's actions and preventing wrong ones by using our system of checks and balances. And I kept thinking how important it is to educate America's children to those values.

II

The Trial

*I*N NUREMBERG, ON NOVEMBER 20, 1945, the trial was about to begin. The International Military Tribunal — "the Court," as distinct from the American prosecution — had its own staff of interpreters with an electronic system for simultaneous translations into English, German, French, and Russian. As a courtesy, I was asked by the tribunal's executive secretary to interpret the opening session from English into German.

There I sat in a glass box, which encased the interpreters, in the courtroom. The four judges and their four alternates were on my left, the defendants and their lawyers in front and to the right of me. The tables for the four prosecuting nations were straight ahead of me, and behind them was an upward-sloping gallery for the press and privileged visitors. White-helmeted armed guards stood against the wall behind the defendants. At that moment, this courtroom was the center of the world, and I was on the hot seat!

The judges looked solemn and, from the first moment of the trial, Sir Geoffrey Lawrence exercised perfect control, despite the irritation of intermittently dead earphones, which he and everyone else needed to follow the multilingual proceedings. During several of these enforced silences, Göring spotted me in the interpreters' glass box and winked at me as though we were buddies.

The tribunal's own chief interpreter was a colonel and a French linguist of renown. He brought trained interpreters with him to Nuremberg, but he asked me to be on his team. During that first session I had to look up legal terms whose meaning I did not understand, and that embarrassed me. I realized how different it would be to interpret in the courtroom rather than in the interrogation suites. There I had asked for breaks when statements became overly long, or I could ask for clarification when a meaning was not clear. Here, the interpreters were physically separated from the speakers and had no opportunity to control the length of pleadings or to ask for corrections. They could only light a red "stop" signal to have a chance to catch up. Then their "audience," most often the presiding judge, would ask for explanations, although the words repeated were often no clearer than those that had caused confusion. The court interpreters had to be true robots — one language in the ears, the other out of their mouths! That did not interest me, and I also knew that the speakers' linguistic versatility and knowledge of legal terms were beyond my capabilities. I declined the colonel's offer to interpret in the courtroom.

Quite unexpectedly, I was awarded the Army Commendation Medal by order of the Commanding General, U.S. Forces in Europe. Justice Jackson assembled members of the prosecution staff and read the citation, which said, in part:

> As Chief of the Interpretation Section, Sergeant Sonnenfeldt [then a civilian, who had been promoted from private to sergeant] took a leading role in the establishment and supervision of an organization of 50 persons. His organization furnished the interpreters for the interrogation of over 75 different major witnesses, including the 21 major Axis leaders, then recorded, transcribed and processed the proceedings of the interrogations as well as the related statements

and affidavits. His section compiled through this work more than 10,000 pages of testimony. Sonnenfeldt recommended policies and procedures concerning the treatment of prisoners during interrogation, and these procedures were found so sound and practical that they were approved and have been used by interrogators to date. Among the personnel in Sonnenfeldt's section were military personnel of grades and ranks higher than his were and civilians of many different nationalities. He handled them with such amazing diplomacy and tact that he managed to enlist their whole-hearted cooperation in spite of so many differences. Through his leadership and devotion, Sergeant Sonnenfeldt has made a valuable contribution to the trial of the major Axis criminals at Nuremberg, Germany. By direction of the Secretary of War, etc., etc.

I was proud of this recognition and treasure the photo of Justice Jackson pinning the ribbon on me.

My decision to turn down a transfer to the court interpreter's team pleased Colonel Amen and Justice Jackson, who did not want me to leave the prosecution team. My role of interpreter had evolved into that of interrogator. I had already started to question additional witnesses who would bolster the case against the defendants.

As the trial got under way, one of my witnesses and I were involved in an episode that was eventually reported to President Truman. General "Wild Bill" Donovan had always wanted Göring, the highest surviving Nazi, to make a public confession in court. Naturally, no one was opposed to that, but meanwhile I continued to look for prominent Germans who might turn "state's evidence" or incriminate Göring. Ideally, these would be knowledgeable former Nazis who would expose the evils of Nazism not only to the court but also and especially to the German people. A public confession by Göring remained a "hot button" for General Donovan, who had initially helped to organize the American prosecution. At Nuremberg, Donovan still had great influence and prestige, but he had no official assignment with the American prosecution. He did interview prisoners and witnesses with his own agenda in mind.

A key figure in Donovan's attempt to wring a confession from Göring was General Erwin Lahousen, whom I had discovered and who was now in the safe house. When I first met him, he was embarrassed because he had no soap and no cologne for his personal hygiene. After I got those, along with shaving soap from the PX for him, he wanted a certain young lady to visit him, and Countess Ingeborg Kálnoky, a Hungarian national who ran the safe house where Lahousen stayed, arranged it (and also described it in her book *The Guest House*). I then interrogated him for many hours to develop his story. He was originally an Austrian military intelligence officer who then had served for many years as deputy to Admiral Wilhelm Canaris, chief of the Abwehr, the German equivalent of the OSS or today's CIA. They, far more than Hitler and his entourage, had the most comprehensive view of the balance of power between the Axis and the Allies. They also knew of the atrocities that went on in concentration camps and the killing of millions of Russians, all contrary to treaties or conventions that Germany had signed. Lahousen was well aware of the parts Keitel, Jodl, and Göring played in perpetrating these atrocities. Admiral Canaris and his circle of intimates also correctly saw each German conquest as a prelude to the involvement of the United States, whose power they dreaded. Abwehr officers knew long before it became obvious that Germany was losing the war. As a last resort, to obtain terms more favorable than unconditional surrender for Germany, Canaris joined the would-be assassins of Hitler, who wanted to sue for a negotiated peace. When Hitler survived the bomb planted under his conference table, Canaris's complicity was discovered, and he was garroted with piano wire, a horrible slow death reserved for Hitler's enemies.

I had found the charred official Abwehr diary and had it partly restored. I knew that General Erwin Lahousen was privy to all or nearly all that Canaris had known, including all of Göring's activities and Keitel's and Jodl's spineless transmission of Hitler's criminal orders regarding the murder of Russians. The fragments of the diary jogged the memory of Lahousen, who was also well aware of Göring's criminal orders to lynch downed Allied airmen.

One evening, I had arranged a session with Lahousen, but he did not appear, and I discovered that he had been taken from the safe house to the residence of General Donovan. On learning that Donovan might be preempting their witness, Colonel Amen and Justice Jackson were livid. When I had Lahousen brought up to the interrogation room the next morning, Amen and Jackson walked in and asked Lahousen indignantly what he meant by sneaking out on me to see Donovan. Lahousen spread his palms and said, "What could I do, a poor prisoner of war, when I was told to get into General Donovan's car?" This incident led to an impassioned exchange of letters between Jackson and Donovan. Jackson then wrote a long report to President Truman, laying out his strategy as the official U.S. prosecutor and complaining that he and his interrogator (me!) had been interfered with by Donovan. Donovan left Nuremberg, and a copy of that report to the president is now one of my mementos of the Nuremberg trials. Lahousen went on to give devastating testimony in court that incriminated Göring, Keitel, and Jodl beyond redemption.

At the trial, Justice Jackson made the opening statement for the American prosecution:

"The privilege of opening the first trial in history for crimes against the peace of the world imposes a grave responsibility. The wrongs which we seek to condemn and punish have been so calculated, so malignant, and so devastating, that civilization cannot . . . survive their being repeated.

(I found it noteworthy that Jackson began his opening statement by referring to the historical importance of these trials before talking about their legal significance.)

Jackson then explained that the war unleashed by these defendants had left virtually no neutrals in the world, and so either the victors had to try the vanquished or the vanquished would have to try themselves. We were never to forget "that the record on which we judge these defendants today is the record on which history will judge us tomorrow. . . . We will not ask you to convict these defendants on the testimonies of their foes."

Outlining the prosecution's case, Jackson declared: "The German people were in the hands of the police, the police were in the hands of the Nazi party, and the party was in the hands of evil men, of whom the defendants here before you are surviving and representative leaders." As I heard those words, I feared that this statement would make Germans claim that they had been duped and bore no responsibility for what happened.

Knowing the evidence that was in the voluminous documents and films showing Nazi cruelties and obscenities, Jackson said: "Our proof will be disgusting and you will say I have robbed you of your sleep."

As he closed, Jackson said:

"The real complaining party at your bar is civilization. In all our countries it is still a struggling and imperfect thing. . . . Civilization asks whether law is so laggard as to be utterly helpless to deal with crimes of this magnitude by criminals of this order of importance. It does not expect that you can make war impossible. It does expect that your juridical action will put the forces of International Law . . . on the side of peace."

I felt like applauding but the decorum of the court forbade it.

During the trial, I sat at the table of the American prosecution to verify that courtroom testimony by witnesses or defendants (in German) was the same as what I had previously interpreted or obtained. Chief Justice Sir Geoffrey Lawrence was unperturbed by blatant lies, brilliant legal maneuvers, or gruesome facts. The witness box was straight ahead from where I sat and the prosecuting attorney's stand was to my right. The defense lawyers would rise to my immediate left. I was grateful not to be behind the glass wall with the tribunal interpreters, who, now proficient in their demanding jobs, did magnificent work in four languages — available to all in the courtroom by turning a button on a little box connected to one's headset.

The scales of justice hung from Athena's arm, high up behind the witness box, as they had in Hitler's day and before. Now, in her shadow, SS killers added up the millions of human beings they had killed. Hitherto hidden secrets of the most evil empire the world had known were bared here, day after day, week after week. Here was meticulously recorded the detailed history of tyranny, organized hatred, and malefaction on a scale never before known to man.

One of the first prosecution witnesses was Otto Ohlendorf, commander of an Einsatzgruppe, an SS formation attached to the German army, whose job it was to track down and murder Jews in the conquered East European countries. Ohlendorf explained how hard it had been for his men to kill 90,000 Jews, a few dozen at a time in its first year of operations. He explained that they had modified trucks by routing the exhaust gas inside and driving the victims until they were dead. Then his men shoved them into mass graves. Another method was to have the victims dig a trench and then stand them up and shoot them in the neck so that they tumbled into the grave they had fashioned for themselves. That had been even harder for his men to do day after day, he complained.

My limited duties in the courtroom allowed me ample time to observe the defendants. Some of them were chummy with each other, while Streicher, the anti-Semitic pornographer, was shunned by all. Once more it was obvious that Göring tried to dominate those henchmen, his fellow defendants. Their fawning subservience to a dictator had brought them to this — their last — state of prominence under the bright lights of the defendants' dock. Göring grimaced during shocking testimony and ogled the women in the spectator's gallery and, once in a while, winked at me.

When movies of extermination camps, including the slaughter of women and children, were shown in that Nuremberg courtroom, gasps and sobs, even by some of the defendants, interrupted an otherwise total silence. So many in the courtroom were visibly shaken when the lights came back on that a recess was needed before proceedings could resume. But not Göring. This time I heard him say that all of this footage was just propaganda, like the propaganda Goebbels had produced for the Nazis. As though the Holocaust were a figment of the imagination.

Finding counsel for the accused had not been easy. Known Nazis were excluded, and distinguished German lawyers had not thrived under the Hitler regime. Nevertheless, even in chaotic postwar Germany two dozen defenders were found, with help from the tribunal in locating individuals not always eager for the job. The counsel ranged in quality from adroit and effective advocates to outright clods.

Of course, they had an impossible job. Of the deeds of their clients there was no doubt, and their repeated challenges of the legality of the proceedings themselves were rejected.

I could now again observe the first defendant to take the stand. He was given two days to make a statement in his defense. After he came to the jail in Nuremberg and was questioned by John Harlan Amen, he realized that he would be treated as a prime war criminal. His attitude had become that of a man who knew he would be hanged. And now he had decided to become a martyr for Nazism.

On the witness stand, the judges permitted Göring to brag about the Nazi seizure of power, which confirmed Göring's role as a principal Nazi conspirator. How well I remembered the Reichstag fire less than thirty days after Hitler's appointment as chancellor, the arrest of Nazi opponents, the subsequent boycott of Jewish businesses, the dismissal of Jewish judges and teachers and the exclusion of Jewish doctors from German hospitals! And in 1935 Göring, as president of the Reichstag, proclaimed as noted the infamous Nuremberg Laws, which terminated the citizen rights of Jews in Germany. He presented himself as largely responsible for Hitler's triumphs in all these key events in the Nazi conspiracy. He did not mention his brazen attempt to take all executive power from Hitler by becoming minister of war, nor his fall from grace as his Luftwaffe was defeated by the RAF and later proved inadequate in relieving Stalingrad. Nor did he relate how Speer as minister of munitions stripped him of all power as economic czar of Germany. Those setbacks had propelled Himmler, Goebbels, and Bormann into the first rank previously occupied by Göring, whom Hitler after 1941 left with his title but little authority.

(A dictatorship depends on at least three important functions: a propaganda machine to keep the people enthused or at least quiet, a party organization to exert control, and a secret police to ferret out and eliminate opposition. Hitler had his Goebbels, who was the master of the big lie; his Bormann, who controlled the Nazi party; and his Himmler, who directed the Gestapo and the concentration camps. These three ran Germany for Hitler from 1941 onward when, believing himself to be a military genius, he spent virtually all his time on the war.)

During his cross-examination Jackson started out well for the prosecution case, but this also suited Göring. Here are some examples:

> PRESIDENT: Do the chief prosecutors wish to cross-examine?
>
> JUSTICE JACKSON: You are perhaps aware that you are the only living man who can expound to us the true purposes of the Nazi Party and the inner workings of its leadership?
>
> GÖRING: I am perfectly aware of that.
>
> JUSTICE JACKSON: You, from the very beginning, together with those who were associated with you, intended to overthrow and later did overthrow the Weimar Republic?

GÖRING: That was, as far as I am concerned, my firm intention.

JUSTICE JACKSON: The principles of the authoritarian government which you set up required, as I understand you, that there be tolerated no opposition by political parties which might defeat or obstruct the policy of the Nazi Party?

GÖRING: You have understood this quite correctly. . . . It was now time to have done with it.

But later Jackson, reading from a document that had been translated by the documentation division of the American prosecution but never seen by me, accused Göring of having ordered the "liberation" of the Rhine River, in violation of the Treaty of Versailles. Göring asked to see the German document and pointed out that it referred to the clearing of ice from the Rhine! That was a big embarrassment to Jackson. In a much more serious flap, Jackson failed to get Göring to admit that he had issued the order for the "final solution to the Jewish question," Nazi jargon for the Holocaust. In pretrial interrogation, that was the paper I had shoved under his nose so that Colonel Amen could record, after endless denials by Göring, that he had signed the order for the Holocaust. When Jackson insisted on "yes" or "no" answers regarding this document, the judges, perhaps suspecting another flap like that pertaining to the Rhine, overruled Jackson to give Göring a chance to "explain."

The judges were so eager to appear fair to Göring that Jackson lost his cool. He never nailed Göring with ordering the Holocaust. I was dismayed that this devastating result of Colonel Amen's interrogation, which I had interpreted, did not become part of the trial record.

We knew that in 1938 Göring had convened a conference of all government departments, at Hitler's behest, to plan the solution of the Jewish Question, then the forced immigration of Jews by destroying their means of economic subsistence. His 1941 order for the Final Solution was a follow-on mission to destroy the Jews. Heydrich, Himmler's second in command, later read Göring's order to the Wannsee Conference, a high-level meeting he called to organize the Holocaust. Again, representatives of every Nazi government department plus railroad management (to take care of transporting the victims to their deaths) attended this conference. The infamous Eichmann, tried and executed in Israel, kept the minutes. No other order for the Final Solution has ever been found and no one has ever claimed that there was one. Göring had sent his own representatives to the meeting, but Jackson apparently also knew nothing about the consequences of Göring's order and dropped the subject.

During the cross-examination, Colonel Amen and I looked at each other. I could read his thoughts: If Jackson had only used the sworn interrogation text showing he had admitted signing the order . . .

In other instances during Jackson's examination, Göring simply denied evidence. For example, Jackson introduced the sworn statement I had obtained from General Halder about Göring's boast that he had torched the Reichstag, the major event on which Nazi power was based. Göring claimed he had never said such a thing. Jackson called none of the available witnesses to that boast.

In an argument over a botched translation, Jackson also failed to nail Göring for having ordered the lynching of aviators.

Much of Jackson's cross-examination of Göring was a disaster, but on the third day Jackson recovered. Göring nevertheless acted as though he had won the contest.

With all those first-rank Nazis now dead, Göring wanted to stand out as the heroic martyr of the Third Reich. He had told the psychiatrist Kelley that his single driving ambition had been to achieve supreme command of Germany. Cowing his fellow defendants by becoming their Führer now was his last try at glory. The court psychologist, Gustave Gilbert, noticed how

Göring used the lunch recess, when they were permitted to eat and talk together, to harangue his fellow defendants into aping his behavior. After he heard Göring say, "I cut quite a figure on the witness stand!" Gilbert arranged for Göring to dine alone so that he could no longer use the communal lunch to intimidate the other defendants into following his example. Thus his last attempt at glory failed like all his prior ones.

The British prosecutors were more effective. They nailed Göring for the murder in cold blood of British airmen. I admired their command of the subject, their cool demeanor, and their velvet courtesy, which often hid the dagger aimed at the accused. Göring paled and trembled under the onslaught of Sir David Maxwell-Fyfe, the British deputy chief prosecutor. The Soviets were largely ineffective in their courtroom maneuvers. While the Americans carried the greatest load, the British were by far the most accomplished.

After his encounter with Göring in the courtroom, the hitherto close relationship between Jackson and Colonel Robert G. Storey, chief of the Documentation Division, soured. Storey's division had been responsible for the botched translations, which had trapped Jackson in his cross-examination of Göring. Storey himself had made a poor appearance in court. Jackson, who had wanted to rely mainly on documents, rarely spoke during the rest of the trial until its very end and, with the exception of Speer, he left cross-examinations to Amen and others. Storey soon left. Some thought that Jackson never recovered from his cross-examination of Göring.

Göring was followed by Hess, who refused to testify, and by Ribbentrop, who babbled endlessly, blaming all on Hitler while trying to deny his own enthusiastic participation in the extermination of Jews in the conquered territories. The military men Keitel, Jodl, Raeder, and Doenitz presented themselves as loyal subordinates of an all-powerful Führer as they had knowingly carried out unlawful orders.

The prison psychiatrist Leon Goldensohn wrote about Doenitz, grand admiral and successor to Hitler, "I don't believe this man has any notion of what is going on in the world. . . . He rejects anti-Semitism, the Holocaust, and the entire modus operandi of the Nazi party. He sees himself innocent of any crime. . . ."

Party and Nazi government functionaries all blamed Himmler's SS and Gestapo for the dirty work.

Albert Speer, not looking like a criminal, well educated and a good speaker, had more than a hundred days to study prosecutors and judges before he was called to testify. He made the most of this opportunity. Speer had succeeded Fritz Todt, the engineering genius who had built the autobahn roads, whose airplane exploded "mysteriously" after he had warned Hitler in 1941 that he was going to lose the war. Speer, Hitler's protégé and architect and later his plenipotentiary for armaments, succeeding Todt, condemned the Nazi regime in Nuremberg for being a stupid form of government. In his testimony, he argued that the Führer Prinzip, the myth of an all-knowing leader who had to be obeyed under all circumstances, led to inane decisions and insane crimes. He condemned Hitler's last order to destroy all things German ("a people so weak as to be defeated did not deserve to live") as criminal. And he described several of his own plans, which were never carried out, to kill Hitler. Speer was allowed to discourse at length on the witness stand about the dangers faced by a world where weapons of mass destruction could be delivered from far away by the push of a button, a catastrophic vision he used to warn against future dictatorships. Though others, like Frank, the murderous governor of Poland, and von Schirach, once the leader of the Hitler Youth, condemned Hitler's immorality and dishonesty in their testimony, Speer confined himself to a purely intellectual warning of the dangers and foolishness of despotism. Speer was never asked how he could reconcile his dangerous trip to Hitler's bunker in Berlin to say an emotional good-bye to him, when he claimed to have seen him as the cause of Germany's collapse. Nor was he ever grilled about his knowing use of concentration camp labor.

The lack of direction of Speer's pretrial interrogations showed up in the shallowness of his cross-examination by Jackson. His questioners had failed to develop the extent of his criminal actions, and they had already gone back to America when he testified. That Speer had employed over five million slave laborers under horrible conditions in his armament factories never became a prominent part of Jackson's cross-examination of him. The key sentence in his confession, if one can call it that, was: "As a member of its leadership I take responsibility for what was done by an evil regime." Also, judges and prosecutors may have been so beguiled by a defendant who condemned the Nazi regime that they did not consider the full extent of his culpability. Speer's fellow defendant Sauckel was hanged for rounding up those very slaves that he delivered to Speer, who only got twenty years' imprisonment.

A recent German documentary raises the question of Speer's guilt and finds him more culpable than the tribunal did. I am one of the few people alive who saw and heard Speer and I expressed my doubts about his honesty, as did two of his own children.

Occasionally there was drama in the courtroom. Hans Bernd Gisevius, an early Nazi state-police official and later member of the anti-Nazi conspiracy against Hitler, had found refuge in Switzerland. He was perhaps the most knowledgeable survivor. In riveting testimony, based on extensive documents he had secreted, he visibly angered Göring and certain other defendants with detailed descriptions of their criminal deeds. Gisevius's testimony, though, favored defendants Hjalmar Schacht and Franz von Papen, who were claiming they had stayed on only to moderate Nazi crimes.

But nothing equaled the testimony of Rudolf Hoess, the commandant of Auschwitz and its satellite camps. Dr. Kauffmann, defense attorney for SS chief Kaltenbrunner, brought Hoess to Nuremberg and called him as a witness. The testimony of Hoess did not help Kaltenbrunner, whom we had interrogated at length. Before he was in charge of the Gestapo, the concentration camps, and the Sicherheitsdienst (the internal spy network to keep party and government officials in line), Kaltenbrunner was the top SS man in Austria, known as the Viennese Himmler. He denied any responsibility for the Holocaust and other atrocities, even when presented with orders that bore his signature. There was enough evidence for conviction.

Kaltenbrunner was a heterosexual athlete. Two of his mistresses had been placed in the safe house to be interrogated as witnesses. That was not productive, because sex was their only connection with Kaltenbrunner. General Halder called these Austrian beauties "buffalo cows" after he saw how they tried to attract some men there.

When Kaltenbrunner's defense attorney brought Hoess to the Nuremberg jail as a defense witness, Sender Jaari, a military intelligence officer, recognized his value to the prosecution: what we could do with him in cross-examination. We found out that Hoess had met Kaltenbrunner, second only to Himmler, in the extermination area of Auschwitz, and the defense attorney did not seem to realize that his testimony would seal the case against Kaltenbrunner, his client. We interrogated Hoess at length and I spent many hours with him alone.

In court, Hoess was cross-examined by Colonel Amen, using a sworn deposition taken by his deputy, Lieutenant Colonel Smith W. Brookhart. I had gone over an English version of the Hoess statement with him to be sure he understood and agreed with it. Hoess had an extraordinary memory, and he answered in court every question exactly as he had answered us.

In pretrial conversations, I had discovered that in the 1920s Hoess had been a right-wing assassin who had served out a maximum-security jail sentence. The SS recruited him as a driver before Hitler came to power. Hoess got his basic management training in Dachau, one of the first concentration camps. After the war began in 1939, the term "enemy of the Fatherland" was applied to all individuals whom the Nazis wished to destroy. They made mass extermination of Jews into a patriotic duty for SS men and women. Hoess did his duty.

Humans and corpses were mere numbers to him, all neatly filed away in his memory. Hoess had been the world's most deadly efficient professional exterminator of innocent human beings. Yet Hoess was so undistinguished in appearance and ordinary in manner that I wondered whether he had ever had an original thought. Although his admissions surely tied the hangman's noose around his neck, he never gave a sign that he was talking to relieve his conscience. Nor did he ever brag.

Hoess was visibly angered when I asked him whether it was true that he had exterminated three and one-half million human beings. "No," he said. "Only two and one-half million. The rest died of other causes."

" 'Other causes,' Herr Hoess?"

"Yes, illness, epidemics that we could not stop, and starvation causing physical collapse when we could not get food for them."

"Why did the Nazis place their principal extermination camps in the occupied territories?" we asked Hoess.

"So the German people should not know what was happening. No more than two hundred fifty SS men knew," he claimed.

He had heard Heinrich Himmler, the man in charge of the SS and the Gestapo, address SS leaders in Krakow: "I shall speak to you with all frankness of a very serious subject. We shall now discuss it absolutely openly among ourselves; nevertheless we shall never speak of it in public. I mean the evacuation of the Jews, the extermination of the Jewish race. . . . This is a glorious page in our history that has never been written and shall never be written, for we know how difficult we should have made it for ourselves, if . . . we still had Jews today in every town. We had the moral right; we had the duty to our people, to destroy this people, which wanted to destroy us. We had to face the question: what to do with the women and children? I was determined to find a clear solution. I did not think I was justified to exterminate the men and to raise their children as avengers. Yes, I had to decide to have these people vanish from our earth."

Himmler's speech was noteworthy in that it did not begin and end with the customary adulation of Hitler! Himmler talked as though he was responsible for the Holocaust.

How did his decision work out to keep the Holocaust a secret?

The total Jewish population of Nazi Germany had shrunk from over half a million in 1933 to 240,000 in 1939, less than one in two hundred Germans. By then, Jews had been confined to ghettos in Germany, isolated from the Aryan population for several years. Starting in 1941, they were rounded up in the small hours of the morning, on short notice, neither seen nor missed by Germans who had no contact with them. The Nazis let it be known that Jews were going to enclaves, in the occupied territories of Poland and Czechoslovakia, where they were reported to have their own symphony orchestras and theaters in pleasant surroundings. In fact, these destinations like Theresienstadt were only way stations to Auschwitz. About 170,000 German Jews were incinerated while fewer than 70,000 survived. The extermination of over five million Russian, Lithuanian, Latvian, Polish, Dutch, Belgian, and French Jews was carefully kept secret, because Himmler's SS and Gestapo ruled supreme in these conquered lands. Word of death factories did not reach the Western allies until millions had been killed, and the true numbers were unknown to the world until April of 1946, when Hoess testified in Nuremberg. Unfortunately there was no live broadcast of his testimony for Germans and their conquerors to hear the true story of the Holocaust from one of its main executioners. But I heard it with my own ears as we interrogated Hoess and again as he testified in court.

Hoess confirmed that to keep secret a Holocaust of vast proportions, a dictator must punish everyone for asking questions. When Jews were herded aboard trains in German-conquered areas, only a few SS thugs knew where they were headed. As is known, these victims went directly from their hometowns or other collection points on long and killing journeys in cattle cars to Auschwitz or one of the five extermination camps in Poland, not knowing what was in store for them.

After exhausting trips that lasted several days, with deaths of babies and older people common, their SS guards told the hapless travelers at Auschwitz that they were going to shower rooms before being fed.

"Why shower rooms, Herr Hoess?"

"We wanted no panic. These people were dirty, exhausted after days in freight cars, befouled by their own excrements. We told them gently to undress because they needed to be clean and disinfected before getting their new clothes. They would have rioted had they known where they were going."

"And where was that, Herr Hoess?"

"I didn't want to have riots with wounded and dead bodies all over the place," explained Hoess, "so we made the gas chambers look modern and clean, with tiled floors and walls and shower heads."

"And the shower heads were nozzles for Cyclone B?" we asked.

"Yes," he said. "At first there was a lot of panic when the gas worked too slowly and prisoners realized it was not hot water coming out of those shower heads. They stampeded to break open the locked doors and trampled each other to death. Later, we learned how to make the gas work much faster and prevent those terrible messes that took a lot of time to clean up before the room could be used again."

The bodies of the victims were then carted out of the showers by other inmates, who were allowed to live until they, too, were killed. The remains were taken to the ovens. "The heat of thousands of burning bodies was more intense than that of steel making," said Hoess. "It took a long time to get good ovens."

"Did the manufacturers know what their products were used for?"

"They must have known," said Hoess.

Nor was this commandant with the perfect memory hesitant to describe how his men extracted gold from the teeth of the dead (and sometimes the living), and how they collected jewelry to be processed, packaged, and indexed for depositing in the special SS Reichsbank vault in Berlin.

"Were any of these valuables ever stolen?" we asked.

"Yes," Hoess said. "Once we caught several SS men with gold taken from victims' teeth and jewelry. I sent those criminals to a special concentration camp for SS men where they were punished, worse than in Auschwitz. We never beat our prisoners at Auschwitz," he said.

Before he appeared as a witness, I asked him whether he had ever enriched himself with victims' possessions. Hoess was visibly angry. "What kind of a man do you think I am?" he asked in a hurt voice.

"When you and your family were living near Birkenau, part of the Auschwitz complex, your wife constantly complained of the stench in the air. What did you tell her?"

"I told her it was a glue factory."

Not bad, Rudolf! I thought. It was a glue factory all right, but you did not tell her the glue was made from human bodies.

"Do you recall the time when a visiting dignitary, the Gauleiter of Thuringia, chatted with your wife about your getting rid of enemies of the state? That you had already killed over a million?"

"Yes."

"When your wife complained that you had never told her what you were doing, what did you tell her?"

"I told her the truth when we were alone."

"And then?"

"She moved out of my bed and never let me touch her again. But I found a young camp inmate, Eleanor Hodys. She asked no questions." The mention of this mistress brought a faint smile to his lips.

Who was she? I wondered silently. How did she feel about letting this monster kiss her, embrace her, and penetrate her most intimate parts?

I found it interesting that in his autobiography, written in jail before his execution in Auschwitz where he had reigned, Hoess bragged about his warm marital relationship and never mentioned this episode. I suppose that even in the breast of this monster there lay a desire for a posthumous image of bourgeois decency!

One incident involving Hoess impressed me especially. An SS sergeant was known as the butcher of Auschwitz and, notwithstanding the denials of Hoess, had beaten and tortured prisoners. This sergeant, with a body like a barrel and a face like a piece of raw meat, was now a prisoner at Nuremberg, but he refused to talk. We wanted him to tell us which of the top Nazis, who denied ever having been there, he had seen visiting Auschwitz. When we stood him up before his former commanding officer, he saluted. Hoess told him to talk, and only then would he answer our questions. I saw that familiar superior/subordinate relationship. *Gehorsam* (obedience) *über alles! Befehl ist Befehl!* (Orders are orders.) And suddenly I realized that perhaps Hoess now considered us his bosses, since his old ones were dead!

"And how did you like your job as champion of extermination?" I asked Hoess.

"I wanted to get out of it for years. I repeatedly asked for a transfer to the front to fight and die like a soldier, but Himmler told me I could not be spared. I was doing more valuable work for the Fatherland. I had to fulfill my oath to Hitler and Himmler to carry on," he complained.

Himmler fainted when he saw Jewish women and children being murdered. I asked Hoess, who was made of sterner stuff, "Did you believe what Himmler was saying?"

"At the time, absolutely," said Hoess.

"And now?" I asked.

"Himmler was a coward and killed himself, and now one hears different things. . . ."

Thus were mass murderers turned into heroes of the Fatherland! I thought silently.

As the examinations and cross-examinations went down the list, I heard Schacht defend himself. One of the accusations was that his wife commissioned a brooch in the shape of a swastika and kissed Hitler. Schacht countered that he had divorced her to marry a much younger woman. Hitler had eventually incarcerated him in a concentration camp during the last year of the war, on suspicion that he was involved in the plot to kill him. Schacht, as president of the Reichsbank, had been an early and enthusiastic supporter of the Nazis as long as Hitler listened to him. But after Hitler ignored him a couple of times, as his power increased, Schacht became disenchanted. He left the regime, out of pique I felt, at being slighted rather than for political or moral reasons, and I always wondered what he would have done had he continued to enjoy controlling Hitler as his banker. Schacht had boundless ambition and questionable morality. He was exonerated in Nuremberg because his break occurred so early that he did not participate in war crimes.

The evidence against the guilty was overwhelming. Not one of them offered a defense of Nazism or even tried to explain what it was. The case against them was solidly based on Nazi documents signed by the defendants themselves and validated by multiple witnesses, who laid out the macabre, incredible tale of Nazi cruelty, crime, and corruption.

The trial ground on to its end. In his summation, Jackson said that Göring "was half militarist and half gangster. He stuck his pudgy finger in every pie. . . . He was, next to Hitler, the man who tied the activities of all the defendants together in a common effort." Jackson sketched "the ridiculous composite picture" offered by the defense:

Of Göring, "A number-two man, who knew nothing of the excesses of the Gestapo which he created, and never suspected the Jewish extermination program, although he was the signer of over a score of decrees which instituted the persecution of that race";

Of Hess, "A number-three man, who was merely an innocent middleman transmitting Hitler's orders without ever reading them, like a postman or delivery boy";

Of Ribbentrop, "A foreign minister who knew little of foreign affairs and nothing of foreign policy";

Of Keitel, "A field marshal who issued orders to the armed forces but had no idea of the results they would have in practice";

And so on down the list.

"They stand before the record of this trial as bloodstained Gloucester stood by the body of his slain king. He begged of the widow, as they beg of you, 'Say I slew them not.' . . . If you were to say of these men that they are not guilty, it would be as true to say that there has been no war, there are no slain, there has been no crime."

The defendants had some last words. Göring was the first to speak and he, the man who had signed the order for the Final Solution of the Jewish Question and for the lynching of Allied airmen, said: "I especially denounce the terrible mass murders, which I cannot understand. . . . I never ordered any killing or tortures where I had the power to prevent such actions! . . . The German people trusted their leader and because of his use of authority could not influence events. . . . The German people are innocent! . . . My only motive was my complete loyalty to my nation for its liberty and good fortune." Hess, the second one to speak, babbled nonsense, to the consternation of all present. When brought up short by the presiding judge, he assured the court that if he had the opportunity he would do everything again, just as before.

Ribbentrop said: "One holds me responsible for the conduct of the foreign policy of another. . . . I was trying for friendship with Russia, but this is now the problem of the Western allies, and I hope with my whole heart that they will be more successful than I was." Not one word from him about his enthusiastic participation in the extermination of the Jews.

Keitel, Hitler's general, on whose orders millions of Russian prisoners died, was more honest than those who had preceded him. He said, among other things: "I believed [Hitler] and I was wrong; I did not prevent what I should have prevented."

Kaltenbrunner, who had all the concentration camps under him, denied knowing anything about the Holocaust.

Frank, once Hitler's chief legal officer and later governor in Poland, said: "I hope that the German people will abandon the path Hitler — and we — showed. I beg of our people to take not one step more in this direction."

Baldur von Schirach, the leader of the Hitler Youth, intoned: "I want to affirm that our young people bear no part of the guilt for the horrible excesses of the Hitler regime. . . . They knew nothing of the horrible events unleashed."

I was also present when Speer spoke: "The German people will condemn Hitler as the proven cause of its misfortune. The world will learn not only to hate dictatorship but to fear it." Here again, he never referred to his own actions when he employed millions of slaves to make Germany's munitions.

Schacht, von Papen, and Fritzsche protested their innocence of the charges against them.

At the end of the defendants' statements, the judges retired to consider their verdicts. There was a hiatus of several weeks.

As we waited for the verdicts, I indulged in some social life. Among other responsibilities, I had been acting as liaison officer for the American prosecution with other delegations to the trials. Down the hall from me were the offices of the Russian prosecution, which included a buxom blond lieutenant with a country girl's face and a bright come-on smile. One day I met her in the hall, and, though she spoke no German, English, or French, I decided to date her anyway. I drew her a picture of the Grand Hotel, the center of social activity, and the picture of a clock with the hands at six. She nodded and smiled, and I was excited and anticipated a great time later that evening.

Less than an hour later, a Russian colonel came to my office, shook hands, and sat down. He then drew a picture of a woman with a Soviet lieutenant's insignia, a clock with the hands at six, and a picture of a house. He wrote down an address. I recognized it as the residence of the Soviet prosecutor. He said, "Da?" and I said, "Nyet." I was not about to have a chaperoned date in a Soviet general's house. Obviously, the Soviets looked upon my would-be romantic date as an affair of state. The lieutenant and I smiled at each other whenever we met in the hall after that, but we never met anywhere else.

But there were other attractive women at Nuremberg: British, French, Danish, American, civilians on service with the military, journalists, secretaries, interpreters. I made many good and close friends, male and female, among the various delegations. Some of these friendships endured for decades. But most of these friends are gone now, because I was so much younger than they.

I had become especially friendly with Poul Kjalke, head of the Danish delegation, who had been chief of the underground in the Danish police during the Nazi occupation of Denmark. Poul and his wife had risked everything to be true to their beliefs when they could have been collaborators.

The Danish delegation appreciated some help I had given them in finding war criminals, work that was in my line of duty. I was invited to Copenhagen to meet the royal family, Poul's family, and their resistance comrades. Justice Jackson's pilot flew us to Copenhagen in his C-47. On the way, we circled Poul's home, and I saw his wife and children standing in front of their house waving us on to Copenhagen. That was a big event in their lives!

I was taken to the Royal Palace for a banquet. I never could have imagined such an event happening to me. During the reception that preceded the banquet, I had a great conversation with a tall, distinguished man in white tie and tails. Finally he said, "Sir, you must excuse me now. I have to wait on table."

During the banquet, I was seated next to a royal prince. After extracting my life's story from me, he said, "What a life you have had! And to think I have spent my entire life as a prince and mostly in this palace!" All I could say was, "Well, it was fate for both of us."

We were served a feast. The Danes had obviously hidden a few things from the Germans! Soup, salad, fish, meat, sorbet, each course better than the last. It was all washed down with iced aquavit and beer, with many toasts to the Danish royal family, President Truman, General Eisenhower, Prime Minister Churchill, and Justice Jackson. Finally, there was a toast by Poul Kjalke to me, as a great and good friend of Denmark.

I assumed this was the end of the banquet, but I was wrong. After a pause, we were served huge dishes of strawberries, whipped cream, cake, coffee, and cognac. I was ready to burst because, not knowing what was to come next, I had eaten each course as though it were the last. I now understood the saying "He lived like God in Denmark." The informality of the occasion and the easy charm of the Danish royal family was infectious.

When the festivities were over, Poul brought up a police sedan, escorted by motorcycle riders, to take us to his home. His wife had prepared yet another feast of which I sadly could not eat one bite, so full was I from that royal banquet. In the following days I was feted as a conquering hero, when in fact I had performed only modest services for Denmark. There and then, I formed a lifelong attachment to people who became dear friends and to a wonderful country, to which I returned many times in my later life. Poul and I remained close until he died in 1993.

The Danes, a small and defenseless people, resisted evil when they could have been collaborators. The king of Denmark wore a yellow star, making himself an honorary Jew. That infuriated the Nazis, who had neglected to make it illegal for non-Jews to wear the star. They could not arrest the king. These most Nordic of peoples despised racism.

When the tribunal handed down its verdicts in the fall of 1946, I was an engineering student at Johns Hopkins, grateful to be alive, still trying to digest all that I had experienced. I had been lucky, miraculously fortunate — so much better off, in fact, than an Aryan boy in Gardelegen, who would have been sucked into Hitler's maelstrom. I was happy and proud to be an American citizen, appreciative of the values and ideals of this land of freedom, and optimistic about my future.

I have often been asked whether I thought the Nuremberg verdicts were just. Hjalmar Schacht, Franz von Papen, a German chancellor before Hitler, and Hans Fritzsche were exonerated. A savvy and sneaky diplomat, von Papen claimed he had tried in positions of ever lesser importance to moderate Hitler's behavior. Von Papen struck me as a man not to be trusted.

The least important defendant before the tribunal was Hans Fritzsche, who had been in charge of radio news under Goebbels. The Nazis hid all public evidence of the Holocaust and mistreatment of prisoners from their own people. That, however, was no evidence that Fritzsche had incited or committed crimes.

Göring, who killed himself with a cyanide pill after being condemned to death, should have been hanged. I thought he killed himself less out of fear of the noose than as a last act of defiance to his executioners. Ten Nazis were hanged. Seven of the defendants received jail terms, and three were exonerated. If there were any errors, I felt they had been on the side of lenience.

The crimes of which the defendants at Nuremberg were convicted were crimes punishable under any national law. Hitler had never bothered to repeal the German Articles of War, which German soldiers had not observed, nor the German constitution, which Hitler had ignored.

I considered then what to do with my life. For the first time, the choice was finally mine; I no longer needed to plot how to escape from yet another looming disaster or bet on the luck of the draw. I had offers to continue in government service. When Johns Hopkins University accepted me as a regular full-time student, I was excited and decided to enroll in its electrical engineering program. I had been drawn to things mechanical and electrical since I was a kid, and engineering also denoted a return to normalcy, which had eluded me for thirteen years, more than half my life, ever since I left Germany, where I grew up.

III

Family

*A*FTER TWENTY-THREE HOURS OF LABOR, I was still anchored so firmly in my mother's womb that forceps were needed to pull me into the world. When I was old enough to understand, Mother always let me know that she loved me despite the agony my birth had caused her. I was born on July 3, 1923, when Germany was in the throes of the worst inflation ever and most Germans, including my parents, were hard pressed to make ends meet. I was named Heinz Wolfgang Richard Sonnenfeldt, a long name, perhaps because I took so long to arrive!

To have her babies Mother went to Berlin, the *Grossstadt* (metropolis), from Gardelegen, the *Kleinstadt* (our country town). In Gardelegen birthing normally took place on kitchen tables, presided over by midwives of hefty build. If complications arose, there were no obstetricians to summon, only family doctors like my own mother and father. The most difficult births went to the local hospital, not always with happy results. So Mother, unlike anyone one else from Gardelegen, went to the most progressive clinic in Berlin, where she herself had trained.

Three years later, in better economic times, my only sibling arrived, also at Dr. Strassmann's clinic. Before Helmut's birth, my parents told me that the new baby would come out of Mother's belly, not from the stork, but they made me promise to keep this special knowledge to myself.

After Helmut's birth Mother developed melancholia, now called postpartum depression. Mother, Father, brother Helmut, and a live-in nurse went home to Gardelegen, while I was left to stay with Grandmother Martha and Grandfather Max Sonnenfeldt, who shared a large apartment with my aunt Kate and her husband Fritz in the posh Tiergarten quarter of Berlin.

Grandfather Max was a stout, bullet-headed man with a moustache and stubbly gray hair. He prided himself on his physical prowess, which he showed, even when nobody challenged it, by flexing his biceps. He wore shiny black ankle boots with laces tied in symmetrical bows, shirts with detachable, starched white collars, and a stickpin, always, in his preknotted tie. Around his rotund middle was draped the gold chain from his vest-pocket watch, which he adjusted every day on the stroke of noon. Grandfather Max kept a list of friends and family members with whom we were allowed to talk and a second list of those we had to shun. We had to be current with his list or we would be in trouble.

Grandfather was proud of his Prussian military training. At home he applied it by using his walking stick as a straight edge to detect any wrinkles the maids left after making the beds. Grandfather taught me how to wash myself from the bowl that was kept in the bedroom: first the face and, after two snorts, the chest, arms, hands, armpits, and crotch. Then wring out the washcloth before using a similar ritual to rinse off, snorts included.

Grandmother Sonnenfeldt had been born Martha Caro. Her family came from Breslau in Silesia (current-day Wroclaw, Poland). They traced their ancestry back to Martha's great-grandfather Nathan Steiner, who became a Prussian citizen by royal proclamation in the late eighteenth century as a reward for fabricating wicker ammunition baskets on credit for the king of Prussia. At the turn of the nineteenth century, the Caro family moved west to Berlin, which was then the fashionable place to live for German Jews.

My grandparents' third child, Aunt Kate, lived with them. She was prissy but nice. She had married Uncle Fritz, who had been orphaned at a young age. Too poor for a university education, Fritz was apprenticed at age fourteen to become a *Geschäftsmann* (trained business clerk). One day his boss sent him to the venerable Reichsbank to cash the payroll check. Fritz told the teller he had given him one hundred marks too much, whereupon the teller replied, "Run along, you young snot. A teller of the Reichsbank does not make mistakes." My uncle remonstrated once more, to no avail, and then did indeed run along. A week later, an obituary reported that a teller of the Reichsbank had committed suicide after auditors found a shortage of one hundred marks in his accounts. As Uncle Fritz later told this story, I realized that he was cut somewhat from that same cloth: a perfectionist and a bit of a tyrant. He dominated my aunt Kate as much as he spoiled her.

On Friday evenings in Berlin, although I was only three, I was allowed to eat at the great dining-room table with the assembled family. The Sonnenfeldts were no longer observant Jews, but they still congregated on Friday nights. The huge chandelier over the table had clear bulbs with pips at their ends and trembling, glowing yellow filaments within. We stirred sugar cubes in tall tea glasses with silver holders that kept the tea warm. When nobody was looking, I would suck on a sugar cube before secretly putting another one in my tea. From gilt picture frames on the walls, buxom, décolleté, long-necked, pale ladies made eyes at me. Some had elegantly dressed male companions gazing at them. Berlin was so different from Gardelegen.

Besides Aunt Kate, Father had another sister and a brother who usually joined us for Friday dinner. Aunt Erna, the oldest, had a heart of gold and a sunny disposition, but Mother mocked her so much and so unjustly for being stupid that I often felt protective of her. Uncle Hans was the youngest of the four Sonnenfeldt children and an enfant terrible. He had a huge *Schmiss*, a scar from a sword cut to the face, on his right cheek. The head of a so-called Germanic (a code word for anti-Semitic) fraternity had challenged Uncle Hans to a duel by uttering a slur on Jews, and then cut him across what he called his "big yap of a mouth."

Uncle Hans studied chemistry and opened a soap factory, which failed. His next attempt, making chocolates, was no sweet success either. He then studied *Volksökonomie*, a mixture of economics, tax, and constitutional law, in which he earned a doctorate. My mother always swore that the degree involved some trickery with his thesis.

As an unemployed Herr Doktor in the 1920s, Hans read about the gigantic Stynnes Company bankruptcy, which involved the loss of billions of marks. Armed only with his newly acquired academic knowledge of tax law, Uncle Hans persuaded the creditors of Stynnes to retain him. He won them a tax refund of over eight hundred million marks by representing them before the highest German court. His commission was eight million marks, more than two million dollars, then a huge sum in impoverished Germany.

Hans put eighty bundles of brand-new one-thousand-mark notes in a suitcase. In front of assembled parents, siblings, cousins-in-law, maids, and the elevator operator, he opened his suitcase and said to his father, "Count." Hans took care of the neediest who were there by his invitation. From that time until he left Germany eleven years later to escape the Nazis, he was known as the man with the golden touch. Well, not all he touched turned to gold, but he knew how to make things glitter.

My father, Walther Herbert Sonnenfeldt, grew up in Berlin amidst his middle-class Jewish family. He was the first person in his father's family to attend a university. His fraternity required each member to fight a duel; father's *Schmiss* was well earned.

Father was a third-year medical student at the outbreak of World War I in 1914. Along with most Germans, he volunteered for service in the Imperial German Army. Since he was not yet a licensed physician, he served as an "army doctor under supervision" for four years, on the western and eastern fronts, and he earned the coveted Iron Cross for valor under fire. After the war, when allegations circulated that German Jews had shirked military service in World War I, Father was always proud to recite statistics proving that, proportionately, Jews had suffered greater casualties than the general population.

During World War I, while tending tens of thousands of wounded and sick soldiers, Father gathered and honed the priceless medical experience that made him such an outstanding family doctor. There he developed his medical philosophy: "There are those who get better and there are those who will not get better, no matter what I do. A few I can help with medicines and by keeping them in bed. I am here to give people comfort and hope, and help them recover." Of my father it was said that he could help patients just by laying hands on them. To give patients confidence that they would get well without making promises that could not be kept was then the physician's art, and my father was its master.

While on leave from the Kaiser's army, Father visited his professors at the medical school in Berlin and met Mother, who was also a medical student. In the best tradition of German soldiery, he kissed her under a streetlamp. They were engaged not long after that. Father received extra academic credit for his military service and was exempted from a formal internship, and he graduated two years ahead of Mother.

Father became a doctor because he believed in service to humanity, and he settled in Gardelegen because a doctor was needed there. He and his mother, Martha, believed that people must never compromise their integrity, that they must bear misfortune and injustice silently and with dignity, and that good fortune was to be enjoyed with humility. One never bragged; it was for others to discover and extol one's good qualities. Father taught me, by example, to be accountable for my actions and never to blame anyone else for my deficiencies. He accepted Prussian mores, but he practiced them with modesty and gentleness, not showmanship or arrogance. It was easy to overlook what a strong character he had. Although he was usually mild in his expressions, he could fly into a frightful rage when sufficiently provoked.

One of the most wonderful experiences of my childhood was accompanying my father on his rounds. Carrying his doctor's bag, he visited many patients on foot. While we walked, he would give me mathematical puzzles to solve or talk to me about history and his own childhood. On those walks a bond formed between us, which lasts to this day. Though Father punished me for misdeeds when I was small, he and I never had a serious disagreement, never an argument when I was grown.

My relationship with my mother was far more complicated. Mother had been born Gertrud Liebenthal. Her parents lived in Brunsbuettelkog. An only child, she always believed her father had wanted a boy. She grew up to become a redheaded, statuesque lass. In her teens she secretly trained to be a Wagnerian soprano, but her father forbade an operatic career. "No child of mine will ever appear on a public stage!" he said. Though Mother never became a professional singer, she had a voice, with never a false note, that could shatter glass. I can hear her today, singing at the piano to her own accompaniment or in the choir, where her voice always stood out.

Mother was determined not to be a hausfrau like her mother, and decided to become a doctor "to show him," as she told us. This ambition was highly unusual for a woman at the time of World War I, but after her successful preparation at the University of Rostock, her father let her attend the famous Berlin University Medical School, considered perhaps the most famous in the world. She talked about her student days quite freely, frequently mentioning her strong *Geltungsbedürfnis* (the need to be important or be noticed), which to her was an immutable condition that had to be satisfied. At the university, Mother attracted animosity and admiration, as she did all of her life. Though she venerated some, she considered few to be her equals. She had admirable values and intentions, but she also caused a lot of friction and anger. From her tales of her life at university and the life I observed as her child, she was always involved in good deeds, heated controversies, and several spats, all at the same time.

Mother liked to tell stories about her family. She extolled Grandfather Hermann, her father, as the smartest of four brothers, even though he did not become a Herr Doktor like two of his siblings. Grandfather Hermann served as head of the city council at Brunsbuettelkog, a city at the North Sea end of the Kiel Canal, once considered as vital to the German navy as the Panama Canal was to the U.S. Navy.

Grandfather Hermann had become an incurable asthmatic during one afternoon of stubborn teenage anger when he ran twelve miles to beat home a horse-drawn stagecoach from which he had been ousted unjustly. When his gallbladder had to be removed later in life, he could not have general anesthesia because of his asthma. Instead, the surgeon applied local anesthetics progressively as he cut deeper. Hermann asked for a mirror to be mounted over his head so he could watch his own operation, slice by slice.

Grandfather Hermann survived World War I and the end of his beloved German monarchy by only three years. Though he was of Jewish origin, there was no nearby Jewish cemetery, and upon his death the local Protestant and Catholic ministers vied for the honor of burying him. The Protestant minister won and gave him a loving eulogy for which he was severely chastised by his bishop. This minister then rebuffed his bishop publicly for his lack of Christian charity.

Mother's mother, Grandmother Millie, lived in the shadow of her husband and received more affection from my father, her son-in-law, than from her husband or her daughter.

The uncle that Mother talked about most was Onkel Emil, a renowned physicist. He nearly became director of the Kaiser Wilhelm Institute, the leading German research facility, because its patroness, the empress of Germany, wanted him to head it. Naturally, she asked him to be baptized, since only Christians could hold positions of eminence in imperial Germany. Though

Uncle Emil was an agnostic and had married a Christian wife, he refused and was passed over.

It was explained to me that during the monarchy, which ended in 1918, Jews could not be commissioned officers, civil servants, or regular university professors unless the ruling monarchs granted them special privilege. Jews could earn this royal exemption by extraordinary efforts and by agreeing to be baptized, at which point they were usually regarded as hypocrites and careerists. In their ordinary lives, Jews admonished each other, "*Mach kein Risches*" (don't appear to be pushy). When I first heard that word *Risches* I was far too young to understand the duality with which German Jews viewed their lives: impress those above you but don't be too obvious about it!

In quite another vein, Mother also spoke proudly of her maternal grandfather Rosenbaum, a diminutive man. One balmy summer evening late in his life, he was sitting with his family in front of his house. A strapping young man passing by pointed to some rose bushes and teased the old man with a poem: "*Baumelein, Baumelein, du bist zu klein ein Baum zu sein*" (Little Rose Tree, Little Rose Tree, you are too small to be a real tree). At this, my octogenarian great-grandfather rose and broke the young man's arm. He was exonerated in court, on the grounds of "justified anger."

Friction often arose between Mother and my father's siblings. His sisters, Mother felt, paid insufficient homage to her university education, which they lacked. Sparks also flew between Mother and my uncle Fritz, to whose manly opinions she did not defer. As for Uncle Hans, Father's youngest sibling, he refused to take Mother seriously. When trying to lecture him, she once said to him, "Hans, I only tell you this because I am so outspoken!"

Frequently Mother directed her prodigious energy toward improving the behavior, appearance, or accent of others. And did she know how to make an entrance! Sweeping into the middle of a group, she expected all conversation to cease and for someone to rush up to her and take her coat and hat. She often carried her doctor's bag, even when there was no need for it. People had to know that she was not just Frau Doktor, the wife of a doctor, but a Doktor in her own right. As a child I knew instinctively that my mother would always take care of me, but her personality was so overpowering that I spent a lot of energy getting out from under her. I rarely felt comfortable in her presence.

But Mother was wonderful with patients who needed support and with anyone who sought guidance on any subject. In real emergencies, Mother could be uniquely effective. Our family would undoubtedly have perished in the Holocaust without her energy, courage, and ingenuity.

IV

Childhood

*W*HEN MOTHER RECOVERED FROM HER MELANCHOLIA, after my brother's birth, I returned to Gardelegen, where indoor toilets were rare, bathtubs with hot water practically unknown, and apartment houses did not exist. In Berlin, the telephones had dials, but in Gardelegen, phones still had cranks to ring chatty operators, who would call us back after they placed our call. In the 1920s, the primary means of communications were the postcard and the letter, not the expensive phone.

My first day of school was April 1, 1929, when I was nearly six. Without nursery schools or kindergartens in prewar Gardelegen, parents trained their young children to be ready for learning and to listen to the teacher.

There were forty-seven boys in my classroom. Herr Horn, the teacher, showed us how to blow our noses. "Hold your thumb over one nostril, blow hard out the other with all your might, and make sure you catch everything in the handkerchief, and then do the same on the other side and catch it. I don't want to see any snot at the end of anyone's nose," he said. He then inspected our faces, hands, and handkerchiefs to make sure that we had learned our lesson. To ask to go to the toilet during lessons was called *austreten* and was *verboten* (forbidden). Finally, he made clear that there would be no *schwatzen* (talking to one's neighbor) during class. The nose, the toilet, and *schwatzen* were the lessons for our first day. When my parents asked me how I had done, I said, "I passed."

Disciplinary problems were actually rare except with boys who failed to understand what they were supposed to do. For minor offenses they were rapped on the knuckles. For serious offenses, Herr Horn pulled down their pants and underpants and caned them while he showed their naked behinds to the class. Most of my classmates' parents had left school at age fourteen to work. I already knew, from my own parents, almost everything that was being taught in first grade, so Herr Horn regularly sent me on errands to the bank and the shops to cash his checks, pay his bills, and order bread and meat. Sometimes he sent me to visit his home and report back to him what his wife was doing.

My parents, like their contemporaries and their parents before them, convinced they knew what to do in every situation, never asked anyone for advice in raising their children. Basically, children were to suppress all kinds of urges that did not fall within the rules of good behavior. "Penis envy" and "sibling rivalry" had not yet been introduced to Gardelegen, though selfishness was known. Learning disabilities, attention deficit disorder, and other latter-day afflictions, even physical handicaps, were then characterized as bad habits, to be overcome by routine correction and hard work. When I complained about something, my mother or father would say, "Try harder." Individuality could be acquired by developing particular skills or by excelling in school or in sports, but not by what we would now call personality development. My parents, my mother particularly, made clear that I had to be best in everything if I wanted love and admiration, which had to be earned.

In those days, folk wisdom and maxims dictated how everyone, especially children, should behave. We grew up with "*Klage nicht, du musst dich abhärten*" (Don't complain; you must learn to be tough) and "You are noticing the speck in somebody else's eye and missing the ugly blemish in your own." We learned to accept that medicine was supposed to taste bad, like cod liver oil, to be effective. I remember a story about my grade-school superintendent, who got his daughters all dressed up for a Sunday outing at a country inn and then canceled it solely to teach them "frustration tolerance." The pedagogic principle involved was never questioned, although the fact that the father had lied to his daughters was talked about. In Gardelegen in the 1920s, obeying "the rules" was all-important. This attitude is exemplified by the old joke about the righteous German pedestrian who longed to be hit by a driver running a red light.

I had the reputation of being stubborn. Once, when trying to discipline me, Mother hit the corner of the dining room table instead of me and broke a bone in her hand. By contrast my brother, Helmut, a diplomat even at a very early age, had a way of deflecting Mother with wit. After his first music lesson he referred to her as *Die Dominante*, that musical term for the note that anchors melodies.

At home my parents would say, "Children are to be seen but not heard." Our dining room table, an ornate, rococo, ebony monstrosity, had bare-breasted women, like those on ship's prows, projecting out at the upper ends of the legs. The table had been inherited from my paternal grandparents and the linens upon it came from my mother's side of the family. While the adults talked, I remember running my fingers under the white linen tablecloth over those wonderful female bosoms, until my mother commanded, "Always keep your hands on the table!"

Although Mother never hesitated to correct us, she let Father mete out punishment for major infractions by us children, just as her father and his father had done. "Wait until your father hears about this," she would say. Of course, "waiting for Father to hear" was part of the punishment. Gentle as he was, Father did not hesitate to spank my behind. I can still hear him say, "Better for me to teach you what is right than for strangers to do it!" No parent feared that "punishment befitting the crime" would ever

produce bad results. On the contrary, punishment was a necessary and valuable learning experience, and my parents meted it
out, convinced it was beneficial.

My parents were without guile. They taught me how repre-
hensible it was to steal or to lie. I was told that all varieties of dishonesty were bad, including insincerity and pretense. I was taught
to confess and atone if I violated these precepts. I never heard my
parents trying to con anyone, though they may have made the
truth less shocking when dealing with incurable illness. They
impressed on me that carelessness might permanently damage
my health and that sexual promiscuity would cause irreversible
damage.

My parents' beliefs were an amalgam of Judaic morals and
Lutheran ideals. But their everyday actions were more Prussian
than anything else. You did not spend money on frills! You saved
wherever you could! You mended things before throwing them
out! You labored to achieve! You never bragged about having
money! You suffered without complaining! My parents had grown
up revering Prussian virtues, and to them it was a labor of love to
inculcate their children with the virtues they had been taught.

The one activity my parents and teachers left strictly to children was play. I don't ever remember a sympathetic adult presence when playing with other children. We were mostly told not
to make too much noise. Left to ourselves, our play often boiled
down to dominance of the fittest. When the less fit went bawling
to their mothers, the more fit were sometimes spanked. We established our own social order based upon physical strength, en-
durance, verbal skills, how many marbles we owned — and the
perceived rank of our parents. I was strong and smart and I exercised the Gardelegen prerogatives of a doctor's son who was
playing with children of parents with lesser rank. It was expected
of me to be the leader of the band. Today I marvel at the social
skills and graces of my grandchildren, who are trained at a very
young age to "share" and "take turns" in the supervised play of
nursery school and kindergarten.

On the sidewalk in front of our house, we played hopscotch and catch, shot marbles with the kids on the block, or walked on homemade stilts. Later, when we were eight or older, we played cops and robbers by the Wall, the remnants of a three-hundred-year-old rampart that surrounded the town. One section that drew us was the Salzwedeler Tor, a fortified portal whose crumbling parapets were off limits to us, but which we climbed nevertheless. Once a policeman saw us there and chased us. He came to the house, notebook in hand, to tell Mother. She put on her inquisitorial face and asked me to look her in the eye. "What were you doing on that forbidden parapet?" she asked. "That was somebody else, not me," I lied. Afterwards, I felt guilty but also a little pleased that I had gotten away with it.

Across from our house was a school for girls, but they might as well have lived in another world. Boys who played with girls were called sissies. I never attended a birthday party with girls and I never even talked to girls until I was fourteen.

By the time I was ten, I was allowed to play outside the walled town. Once, out in a grazing field, I climbed a tree to escape a bull. Perched in the branches, I had to wait till evening for the farmer to drive his herd back to the barn before I could get down. In the spring, the meadows were abloom with delicious wildflowers. I would lie there on the soft ground, with sweet-smelling grass, yellow buttercups, and fragrant violets all around, and dream the hours away as I watched towering bright white clouds drifting by in a blue sky.

To teach me about the harsh lives of our farming neighbors, when I was in fourth grade Father sent me to live a week with a peasant family in a neighboring village. Their house had a thatched roof, no running water or indoor toilets, no gas or electricity. The light of candles and kerosene lamps was too dim for reading after it got dark, but that did not matter, because the Bible was their only book. I was roused at four in the morning to help feed the pigs, cows, and chickens, all living under the same thatched roof with us. After a breakfast of black bread with lard and "malt" coffee, I rode on an oxcart with my hosts out to the fields to grub for potatoes. For lunch we ate more dark bread with salami or liver sausage, washed down with water from the pump. We drank out of metal mugs pocked with age. By then my back hurt so much I could hardly stand up. Back at their house for supper at five, so tired I could barely finish my meal, I was ready to go to sleep on a potato sack stuffed with straw. On Sunday, the animals still had to be fed at dawn, but the family stayed home to repair gear, cook for the week, wash bodies and clothes, and get ready for Monday morning. My hosts spoke that German peasant patois Plattdeutsch, which has now disappeared and which I have long since forgotten. These peasants never complained, they even sang when they labored. I learned to appreciate how much easier my life was in Gardelegen.

In autumn the winds came up and we flew kites, taller than we were. The old men who had nothing more important to do taught us how to build and fly those kites from the meadows outside the Wall. We could make them rise, dive, recover, and rise again, high over the town. There were crashes, of course, and kite wrecks could be seen every autumn on roofs, in trees, and even on the high steeple of the church.

After some older boys told us where to buy gunpowder ingredients, my friend Willy Grueder and I, then ten, built a cannon in my backyard. We felt like soldiers! First we dug a hole and embedded a piece of iron pipe in it. Next we dropped the powder charge and a big round stone down the tube, and then we lit the fuse, a waxed string. Fortunately, we had enough sense to run into the woodshed and wait for the big bang. When we came out, our entire "cannon" was gone.

We then heard a great commotion. "Something" had gone through the roof of the girls' school across the street and pierced the water tank in the attic. Water was pouring into the school below, although no one was hurt. Willy ran home and I went to my room. Soon after, Father came home and said, "Can you imagine what happened at the school?" I replied, "No, Father, I can't."

But there was that big black spot in our yard, and I confessed. I was spanked and had all of my privileges cancelled for many weeks. Willy and I were supervised more closely after that.

In winter we played ice hockey with homemade sticks and skates clamped to the soles of our high-laced boots. Once the steel runner of a sled ran right over my thumb, which became so infected that the nail had to be removed. My parents laid me on their bed, put a cotton mask over my face, sprinkled it with ethyl chloride, and told me to start counting. Now, more than seventy years later, I still remember the awful sweet smell of that anesthetic as I counted to eight and heard bells ringing in my ears. When I woke up, my thumb, minus the nail, was already neatly bandaged, and I heard Father say, "This ethyl chloride is really wonderful. He does not even have a hangover." With this I acquired fame of sorts, because none of my friends had ever been "put under." Usually my father reserved anesthesia for setting broken bones or working on dislocated shoulders. Carbuncles, furuncles, sprains, and strains rated no anesthetics or even painkillers in those days. People had to summon their courage before going to the doctor.

Every winter in Gardelegen senior citizens died of pneumonia or "grippe," the dreaded flu, and children succumbed to diphtheria and scarlet fever. In the cold months Father saw two dozen or more patients in his office before starting on his rounds, when he visited many more in their homes. Helmut and I were kept away from the sneezing, wheezing, feverish patients on the first floor of our house, and fortunately we were spared diphtheria, scarlet fever, and typhus, all quite common in those days. We were vaccinated against smallpox, but we did have the usual childhood diseases — measles, German measles, chicken pox, and whooping cough. When we ran a fever, Mother wrapped us, head to toe, in towels soaked in ice-cold water. As our body heat warmed the towels, we sweated profusely for the prescribed hour. We were then toweled off and put in clean pajamas to go to sleep. For high fevers, this treatment was repeated several times daily. I hated and dreaded the treatment even more than the diseases it was supposed to cure.

When I got the cold towel treatment in the 1920s, physicians had only a limited arsenal with which to combat disease. There was aspirin for everything, and morphine was dispensed generously to ease acute suffering of the terminally ill. There were liver pills, castor oil, and insulin, which had just been discovered to control diabetes. Ultraviolet radiation was used for everything from tuberculosis to acne. Foul-smelling black ointments, with ingredients from faraway countries, were smeared on the skin to cure infections, and later there was protection against diphtheria. Yet in those days, patients, even those who had to be washed before they could be diagnosed, had absolute faith in doctors, who needed real talent to give patients confidence and help them recover without making promises that could not be fulfilled.

People then simply accepted that serious diseases might not be cured. Father once cautioned the family of an elderly pneumonia patient that he might not live through the night. Next day, he saw a coffin in the family's living room. As he started to express his condolences to the family, the son told him, "No, no. Father is still alive, but we found a bargain for the coffin." The father went on to live several more years. I always wondered what they did with that coffin.

What did people do all day in Gardelegen? Plain living took a lot of time in those days. Cooking, baking, cleaning, shopping, and a little gardening kept the hausfrau busy. Most residents grew their own vegetables, either behind their house or on a plot near the town limits. Many families kept chickens and rabbits. There was always work to do.

Townspeople did have some leisure hours. Mother sang in a choir called the *Liedertafel*. Women also played cards, dominoes, or mah-jongg. There were kaffeeklatsches in the afternoon. Men favored bicycle and motorcycle clubs and hunting, while numerous political parties held meetings in the evenings. Most families had no radio, and the local newspaper took about an hour to read. Even mechanical gramophones were a rarity.

Privacy was scarce in Gardelegen. Houses joined each other, wall to wall, in long rows, and there was no place to hide except in the recesses of one's home or in the bushes outside town. Some houses even had large oval mirrors mounted on swivels outside their windows. By peeking into the mirror from inside, one could observe one's neighbors on the sidewalks without being seen. These mirrors were called *Spione*, spies, and what was seen in them was whispered about. Summer evenings, people sat in front of their houses and chatted with their neighbors while watching passersby. Reputations and nicknames, once acquired, were never shed. Everyone knew what to expect from everyone in town.

Our street was named Sandstrasse. We owned a large two-story stucco house that fronted a street corner. Its walls joined those of our neighbors. The house had a finished attic and a deep cellar. From the cellar, a secret passage joined others that led to the town hall, remnants of defenses built during the wars of the Middle Ages. On the ground floor were my parents' offices, quarters for our live-in help, and a large hall where we kept our bicycles, sleds, and bad-weather boots. Our living quarters were on the second floor. Behind our house were sheds for tools and firewood, a so-called laundry kitchen, and a huge pit for garbage and ashes.

Stoves heated our home and in the morning, to keep the ashes from blowing about, we always splashed water on them as we carried them through the house to the large trash pit in the backyard. There was no regular garbage collection in Gardelegen. Every few months the horse-drawn *Müllwagen* (trash wagon) pulled up and the garbage would be shoveled out of the pit into wheelbarrows. Huge rats would scurry around as I tried shooting them with my air rifle.

Our indoor toilets were considered very advanced. They were in the coldest and draftiest of cubicles, and the water reservoirs, high up on the wall, always dripped, while the lead pipes sweated and leaked at their joints. Most people did not use toilet-paper rolls, but cut newspapers into squares and hung them on a nail by the toilet. That is what our maids used; the family used real toilet paper.

In the winter we wore heavy woolen sleeping suits to bed. Before going to school in the morning, five full days and a half day on Saturday, Helmut and I washed, or at least we were supposed to wash, using water from a ewer that sat in the porcelain washbasin on top of our chest of drawers. The last thing we did was brush our teeth and spit into the basin. I can see that gray soapy water now. On some winter mornings the water froze in the pitcher. We had no antiperspirants — they did not yet exist — but the summer climate in Gardelegen was more moderate than in America, so we sweated less. We used tar soap, lava stone, and stiff-bristle brushes for stubborn dirt on the hands.

We changed underwear and bathed once a week. I remember our young maid, Marta, and getting close to her when she hid under the bed with me while playing hide and seek. By midweek I could smell her body odor as a mixture of something unpleasant and strangely intimate. Our house had a full-size bathtub, unusual for Gardelegen, and a wood-fueled hot water heater, which was fired up and kept going on Saturday afternoons for the family to take baths, one at a time. Our two live-in maids went last. The bathroom adjoined the room I shared with my brother Helmut, and the door between the rooms had a keyhole — you remember those big old-fashioned keys? Helmut and I took turns and vied to observe our nude maids through that keyhole until they got wise and hung a towel over our observation post.

On the first Monday of the month, the laundress came in to wash our clothes in the laundry behind the house. A huge woman wearing wooden clogs, she scrubbed everything on washboards before boiling the laundry, whites first, in huge kettles heated by a roaring wood fire. Sheets and other flat pieces were run through our own hand-cranked "cold" press or taken to a steam-heated clothes mangle that was run by two jolly women down the street. Everything else was pressed with heavy irons, one of which was heating on a coal fire while its mate was in use. Later we got a gas stove that would heat irons without covering them with soot. Doing laundry took several days. Clothing we outgrew was passed on to needy children in the neighborhood.

Once a year, mother bought a live pig for *Schlächtermeister* (master butcher) Fritz Schulz to slaughter in our backyard. After pulling the pig from his oxcart, he coaxed the porker through the front door of our house, past my father's office, and finally out to the backyard. The pig squealed all the way to its impending execution. My mother and the maids had already prepared huge kettles of boiling water. Master Fritz placed a pipelike device, with a charge inside, on the pig's head. Then he banged its top with a hammer, there was an explosion, and the pig squealed loudly and repeatedly before toppling over. Its legs would twitch for minutes before Fritz would cut its throat and catch the warm blood in a pot for use in sausage and other delicacies. This technique was considered more humane and certainly was less messy than the old way of slitting the live pig's throat and bleeding it to death, while everyone held on as it struggled to get away.

Cutting up the pig, boiling various parts, saving the skin for the tanner, cutting off the tail for the kids to play with, and discarding the refuse took all day. The crows circled overhead, waiting to dive for a morsel, while neighborhood cats and dogs lay in wait for a chance to dart out suddenly after a piece of meat or offal. Mother and the maids, in blood-spattered aprons, worked alongside Fritz. Afterwards the inspector would arrive and put his blue stamp on the meat, certifying it was free of trichina parasites. He would get a schnapps, German potato spirits, for his efforts. Pork made up a significant part of our diet. In our deep cellar we hung dozens of smoked sausages and preserved salted meat in barrels. Although the backyard was hand-scrubbed when all was done, the smell of butchering lingered for days. Father and I hated it.

The horse-drawn milk wagon came by our house every morning, with the dairyman ladling tepid milk from his tall tin cans into our tin pitchers. Raw milk, as it was delivered, was not safe to drink. It was boiled at home in a huge iron pot to kill tuberculosis bacilli. I hated the skin that formed as the milk cooled, and always longed for the bottled milk of Berlin.

In the 1920s, the dozen automobiles in Gardelegen were never used for anything that could be accomplished on foot or by riding a bicycle. To start cars in those days, motors had to be hand-cranked and then idled to warm up, or they would sputter and stall. An American car with an electric starter was the height of luxury. In winter the drivers would cover the radiators with blankets. When the weather was bad, plastic side curtains kept most of the rain, cold air, or snow out of the passenger compartments of so-called cabriolets, enclosed cars without metal roofs in which we sat with rabbit fur "touring rugs" draped over our knees.

To avoid the endless, bone-smashing hand cranking in winter, one of my father's drivers kept a horse to start the car by pulling it. If the motor caught but stalled again as the driver let out the clutch, the straining horse would be brought to a sudden halt, his hoofs slipping on icy or wet pavement. If the motor kept running, the car would often lurch forward and hit the horse in the rear. When the driver braked, the motor would die again. Then, to the delight of gaping bystanders, the entire sequence would be repeated, with much neighing, snorting, and rearing of the horse, which, now wise to the scenario, needed to be whipped to pull the car again. That spectacle always brought the burghers out of their houses.

Like my parents, most of our neighbors lived above their businesses. Next door to us lived *Mahlermeister* (house painter) Fehse and his sister, Anna. She wore dark and bulky skirts with bodices to match and wooden clogs, year in, year out. She always smelled of kitchen. He was unkempt, with paint drippings all over his clothes, and he usually tumbled about, slightly drunk. Next to Fehse was the bespectacled carpenter Schuehler, whose shop smelled of glue he prepared by boiling horse and fish bones in a pot atop a coal fire.

Next to Schuehler was Gaede's bicycle shop. Gaede wore blue mechanic's clothes, and his iron gray hair had a parting that seemed to be laid down with a ruler. Bicycles were the universal mode of transportation. Mine had a heavy frame with balloon tires and a carrier on the back. Gaede let me help him after school when I was six, and my mother got me a special blue shirt for this. I worked on those old bikes that did not coast, even when going downhill. I learned how to repair punctures and even how to put spokes in wheels. I couldn't wait to come home from school to work at Gaede's.

Down the street from Gaede's shop was a ladies' hair salon. I used to hate the smell of the burning wood alcohol that heated the dryers and curlers mixed with the scents of baby powder and lilac that clung to the coifed ladies as they emerged. Across the corner was Behrens's motorcycle and auto shop, with a gasoline pump out front with huge glass jars that metered the Leuna Benzin, as we called the pungent synthetic. When I was eight, I graduated from Gaede's bicycle repair to Behrens's motorcycle shop for after-school work. Later I was allowed to tag along with the electrician and the plumber, and helping them, I realized later, was handy training for the future.

Adjoining Behrens's was Mangelsen's bakery, with its delicious aroma of yeast and dough. Mangelsen baked crispy rolls that his daughter brought to our doorstep each morning. He also made that delicious German peasant bread, baked with water, which smells so good when fresh. Farther down the street, Garley beer, dating back to 1459, was brewed. Beyond the brewery lived *Gewittermahler* (thunderstorm painter) Huesch, so known because dark clouds and lightning were his favorite — perhaps his only — subject.

Also in our neighborhood lived a wagon-wheel maker, who fashioned hubs, spokes, and rims by hand, the way they had been made for centuries. Down the street a tailor sat sewing our clothes, hunchbacked and cross-legged, among his steaming irons. He had tuberculosis. "Don't let him breathe on you!" Mother implored. Nearby were a *Kneipe* (modest pub), a shop for wooden barrels, and a smithy, where horses were shod to the hiss of the bellows. I can still see the roaring flame and hear the clang of the heavy hammer swung by the musclebound smith, his naked perspiring torso protected only by a leather apron as he pounded the cherry red iron. I would recognize today the smell of smoke from a charred hoof, accompanied by the neighing and stomping of the horses.

Two doors down from ours along the smaller of the two intersecting streets, the narrow Rendelbahn, lived a woman with two daughters. My bedroom window was close to their house and sometimes I heard screams and shouts in the middle of the night and the slamming of doors. The women were never seen on the street during the day but often leaned out of the windows. My parents explained to me that they had many boyfriends who came to visit them. That was a normal part of life in Gardelegen.

Traffic was banned from our street when peasants congregated for the monthly *Pferdemarkt* (horse market). By midmorning the pavement was loaded with steaming droppings, from which sparrows picked out morsels of half-digested horse feed. The horses snorted as traders wrenched their jaws open to inspect their teeth before haggling over price. On other days there was a cow market. The ground was then covered with green manure and cats tried to catch a little milk from dripping udders. Late on market afternoons, after business was concluded, boisterous traders celebrated at Kroekel's pub, three houses down from ours. After downing gallons of beer, they would emerge to urinate in the street's gutter. The reek of beer and urine mingled with the lingering smell of horse or cow excrement made for a brew both repulsive and hearty.

Smells permeate my childhood memories of Gardelegen. Today, seventy years later, I instantly recognize the smells of cows, horses, and pigs; the scents of pines, cedars, freshly picked mushrooms, and potatoes; the odors of coal and wood smoke from our various stoves. I vividly recall the smells of our bakery, the butcher shop, the smithy, the hair salon, and the drugstore. Nor will I forget the odor of the public soup kitchen during the worst Depression years: the aroma of potato soup mixed with the stench of the unwashed, destitute crowd.

V

Rise of the Nazis

*A*T KROEKEL'S PUB, where I went to fetch my father's evening draft beer, I heard coarse jokes and habitual xenophobic comments. The pub itself had a tile floor and stone walls that had once been whitewashed and were now a peeling gray. The owner, a giant of a man in corduroy pants and a dark shirt covered by a blue apron, worked behind a crude bar with three big porcelain-topped tap handles. The men, in sweat-stained working clothes, stood by the bar or sat on hefty wooden chairs around pine tables whose tops had crude pictures of naked women and ditties smeared on them. Chunks of wood had been carved out of the tabletops with pocket knives or daggers. There were no women patrons at Kroekel's, only a hefty fat-faced barmaid wearing woolen knee socks on legs that looked like tree stumps, shod with wooden clogs. She wore a spotted apron, once white, that bulged over her chest, and she screeched when patrons tried to grope her. Once I saw her swing a mug of beer into a man's face.

At Kroekel's *Kneipe*, the conversation for the most part had an undertone of schadenfreude. The crowd maligned and derided those whom they blamed for tough times, usually the current German government, and declared that nothing was as good as German food, clothing, literature, or "German blood."

In Kroekel's pub and everywhere else around me, there festered a contempt and hatred for anything foreign. Russians were considered inferior and brutish; Poles were derided as slovenly and backward; Austrians and Italians were untrustworthy and artful. The French were degenerate, Bavarians were inferior to Prussians, and as for Jews, they were dirty, sly, and deceitful. In Gardelegen only the English and the Scandinavians were exempt from contempt. The former, though regarded as perfidious, were viewed with awe because of their age-old habit of winning wars and their penchant for staring down Germans. There was nothing good-natured here, only the hard-edged prejudice that fueled not only German but European ethnic hostilities for centuries and still does. Chronic xenophobia reached a crescendo after Germany's economy tanked in 1931.

During the Great Depression of 1930–33, the unemployment rate in Germany was more than twice that of America. Father and Mother became known as "the paupers' doctors" because they did whatever was needed even when they did not get paid. A farmer once gave Mother a dozen eggs instead of money for a house call. While crossing the farm's courtyard, she spilled the eggs out of her doctor's bag onto a pile of cow dung. She gathered up the unbroken eggs, wiped them, and put them back in her bag to bring home. Nothing was wasted in those days. Even apples on the verge of rotting were stewed and baked into pies. However, my family never went hungry. My typical lunch at school was peasant rye bread with lard and home-smoked pork sausage. No fruit or cake. I got water to drink from the pump in the schoolyard. We were relatively well off!

Mother's charitable impulses were strong during the devastating Depression. *Schnorrers* (transient beggars) often rang the doorbell of our second-floor living quarters. Some were penniless Jews who had made their way to Gardelegen from "the East." (It was made clear to me that we were far superior to them.) Mother usually offered the schnorrers food to be eaten on a chair outside the door. Once a beggar reluctantly accepted some freshly made pea soup and later rang the bell to return a very clean plate with thanks. The next day, when Mother took her umbrella from the stand outside the door and opened it, she was showered with cold pea soup. Evidently, not all charity was rewarded.

In the Germany between World War I and Hitler's Third Reich, equality among Germans was more slogan than reality. "Germans are either at your throat or at your feet" was best illustrated by Germans assuming the roles of inferiors or superiors, changing their miens and postures instantly when they turned their backs on an inferior to address a superior.

I noticed that when my mother met someone she considered of superior rank, she would switch to the diffident demeanor she expected from beggars; she would become attentive and respectful rather than assertive, and would speak in a small voice. I noticed the same dual mode of behavior in everyone else. Thus I learned the exact pecking order among our neighbors. I also noticed that my father never changed his dignified demeanor, no matter whom he talked to, but workmen took off their hats or caps when they talked to my father, the doctor — before he became a despised Jew.

A man who owned a tractor became *Herr Traktorbesitzer* (Mr. Tractor Owner) and the baker was *Herr Bäckermeister* (Mr. Master Baker), but the common worker was not even addressed as "Herr."

During the Weimar Republic (1919–34), class and rank were nominally based on education, not overtly on inherited titles and wealth as had been the case in imperial Germany. Education, though, still depended on a family's wealth. A high school education not only cost parents money but also meant the students couldn't work full time to support the family, as they could if they legally left school at age fourteen. In the Weimar Republic, the proletariat could rise in political parties, but those without money to acquire higher education remained economically and socially disadvantaged.

Intellectually, my parents rejected militarism as befitted their political liberalism, but our society had not yet shed its traditional reverence for uniforms, heroes, and victories. And we, like most Germans, resented the injustices of the Versailles treaty with its reparations and prohibitions of national equality. My family owned huge, ornate, cloth-covered books depicting heroic military events in German history. There were lithographs of Prussia's Blücher defeating Napoleon at Waterloo, although England's victorious Duke of Wellington was not mentioned. There were stirring pictures of Prussian victories over Denmark, Austria, and France, wars won by Bismarck, who fashioned the Second Reich, or German Empire (1871–1918), from a collection of principalities. Paul von Hindenburg, a hero and our current president, was shown on his horse with saber in hand, defeating the Russian hordes in 1914.

With a flashlight under the covers, I read glowing accounts of Germany's victorious march into Belgium and France at the beginning of World War I, but not one word about the surrender of German generals in 1918 as they tried keeping the Allies from advancing onto German soil. No, I believed that a traitorous left-leaning government had forced German generals to capitulate and accept *"das Diktat,"* the Treaty of Versailles. The lie that Germany's army was stabbed in the back and forced to surrender by a Jew-dominated government was endlessly repeated by the Nazis and the Right. The moderates who knew that the Kaiser's generals had capitulated did not want to be tarred with signing the surrender. Yes, most Germans in those days believed that they had been cheated of victory by treachery! When I was reading those books by flashlight, under the covers, Germans were thirsting to restore their pride and erase their unfair humiliation.

The Treaty of Versailles condemned Germany as the sole instigator of World War I (a questionable proposition) and deeply humiliated this nation, which treasured its martial prowess. Anger and humiliation were compounded by economic disasters. Runaway inflation in the 1920s, when I was born, rendered German currency worthless, while the Great Depression of the 1930s left millions unemployed and hungry, and hundreds of thousands homeless. Germans wanted to be freed from the treaty's provisions, on which they blamed Germany's lack of international bargaining power. And, as far as a child can feel such things, those feelings were mine.

My heart beat faster when in fourth grade gym class I was taught to march like a soldier, with a stick on my shoulder representing a rifle. My family grieved over lost German glory and longed for the resurrection of German pride. In fourth grade, when I was ten, I increasingly began hearing Adolf Hitler's name. He was a veteran, a brave and decorated volunteer lance corporal, who had suffered gassing in the trench warfare. He proclaimed over and over how much he hated war. From him we heard promises of food and work for the German people and a pledge to restore German national pride and honor. During the Weimar Republic which followed the Kaiser's rule, Germans yearned for their past days of glory and might, and many associated it with imperial Germany while democracy meant poverty and humiliation.

I remember the never-ending election campaigns of the early 1930s. Germany was torn by bitter, often lethal, strife in the streets. The Left (the Communist Party and the Social Democratic Party) fought the Right (the Nazis and the monarchist German National Party) with fists, with bats, and sometimes with guns. The Zentrum, a Catholic-based moderate party, was not strong enough to balance out the extremists. Although Hitler already had the Right in his corner, he needed to acquire centrist support to be appointed chancellor, and so he moderated his message. In 1932 and 1933 he did not often mention the vicious race hate he espoused in *Mein Kampf* and later practiced with such devastating effect.

My family owned one of the few radio sets in Gardelegen, and Father invited the Protestant *Pfarrer* (pastor) and the Catholic *Vater* (priest) to listen to the 1932 election results. As far as I know,

105

these two churchmen met socially only in our house. Strange now to think that I heard my Jewish father saying, "That man Hitler sounds like a pretty sane man," while the two Christian clergymen objected.

In the mid-1932 election, Hitler won less than 35 percent of the votes, and for the next six months he contributed to the failure of successive coalition governments from which he was excluded. Finally, on January 30, 1933, President Hindenburg appointed Hitler chancellor, giving him a turn to head yet another coalition government. The heads of all other parties had failed to put Germany back on her feet, and everyone I knew expected Hitler's turn to fail. "Give him enough rope and he will hang himself," it was said, "and then we can finally have a sensible government."

Within four weeks of Hitler's appointment as chancellor, on the evening of February 27, 1933, the empty Reichstag building, the physical home of the German Parliament, was set on fire. I remember hearing it on the radio. The Nazis blamed communists for the arson. Hitler then persuaded President Hindenburg to declare an emergency and issue a decree, as authorized by the Weimar constitution, "to avert anarchy and to preserve democracy in Germany."

It has been suspected that the Nazis set the fire and Hindenburg's decree gave the chancellor, Adolf Hitler, instant, unlimited, and unchecked powers. Hitler used them to suspend civil liberties and void the power of the courts to review as well as reverse government action. Göring, then the lone Nazi minister in Hitler's cabinet, headed the police, and he deputized 70,000 storm troopers as auxiliary policemen to arrest opposition leaders "for their own protection," as the Nazis proclaimed. Göring instructed the Brown Shirts to shoot first and ask questions later, and quite a number of killings followed. Hitler then called for new elections on March 5, 1933, earning only 44 percent of the votes. Now the Nazis imprisoned enough additional opposition delegates to maintain a bare quorum while guaranteeing themselves a two-thirds majority in Parliament.

On March 24, 1933, less than two months after becoming chancellor, Hitler had the parliament that he had just denuded of opposition vote him unlimited powers over all aspects of German life, and send itself home. Goebbels, the Nazi propaganda minister, recorded the triumph in his diaries: "We always wanted to come to power legally, but not use it legally, once it was ours!"

There is a German word that has no precise equivalent in any other language: *Zivilkourage*. It means the courage to stand up for what is right, as distinct from the soldier's courage to face death. Long before Hitler demanded total obedience, Germans were loath to stand up against anyone in authority or, God forbid, defy a uniformed representative of the State. When rank or authority should have been challenged, deference and hypocrisy and submission, not *Zivilkourage*, were the norm.

At the time, I was too young to grasp that Hitler had conquered Germany. I doubt that many adults understood. In fact, the Nazis were joked about. Hermann Göring was referred to as "Gering," a German word meaning "little nothing," a play on his enormous girth, and Joseph Goebbels, the propaganda minister, was nicknamed "Gebells," meaning "yapping little dog."

On April 1, 1933, the Nazis ordered a nationwide one-day boycott of Jewish stores and professionals. When our senior maid brought me home from school that afternoon, two Nazi storm troopers were standing in front of our house in their brown uniforms, jackboots, and military caps. Others stood in clumps up and down the street. But the Gardelegen police, armed with revolvers, stood by and preserved order. Many of Father's patients, even those with no illnesses, came to his office that day to show their loyalty to him. Father noted in his diary that his practice continued to grow for two more years until 1935, as he and Mother were the most popular doctors in a town that needed them. But by 1935, people in Gardelegen no longer dared demonstrate against the Nazis, even as mildly as visiting their doctor.

Up to 1933, I had never attended a Jewish religious service or a ceremony in my home. I knew I was Jewish mainly because I had noticed I was circumcised while other German boys were not. On that day of boycott in 1933, my parents called on all the other Jewish families in Gardelegen, including several they had assiduously shunned for years. The Jews of Gardelegen had never been a cohesive community, but on that day they shared their misery.

April 1, 1933 was a turning point in my life. Until that day, I had been a German boy, a doctor's son, the smartest in my class, a natural and popular leader of kids around me. Suddenly I was denigrated as a member of an allegedly odious race to which were imputed heinous crimes against Germany. My family was vilified by our government as enemies of the people.

Yet, incredibly, then and for at least two more years, we believed that the Nazi government was only temporary and that President Hindenburg would restrain Hitler from going too far. I can still hear the adults, Jewish and gentiles (those who still conversed with us), proclaiming that Hindenburg was only giving Hitler enough rope to hang himself. There was no "hangman," no one with the power to remove Hitler.

My world began to change, slowly at first. In 1933 I began *gymnasium* (high school) and I had my last pleasant experience. We were taken to a swim test, and I was the only one of my age to dive head first off the high board. Before everyone realized that it was I, the Jew boy, they applauded. Soon after, I sat by myself in class, and fellow students shunned me during recesses and vacations. I began to hate school.

One of the first clicks of the Nazi ratchet was the establishment of the Hitler Youth. Already trained at home and in school to obey and perform as commanded, many of my classmates joined for the camaraderie, the engraved dagger with a swastika, and the new uniforms. The boys went to rifle ranges to practice gunnery, sports, self-defense, and hand-to-hand fighting. The girls joined the BDM (*Bund Deutscher Mädel*, the Association of German Girls) and they, too, trooped through town while they sang patriotic songs as they headed for camping and games.

Hitler Youths were forbidden to play or converse with Jews. Years later, Mother recalled how Helmut, then only seven, stood behind the window curtains, upset he could not join the Hitler Youths singing and marching in the street below to rousing music, ignoring the anti-Semitic venom that fanatic counselors drilled into those young minds. I still remember one song, "*Und wenn das Judenblut vom Messer spritzt*" (When Jewish blood spurts from my knife), sung to a cheerful fast march. Still, so far, those were only words.

In 1934, President Hindenburg died suddenly. Hitler gave him a Wagnerian state funeral, and then cast aside the constitution. He abolished the presidency and appointed himself supreme leader of Germany. All public employees — the military, the civil service, police, teachers, and the judiciary — now had to take a loyalty oath not to the constitution, not to their country, but to Hitler, the Führer. The Nazis' top jurist proclaimed, "In the old days we used to ask, 'What is the law?' Now we ask only, 'What does the Führer want?'" Thus Hitler became the State. And Germans transferred their customary deference and loyalty from the German nation to Hitler personally.

Though nobody was threatening Hitler, he needed what every dictator needs — enemies. He began to pour verbal abuse on England, France, Poland, and Czechoslovakia, although he saved most of his wrath for the Soviet Union. He looked for enemies inside Germany, too. Having already destroyed his political opposition, Hitler now targeted Jews as his domestic enemies. The odious hatred, the envy and falsehood, the half-baked distortions of history, and the venom of a spurned artist, all that he had spelled out in *Mein Kampf*, were now unleashed, however gradually.

Meanwhile, Hitler's popular support was broadening between

1933 and 1935. He was accomplishing for the German economy what Roosevelt was accomplishing for America: pulling his country out of the Depression. Incomes were rising, unemployment was dropping as deficit spending created work.

Neither Protestant clergy nor the Catholic Church interceded or voiced moral concerns. The newspapers were in Nazi hands. The Rundfunk, the state-controlled radio, had become Goebbels's propaganda outlet, and listening to foreign broadcasts became a punishable offense. Books that did not conform to Nazi doctrine were burned. Even to question Hitler's actions, let alone to criticize what was happening or to oppose him in any way, became a crime.

Hitler proceeded very gradually, and Jews and others repeatedly deluded themselves into believing that each move Hitler made was the last, and that they could live with it. But persecution of Jews became serious in 1935 with the so-called Nuremberg Laws. Those flagrant violations of citizen rights ratcheted up the Nazi grip on all Jews in Germany by excluding them from money-earning occupations.

In March 1936, Hitler bedazzled the Germans and ignored his own military advisors by marching the German army back into the Rhineland. This was a rich industrial area of Germany that bordered France, Belgium, the Netherlands, and Luxembourg. The Treaty of Versailles had mandated that it be a demilitarized zone. Germany had not yet rearmed, but powerful France and England, well-armed Czechoslovakia, Poland, and the mighty Soviet Union incomprehensibly let Hitler move troops into the Rhineland without serious objections. Germany's archenemies, by their passivity, endorsed Hitler. Hitler's success made him a genuine German hero. By letting Germany break the treaty that the victors of World War I had imposed on her, they allowed German dignity to be restored. People felt as if Siegfried, the legendary German hero, had risen from the ashes! Many Germans started singing songs about the Rhine, the Lorelei, and the Nibelungen. Flags flew across Germany. My family, though outcast by the Nazis as Jews, continued to feel like Germans, and we rejoiced with the rest of Gardelegen. Yes, we still felt like Germans!

With the German state already in his possession, Hitler had now captured not just the Rhineland but the German soul. We should have understood then that there was no one left to remove Hitler. Not his legions of brown- and black-shirted fanatics, not the army whose fears about marching into the Rhineland had been ignored but which was now being rearmed, and not the sixty million Germans who went along for the ride. In 1936, we still did not yet equate Germany with Nazism or Nazism with extermination. And why would we? We still believed that Hitler would calm down, become more moderate. Didn't he promise that each new crisis he created would be the last? The commitment to anti-Semitism asked of Germans up to then involved no outrageous acts by ordinary citizens, only support of new laws. When most Jews were not alarmed enough to leave Germany, why should most Germans have been upset?

Shunned and humiliated but not yet mortally wounded by the Nazis, many German Jews began discovering their Jewish religion. Whether this sprang from a need for redemption, from forced identification, or from guilt, I cannot say. But suddenly I found myself with parents embracing Judaism. I did not find it appealing. After my bar mitzvah in 1936, to which I agreed with no enthusiasm, I refused to have anything more to do with religion. I knew that lack of religious observance by German Jews had not caused Nazism and that a reversion to ancient Jewish rituals would not cause Hitler's demise. I rejected adopting Jewish rituals solely because Hitler was persecuting Jews and demeaning their religion. To me that wasn't "showing" him; it was caving in.

After the Olympic Games in Berlin in 1936, a public-relations triumph that Hitler did not want to spoil with scenes or tales of anti-Semitic terror, the Nazi ratchet clicked more frequently. When patients could no longer collect insurance payments for treatment by a Jewish doctor, my father lost most of his income.

My mother, ever resourceful, converted several rooms in our large house into a convalescent home for Berlin Jews, and she converted another room into a birthing suite, since there were few Jewish midwives. That produced some income.

Between 1933 and 1938, Helmut and I saw all of our friends one by one turn away from us. The livelihoods and social standing of their parents would be in dire jeopardy if the children associated with Jews. "Jews Not Wanted Here" signs appeared in stores, and children jeered at me, calling me a smelly, stealing pervert. Once, a gang of twenty or so boys chased me as the Dirty Jew, until I threw some stones at them and got away. In my early teens, I learned what it meant to be completely isolated from playmates — and to wonder ever so secretly whether there was any truth in the vile epithets that I had to endure. With no friends, I developed hobbies like building radios for my family.

In the summer of 1937, Helmut and I briefly escaped Nazi society. We spent our vacation at the home of an old friend of Mother in Danzig (now Gdansk, Poland). The Treaty of Versailles had established Danzig as a free city under the supervision of the League of Nations. While its residents spoke German and followed German customs, only a minority belonged to the Nazi party, and the city was not subject to Nazi laws. I idealized life in Danzig. At fourteen, I also had my first romance there. Her name was Marianne. She was a niece of our hostess, a little older than I, and she looked good in bathing suits. We grew inseparable and, in the manner of young lovers, talked endlessly, for which our brothers teased us.

Romance and freedom both ended after that summer of 1937 in Danzig. The only two Jewish girls in Gardelegen were the wrong age and they did not attract me. It was now, of course, illegal for me to date girls who were Aryan — a Nazi word for Caucasian, often Nordic, gentiles — although I secretly looked at some, and some looked at me. Had I become romantically entangled with a gentile girl, I would have gone to prison and the girl would have been spat on in the street as a sluttish Jew-lover. So looks remained secret and were not consummated by dates.

More serious than my aborted romantic life was the fact that in 1937 we finally understood we had to leave Germany if we wanted to live. Mother took charge of our emigration.

She contacted a Jewish family in Baltimore, Maryland, that had passed through Gardelegen a decade before on its way from Russia to the United States. These acquaintances now owned a grocery store in Baltimore, and they invited Mother to visit them in April 1937. There, with the help of a Jewish relief organization, she found the sponsor that was required for an American immigration visa. Mother's return from America was a joyous time, as we could now anticipate getting a visa to the United States in a matter of months. We celebrated in high spirits.

Meanwhile, school in Gardelegen turned into hell. I had a teacher of limited qualifications named Pannwitz; he was an Oberschullehrer, authorized only to teach art and fifth-grade arithmetic, as opposed to tenured gymnasium teachers, who were required to have Doktor degrees.

One day in 1937, Pannwitz began his class with the Hitler salute, that projection of the right arm with hand and fingers extended and eyes raised up to Nazi heaven while shouting "Heil Hitler!" I, the only Jewish boy in the class, did not participate. When Pannwitz screamed at me, I explained, "It is illegal for me as a Jew to give the Hitler salute." (There was in fact such a regulation.) Pannwitz's face contorted and his voice alternated between screams and incoherent gurgles. As he gasped for breath, he yelled, "Go and stand in that dark corner of the hall outside the classroom until I finish the Nazi salute." Now, several times a week, I had to wait while my classmates filed past me into class and gave the salute. Then Pannwitz would have someone shout, "The Jew can come in now." This was great fun for some of my classmates, who enjoyed my distress. I never told my parents.

Pannwitz also announced to my brother Helmut's class, "I

want to tell you about the Jews, and our Jew has to leave the room while I tell you all about it." Helmut, eleven at the time, said, "I want to stay because I want to hear what you have to say." Essentially, Pannwitz told the children that Jews were ugly, filthy, money-grubbing peddlers, baby-killing perverts, international conspirators, wily seducers, and enemies of the German people with smelly breath and devious minds. When he finished, Helmut reputedly said, "Thank you for your explanation, Herr Pannwitz."

Pannwitz was rumored to be the secret head of the local Gestapo. Interestingly, he had an enormous nose with a huge crook, the very personification of the gross caricatures of Jews in Julius Streicher's Jew-baiting newspaper, *Der Stürmer*. I always wondered whether he was such a rabid Nazi because he feared being mistaken by his looks for a Jew.

While my family waited for its visa, Pannwitz and I had another confrontation, whose substance I cannot remember. He gave me a *Tadel*, a formal demerit in the official class book, for "Jewish arrogance." The *Tadel* was also noted on my report card. Compulsory attendance stopped at fourteen years of age, and I told my parents I wanted to leave school. Instead they arranged for my transfer to a Jewish gymnasium in Berlin, which had some of the best teachers in the world. Shortly afterwards Helmut transferred there as well. Our Gardelegen school papers noted that we left to attend a Judenschule (Jew school). That epithet was meant to denote a place of confusion, lacking the authority, discipline, neatness, and cleanliness of a Nazi school.

I was fifteen when I moved to Berlin in 1938. At first I stayed with Aunt Lottie and Uncle Hans Sonnenfeldt. They saw me as a great baby-sitter for their seven-year-old son, but I had other things in mind. My new school was coeducational, there were girls who interested me and vice versa. I managed to move from Aunt Lottie's to childless Aunt Kate and Uncle Fritz's. There I could come and go as I wished, as long as I made my bed, did a few chores, and stayed out of trouble. Uncle Fritz warned, "I never want to hear anything bad about you," and I made sure he did not.

I liked my new school. My favorite date was Fritzie, a well-built girl my age. We went on hot dates to the Wannsee, a large lake outside Berlin, where we could sneak a kiss or a little more. I lost track of Fritzie and hope she did not perish in the Holocaust. Helmut boarded with Aunt Erna, that dear and good soul who supported herself as a seamstress. Erna's sixteen-year-old son, Gerhard, had a girlfriend, and I always suspected that Helmut learned a thing or two in that house. Helmut seemed happy there, but I did not see much of him in Berlin.

How, I have been asked, was it possible to have a good time in Berlin, in 1938, after having been hounded out of Gardelegen? Very simply, in Gardelegen everyone knew I was a Jew, but in Berlin, a city of four million, I was anonymous. I do not remember knowing anyone in Aunt Kate's apartment building. On the crowded streets, wearing a typical student's knee-length lederhosen, knee socks, ankle boots, and short jacket, I drew no attention to myself. At age fifteen, my nose was not so big as it is now, and my ears, which have always stood out from my head, were still not prominent enough to mark me as a Jew. My hair was as brown and no curlier than that of my Aryan contemporaries. Like me, they were also pimply adolescents. My accent indicated that I was a German country boy.

My adult relatives in Berlin were also protected by anonymity. They did not smell bad or have the gross features ascribed to Jews by Nazis. Uncle Fritz, fairly tall with a Roman nose, had been a Prussian soldier, and prided himself on the gait of a military man. Coming home one night, Uncle Fritz got off the S-bahn, Berlin's equivalent of Chicago's El. Two uniformed storm troopers stuck a swastika-adorned tin can with a slotted lid under his nose and said, "Heil Hitler. Give for the Winterhilfe." That was a Nazi campaign to collect donations for the poorest of the poor. Uncle Fritz said, "I am sorry, I am a Jew. I cannot participate." At this, the leader of this duo said, "Come on, pal, don't give me that Jew stuff. At least ten others have already made that excuse today."

Abruptly, my family's situation deteriorated. In the spring of 1938, when we were eagerly expecting our visa to be issued any day, Franklin Roosevelt's government suddenly suspended all immigration for Jews from Germany. The timing could not have been worse. Tens of thousands were seeking to leave. Our expectation of an American visa had fed our hope. Now we had no place to go. We were scared.

One day, when I was home in Gardelegen from school in Berlin, my mother sat me down in the treatment room in Father's office. I can see her today in her white uniform with her serious expression. She asked me how I would feel if we ended our desperation with a family suicide that would not hurt. We would just go peacefully to sleep together.

The idea did not appeal to me and I said, "No." The subject did not come up again. I was pleased that I had been asked for my opinion. Perhaps I was too young to appreciate the full import of that conversation or the desperation that motivated it. Later, I often wondered what would have happened had I said "Yes."

Mother bounced back. Ever resourceful and ingenious, using every connection available to her, she miraculously obtained full boarding scholarships for Helmut and me at the New Herrlingen School in England. We were to start the fall term there in 1938, just two months hence. Meanwhile, our parents would wait in Germany for the United States to reopen its doors to German Jews, perhaps the following year. Then our family would reunite in America. But, clearly, saving their children was uppermost on our parents' minds.

So I went home to Gardelegen for the last time in the summer of 1938. I said good-bye to the few Jews remaining there and to the even fewer non-Jewish Germans who dared to say good-bye secretly. My childhood friends were not among them. Only two of my parents' patients, who ascribed their survival to the medical help they had received from my father, came after dark to say good-bye.

In those last days, I joined a gang of hooligans who lived in hovels near the Wall. Normally I would have shunned these unkempt, smelly urchins whose parents had nothing to lose by associating with Jews. They cared nothing about being "good" Germans. These small-time thugs snitched things here and there, and their lack of bodily and mental restraint especially when their girls were around was quite an education for me. Fortunately, we were not caught in misdeeds that would have put my father in jail or worse.

On August 19, 1938, Helmut and Mother and I boarded the train in Gardelegen. Mother would escort us to England and then return to Gardelegen. Father had been unable to get a temporary visa for England, perhaps because the British did not want to have an entire family, seeking asylum, on their hands. As our train pulled out of the Gardelegen station, Father waved good-bye. I saw him weeping. He had lost control over our fate and did not know whether he would ever see his sons again. That must have been the cruelest blow to this man, who believed love was more powerful than might, and who had an iron sense of responsibility. He had defended us to the best of his ability against sadistic Nazis. Neither then nor later did he ever lose belief in the basic goodness of human beings, even when he looked at depraved cruelty. On that day he cried. I, too, came close to crying but consoled myself with the thought that soon we would be reunited in America.

It took more than twelve hours for the train to traverse Germany, and we wondered whether we would make it across the border. I was soon distracted by anger at my mother. She handed me a blanket and said, "Here, cover yourself or you will catch cold."

Well, at age fifteen I knew whether I needed a cover or not! "I don't want the blanket!" I said.

"Do as I tell you," my mother said, but I refused.

Our argument made the time pass. When the train stopped at the German-Belgian border, Mother and I were still not speaking. First the German border police and then the Belgians examined our papers. The officers were so casual that as the train started forward into Belgium, it was hard to realize we had escaped from Nazi Germany.

We had fearfully wondered whether we would leave Germany alive. Now, as the ferry between Belgium and England rocked in the English Channel, I began to comprehend that Helmut and I were free. It was anticlimactic, because we had not escaped after horrendous suffering. We had experienced humiliation and fear, but bodily harm, in fact, never touched us. Now we could believe that it never would. With the white cliffs of the English coast in sight and the foreign sounds of spoken English in my ears, my anticipation of a new life in an English boarding school was already crowding out the angst of the past.

Both my parents had instilled priceless values in me. Father taught me that bravery, honesty, integrity, and charity were rewarded by a clear conscience, and that service to humanity was an honor. Mother taught me that I could succeed at anything if I really wanted to, and that I was "special." She taught me to be courageous, resourceful, and strong. They both prized sincerity and candor and lived their beliefs. Though I did not realize it consciously then, these were the values I would bring to the new life that was now about to begin.

VI

England

I KNEW LESS THAN A HUNDRED WORDS OF ENGLISH when Mother, Helmut, and I landed at Folkestone after crossing the Channel from Ostend in Belgium. I had barely learned to roll my tongue for English arrs, replacing the German errrhs. And there was that problem with English w's, for vitsch there is no equivalent in German.

From Folkestone we took a train to Faversham in Kent, where we transferred to another local train. On those trains we had upholstered seats, not wooden benches as in the third-class coaches we knew in Germany. The carriages were painted bright green and shiny black, as was the locomotive, which looked so different from the grimy German locomotives. It even had some gold stripes on its sides and around the smokestack. The carriages had brass handles on the doors. It was a very cheery train. I was amazed how fast it started and rolled through the country-side, which looked like a park, so different from the drab potato, rye, and asparagus fields near Gardelegen. The English cows were brown and white and fat instead of the lean black-and-white animals I was used to; there were sheep and goats grazing and horses galloping about in neat, hedged-in fields. The railway stations were so clean, some with flowers. It all had a vacation-like feeling. In 1938, rural Kent was lovely with green leas, white-washed stone farmhouses, neat fences, and chest-high hedges. On that first day of my new freedom in England, the morning skies were blue with fleecy white clouds. I had arrived in a wonderful New World.

A driver, who spoke with an accent I later learned to recognize as "Kent," met us and took us to the New Herrlingen School, at Bunce Court in Otterden, near Lenham. The winding roads with tall hedges on each side led us to the front of a three-story brick manor house with many windows, dozens of chimneys, and a lovely rose garden in front. This was the main house of the school.

A boy my age took me to a two-room hut between the power shed and the chauffeur's lodging. In the past, these huts must have been the quarters of servants employed by the lord of this manor. In our hut were four boys in two rooms. I was to share mine with Gaby Adler, a German boy who had been at the school for several years and spoke fluent English. Peter Morley and another boy shared the other room in these accommodations, which were primitive but very private. My brother was assigned a cot in a dormitory in the big house with the younger boys. They were chaperoned by a teacher and her husband, who worked in the carpentry shop.

In Prussia where I grew up, the English were regarded with awe. Perhaps that was because Germany had never won a war against England, which had prevailed against the French and the Spanish and had been a partner in the coalition that defeated Germany in World War I. In 1938, Britain still had a world empire, something Germany had aspired to but had never attained. That is how Germans ranked nations and their citizens. And here I was in the land I had been taught to respect and admire. I was not sorry I had left Germany and what it stood for; I was excited to be in England!

There was now much to learn and also much to unlearn. Some students at the New Herrlingen School were refugees from

Nazi Germany, like my brother and me, but there were some English boys and girls, and a few Czechoslovakians and Poles. Several students had come in 1934 when Bunce Court opened. While even English children could speak German, all classes were taught in English, which was the official language of the school. I remember being very tongue-tied for about eight weeks after I arrived at Bunce Court. My roommate, Gaby, told me one morning, "You have been talking English in your sleep." He made me try it while I was awake and, suddenly, I was unshackled from inhibitions. I learned most of my conversational English in the next six months at school. It wasn't long before I even preferred this language to German, with its endless sentences where the verb was deferred to the very end. I felt liberated from that Teutonic passion for pigeonholing and qualifying nouns in endless clauses. It was so nice to get to the point more quickly in English.

While I was now well removed from the perils of German sentence structure and Prussian cultural strictures, I was also no longer an adolescent in a German-Jewish family. There, my relationship with my parents had been determined by German mores and seasoned with a tad of Jewish guilt and paranoia: I was pressured to conform to my parents' wishes either by threats of punishment or by withdrawal of love. By contrast, the culture of the school was egalitarian, where the individual was protected by the group and responsible to it, perhaps even more so than in traditional English schools. The school was the only England I knew, and it became a spiritual home I never had known existed, a home I loved then and have loved ever since.

The headmistress, Anna Essinger, of German-Jewish descent, had gone to America in her twenties to earn an M.A. in education at the University of Wisconsin, and had become a Quaker. When she returned to Germany, she founded near her family home in southern Germany a boarding school, the Herrlingen School, dedicated to humanistic principles. One of her goals had been to develop a sense of responsibility and

community in her students, who along with the teachers participated in the life and the running of the school. After she moved
it to England in 1934, the school could afford very few full-time
employees: a half dozen teachers, two secretaries, a gardener, the
chauffeur, and the cook with one helper. They and the teachers
led the students in all of the chores necessary to run the school,
which included washing the dishes, cleaning up, tending the gardens, stoking the furnaces, and, of course, keeping our quarters
(reasonably) neat. There was an explicit commitment to communal morals and to the ideal of eminently qualified mentors
teaching students who were dedicated and eager to learn. In this
community, passionate credos of intellectual freedom, integrity,
and social responsibility were bolstered by the English sense of
fairness and the democracy of a nation that had not been devastated by alien occupiers in recent history. My England, at least as
I experienced it at school in 1938, was not corrupted by those
age-old hatreds that, in victory and defeat, have polluted the nationalistic continent of Europe. While I was there, and forever
after, Bunce Court has been my Shangri-la.

Meanwhile, my parents remained in Gardelegen waiting for
their American visas. They were relieved that their sons were
safe in England, but they soon felt the full and evil force of Hitler.
In November of 1938, my mother sent a telegram to my brother
and me telling us, in veiled language, that our father had been
taken to a concentration camp. This was, of course, a terrible
shock, and we did not know how to communicate back in plain
language with Mother lest we endanger her. Her telegram came
after Kristallnacht, so named because Nazi mobs were commanded to smash the windows of Jewish establishments and loot
them while thousands of Jewish males were incarcerated. There
were frightening reports in the *Times* (of London) and on the radio. My brother and I had hardly begun to cope with this terrible
news when a second telegram from Mother announced that Father
had been released from Buchenwald concentration camp. The
mystery of that unexpected return was not solved for another

seven years. Hermann Göring, the number-two Nazi, had first ordered the arrest of all Jewish adult males and then, in a sudden fit of sentimentality for World War I comrades, released those who had earned an Iron Cross for valor in combat. My father was one of those.

Before my father's arrest, my parents had already seen their medical practice vanish and had to sell their house, which still carried a mortgage, at a giveaway price. They had moved in with an elderly Jewish couple, Lina and Julius Hesse, and the couple's cousin, Lina Riess. We learned later that my parents' hosts perished in the Holocaust.

My brother and I were relieved when Father was released, but we were convinced, at least for the moment, that his imprisonment was just one more warning to Jews. Father had agreed to leave Germany with my mother within six months. The problem was, they had no place to go. The American suspension of immigration remained in effect, and now my parents were staring at a time limit that had a frightening void at its end. Father would surely land back in concentration camp, and so would Mother.

Had we not been young with exciting new lives, we would have been paralyzed with fear.

My daily life in school in England was far removed from the plight of my parents in Nazi Germany. I thought of them every day. They did not, or could not, burden their children with reports of the horrors they were suffering. They might have been arrested had they tried to tell us more. We knew they had reentered that numbing state where German Jews saw no relief and could only fear impending catastrophe. Not until I read my father's memoirs after his death did I grasp the extent of their deprivations, terror, and desperation. My parents' only positive experience then was to know that my brother and I were safe in England.

Helmut and I saw each other every day, but we lived apart in the school. The different grades, or "forms" as they were called, were groups unto themselves. Our days were full. We talked about our parents when we saw each other, especially when the papers reported the plight of Jews in Germany. But our respective lives kept us busy, and we were adolescents.

In 1939, the so-called Kinder Transports were organized to save Jewish youths from Germany, Poland, and Czechoslovakia. Anna Essinger, our ever-resourceful headmistress, raised funds to accept many additional children. And those were from a far greater range of cultural and religious backgrounds than the earlier students in Bunce Court, who came mainly from upper-class German-Jewish families. Other than the beggars who had rung our doorbell in Gardelegen, this was the first time I came in close contact with Jews of Eastern European origin, who brought with them the culture of the shtetl and religious orthodoxy. Their behavior and their looks were different from mine. Despite the latter-day embrace by my mother of Judaism and my father's tolerance of it, it was more difficult for me to relate to voluble Eastern Jews than to reserved English gentiles. Fortunately, these leanings did not lead me to make value judgments. Many years later I married a woman of Russian-Jewish origin and came to love her family. But in 1938 I was confronted with several cultures: that of the English, which I admired and wanted to adopt; that of Eastern European Jews, which I had trouble understanding; and the culture in which I was raised. I tried to separate the good from the bad in order to create my own cultural home.

Studies at Bunce Court concentrated on English language and English literature, history, math, and science. The classes were small, five to eight students, and the teachers were dedicated and superb. To me, English was the most demanding but also the most rewarding subject. Blessed with a prodigious memory, I soon found my vocabulary expanding mightily, and I had less and less trouble reading the works of Thomas Hardy, Samuel Butler, and James Boswell. It was as though this English world had awaited me.

In December of 1938, four months after I arrived in England, Fritz Feuerman, a classmate, and I were invited to spend Christmas and New Year's with an English family in Jarrow, a busy industrial harbor in the northeast of England near Newcastle. That invitation came from a friend of my math and science teacher, Benson Herbert, with whom I had bonded immediately and who gave me private tutoring almost from the day I arrived. A few days before Christmas, Mr. Herbert drove us up to London. From there the old LNER railway ran up to Newcastle-upon-Tyne. It was to be an overnight trip, but heavy snows in the Midlands held up our train. After passing through Durham, where we enviously saw the Flying Scotsman, the fastest train in England, whiz by us, we finally arrived in Newcastle-upon-Tyne, hungry, grimy, tired, and a little apprehensive about our first meeting with English people away from school. Mr. Headley, our host, met us and took us to stay with a lady whose husband was a seafaring man and whose grown daughter lived with her. She gave us breakfast, and then Mr. Headley took us sightseeing, one of the sights being his undertaking establishment. Back in Gardelegen, the corpse remained at home until it was collected in a coffin and carted off to the cemetery. At any rate, I had never seen an undertaking establishment. In an unguarded moment I sneaked into the embalming room to look into one of the coffins and found a real corpse in it!

The people of Jarrow introduced us to tea and crumpets, ginger beer (the first English thing I disliked), steak-and-kidney pie, mutton, porridge, kippers, and mince pie, all of which I loved, and, yes, a little whiskey and port wine on occasion. I found English food, so universally maligned, simply wonderful. And then there were the fireplaces. I had never been in a house with a fireplace. A family with a lovely sixteen-year-old daughter, a picture-book English lass with blue eyes and blond hair and a creamy complexion, invited us to tea. The girl would stand in front of the flaming fire so we could see her legs and body through the lacy white dress she was wearing. A lovely picture indeed! Another friend was a dentist with two young boys to whom he gave a little laughing gas — just for fun. I tried it too, sitting in the dentist chair with a mask over my face. This was a great family, and when I told them about the plight of my parents, they offered them bed and board if only they could get out of Germany. I helped prepare the necessary papers but soon found out that a British visa would take months to obtain.

For Christmas, Mr. Headley packed our hostess, her daughter, himself, and us into a huge, rented touring car and off we went to the snow-covered Lake District to celebrate at a lovely country inn. We figured out that Mr. Headley and the daughter, though discreet, were an item. We took side trips to Durham and Carlisle, and even to Scotland, where my knowledge of German and English allowed me to understand some Scottish words even when my hosts could not! Nobody could ever have been more warmly hospitable to a couple of teenagers than the families of Jarrow.

But it was there that I learned to hate the word "refugee." It classified me by my past, whereas I was going into the future. What future? I did not know. But I resented being tagged by my connection to Hitler, who for me was the past. Except for the constant worry about my parents, my new English life was just great. And I did not miss the past one bit.

While I went to Jarrow for Christmas, my brother, Helmut, went to London to visit an English-Jewish family to whom he was introduced by the same Aunt Erna with whom he had stayed in Berlin. Aunt Erna was now working as a maid. Our cousin Henry was also in London. He had a job with the London branch of the Berlin department store N. Israel. At that time Helmut was much more family-connected than I was, and he enjoyed himself with his hosts and relatives. These were the only relatives we had in England. Our other aunts and uncles had made it safely to America.

Back at school, I soon got out of washing and drying dishes and cleaning chores by volunteering to organize a group of boys to electrify a building known as the cottage, away from the main house. This was the young children's nursery, run by a lovely young English woman, Gwenn, who was blond, blue-eyed, and incredibly enticing to teenage boys. In her quarters she only had candles and kerosene lamps for light at night. I was not yet sixteen, but the headmistress, known as T.A. (which stood for Tante Anna), allowed me to undertake this electrification project after Benson Herbert, the math and physics teacher, who had never run an electric wire, okayed it.

The cottage was more than a quarter mile down the road from the powerhouse. To get electricity there, we had to erect a line of poles with cross arms and insulators. I do not remember who was in my crew other than my friend Peter Morley. We felled trees, removed the bark, and creosoted the trunks to protect them against rot before we put them into deep holes in the ground, which we dug with spade and shovel. Being nimble young fellows, we shinnied up those poles to run the wires. Months later, when all was finished, we installed electric lights in the cottage, bare sockets with bulbs in them. There was such jubilation when they lit up! I visited the school in 1961 when it had been converted to an old-age home. Our poles, wires, and lights, however, were still there as we had installed them in 1939. A friend told me that in 1990 the installation was still there. This is just one example of how we were encouraged to be resourceful and independent. It stood me in good stead.

Electricity in the school was generated by an ancient diesel engine that ran on kerosene. We cranked a huge flywheel, while the compression was released to let the engine turn easily. Then, with the wheel up to speed, the compression lever was closed, and usually the engine would fire, often just as the wheel was spinning down to its last few turns. The engine drove a generator, which charged a huge bank of batteries that supplied electricity to the entire school. In summer the engine put-putted very little, but in long winter nights, it was on for many hours each day. Of course, there were no electric heaters, stoves, fans, washing machines, or dryers, only light bulbs, which by today's standards were dim, mostly twenty-five and forty watts, and a few radios. So the demand for power was not very great. Even though the lights were dim, we got along.

Still, the power was not completely reliable, and the entire school could be plunged into darkness at the most awkward times, like during supper or homework period. These outages were not always to the chagrin of the boys, who took advantage of the situation to chase the girls in the darkness. The girls did not always scream when we caught them.

Life at school was regulated by a big bronze bell that woke everybody for outdoor calisthenics, followed by showers (cold water, of course), breakfast, start of classes, et cetera. Not far from the bell in the great house, there was a tall grandfather clock with a gilt face and pineapple-shaped weights on chains. The clock supplied master time for the entire school. In Kent, during June, daylight begins at four o'clock in the morning. We once advanced the master clock in the middle of the night by two hours and then rang the bell to get everyone up when the clock showed seven, though it was really only five in the morning. We went out with everybody else for calisthenics in the meadow to start the day. One of the teachers looked at her wristwatch, wondering why it was slow by two hours. All the other watches were off, too, except for the master clock.

The headmistress did not ask who had done it. But after that, the access door to the great clock was locked.

We also had sports at the school. They included track, broad and high jumps, javelin, discus, and pole vaulting. I was quite good at running and became the half-mile champion. My best time ever was two minutes and twelve seconds, which did not put us in any world league. Some of the teachers played tennis on grass courts of uncertain manicure. We boys also played field hockey, and that could be very rough. I once hit another boy in the head with the hockey ball. He passed out and I was very scared until he came to. Another time, we played a Maidstone public school (you know, of course, that "public schools" in England are private). We were creamed. When I asked the coach of the other team to critique our play, he said, "You have too many stars," which I realized was his way of saying that we had very poor team play. We had poor team play because we had no coach.

I loved the food at Bunce Court. Today my family would call it plain, and that would not be meant as a compliment. But I loved steak-and-kidney pie, especially if I could get the serving spoon under the crust to fish out the most delicious kidneys and the best cubes of steak. Or hot oatmeal on a cold morning. We called it porridge. After it stood for a while, it looked to me as though somebody had spat on it, but it tasted wonderful. In Germany for breakfast we always had *brötchen*, crisp little rolls with butter or lard (margarine was taboo) but never anything else. Here we had butter, marmalade, and raspberry, strawberry, or blackberry jams made from fruit grown in our gardens. Another breakfast I loved was kippers and bacon and eggs.

And there, with all this great food, was Betty Macpherson across the dining room! One of the English girls, Betty was a tall and pretty blonde with bright blue eyes, and I melted whenever she looked at me. Our eyes met many times before I got my courage up and asked her to go for a walk. We went on many walks, just holding hands, before I kissed her for the first time. I did not feel anything and was surprised, so I did it again. But she did not always want to go for a walk, and that made me angry.

While we were sharing quarters in that little hut, I asked Peter, who sometimes visited his father in London, to go to the Caledonian Market, a sort of super flea- market, to buy used radio tubes (called valves), coils, condensers, resistors, wire, solder, and a loudspeaker. Students were forbidden to have radios, but I built one from these used parts, and my roommates and I listened blissfully, into the wee hours of the night, to jazz from Radio Normandy, a pirate station operating from a trawler in the North Sea. Its signature tune was "Blue Skies Around the Corner." In fact, blue skies were not around the corner. Our radio was confiscated after the headmistress heard the jazz one night when padding around the premises. But I soon built a new radio, this time with headphones.

In April of 1939, before an English visa could be obtained for them, my parents, miraculously, were permitted to enter Sweden, where friends had arranged for them to wait for their American visa. Helmut and I, of course, were relieved and happy they were finally safe and that another step had been taken for the whole family to be reunited in America — our ultimate destination.

During my second year I was moved to the senior boys' house, a prefab hut that had individual cubicles, each with a cot, a tiny closet with a curtain instead of a door, a chair, and a small table and shelf. It was like a cell in a monastery, but having my own room was fabulous. There were sixteen seniors in this hut, which had a small room with a real door at one end for the master, our history teacher, Mr. Horowitz. I never knew his first name. We were supposed to be in our quarters by 9:00 P.M. on schooldays and by 11:00 P.M. on Saturdays and Sundays. Betty Macpherson and I often stayed out beyond the prescribed time and sneaked back later to our quarters, she to the main house and I to my cubicle. Mr. Horowitz pretended not to see me.

One evening Betty came to visit me and stayed after the curfew. Soon I heard footsteps and the voice of the headmistress looking for me. She liked to talk to me, as though I were her equal, about politics, history, and the world at large, and this was an evening she had picked for a tête-à-tête. What to do? I pushed Betty in my closet and drew the curtain. As T.A. came into my room, from the corner of my eye I noticed Betty's feet protruding from under the curtain. T.A., fortunately, had very poor eyesight, corrected by enormously thick lenses. Our conversation seemed to last forever. As it went on, I noticed that the curtain in front of my closet was swaying, apparently in response to Betty's breathing. After a while, when it was quite dark, I offered to escort T.A. back to the main house, a walk of several hundred feet through the dark garden. As she accepted, I noticed an extra wave of ripples in that closet curtain. When I came back, Betty was gone.

In the spring of 1939, I was invited along with Fritz Feuermann, who had been with me in Jarrow, to visit Guernsey. This was one of the Channel Islands, an English-speaking part of the British Empire with its own currency, off the coast of France near St. Malo.

The invitation came about because Edith Clarke, secretary to the headmistress, and I had become great friends. She was a diminutive woman whose father was a Church of England cleric. He had raised three daughters, all of whom led unconventional, though humanitarian, lives. Clarklet, as we called her, befriended Betty and me, and she often included Joyce Wormleighton, the sister of my English teacher, and Peter Ryan, both English students at the school, for Sunday high tea at her tiny apartment at the Wilkens farm. This was an old stone house about a half mile from the school. Our favorite activity was reading plays before a roaring fire, with tea and scones or mince pie and, once in a while, red wine. There I worked my way through many Shaw and Shakespeare plays and discovered Oscar Wilde's wicked humor. It was all such innocent and great fun. And I remember the walks back to school through the Kentish meadows that were full of sheep over which we stumbled in the dark. On other nights there would be cloud castles in the sky, lit by an incredibly bright moon. Betty and I used to walk back together and kiss in ecstasy at the wonder of those lovely meadows. Kissing certainly improved with practice.

Clarklet, a wondrous free spirit, had a sister, Lillian, who lived in Guernsey with Miriam Leale, a native of that lovely island. They invited us to their Channel Islands for spring holidays and Clarklet came along. We took the train to the Weymouth ferry and then had an all-night trip across the widest part of the Channel to Guernsey. I remember, as though it were yesterday, lying on the boat deck and looking at the star-studded sky, which swayed with the motion of the boat. This was my longest boat trip so far.

Lillian Clarke and Miriam Leale, our hosts, lived in a house in Guernsey and they shared a bedroom. They were obviously congenial and did everything together. Lillian worked, but Miriam had independent means. She drove a Wolseley convertible, which had a fantastic lighted white emblem in the radiator grille. Miriam took us all over Guernsey, which was full of greenhouses for growing tomatoes. Early on, and over our protestations, Miriam gave each of us five quid (a five-pound note) "so that you don't have to bother me when you need something."

In my bedroom I found a copy of Havelock Ellis, which I never mentioned to my hosts and which was never mentioned by them. Fritz and I did not know that anything like this existed. At home I had only leafed through my father's tomes, when my parents were away, to study the female anatomy. Now this book was a whole other thing, about sex and how to enjoy it! Fritz and I competed for reading time.

Slowly it dawned on me that Miriam and Lillian were more than just friends. At that time I knew them both as lovely women, quite different from each other, wonderful guides and hosts to us. So I was not shocked by my discovery, as I might have been had Miriam and Lillian been introduced to me as lesbians.

After a few days in Guernsey, we all took a tiny steamboat to the island of Sark, where the Dame ruled as an absolute monarch. Sark (or Sarque as spelled out on its own currency) banned motor vehicles, and there was no electricity or running water on the island. Three other women joined the five of us. We had a grand time, walking, wading, crabbing, and watching the enormous eighteen-foot tides come rolling in. At low tide, we had to watch for giant waves that announced the returning tide. I was nearly trapped once; that was very scary, but I made it back safely, just in the nick of time. In the evenings, by candlelight, we read plays and enjoyed party games like charades and mysteries. I learned how to play whist and bridge. Ah, those were the pleasures of a bygone age! We had such a good time, and nobody ever thought it odd (at least to our knowledge) in 1939 that six gay women and two male teenagers made up a vacationing octet. Fritz and I went back to school with the most pleasant memories.

I felt even greater pleasure when at the end of the next term, just three months later, I was invited back to Guernsey. These were the post-Munich days, when Chamberlain had promised "peace in our time" while Hitler had already decided, of course unbeknownst to us, to start an unprovoked war. My companion from the earlier trip, Fritz, went home in July to visit his family in Czechoslovakia, and I went back to Guernsey.

This time there was a summer camp run by the Reverend Jimmy Butterworth for kids from the slums of London. He was cheerleader, music man, and preacher, all in one diminutive, fire-cracker package. Miriam Leale, who supported him financially, took me to his camp for a dance. These were not like the English I had been associating with. The girls were very forthcoming and the boys very aggressive. They were cockney youths from the slums of London, kids whose fathers or mothers were in jail for stealing or worse, kids who had been kicked out of school or had been in reformatories. Reverend Butterworth offered them fresh air, dance, and prayer, and they were making the most of it. Had I been less shy, I could have made many friends there. I stood in amazement and awe as they cavorted with each other. Nobody paid any attention to me until a red-haired girl with a funny turned-up nose and bouncing boobs asked me to dance with her. I did not know how to dance, but I loved it. She snuggled right up to me as no other girl had ever done, and that was a thrill. Eventually she kissed me good night and said, "See ya, Heinie. Come back to me." Ah, my German accent was not completely gone yet!

Back at school, I was determined to work on my accent and my English vocabulary, which was still improving rapidly because Norman Wormleighton, our English teacher, had us memorize several pages of the *New Oxford Concise Dictionary* every day. But momentous events were just ahead.

I returned from Guernsey just two weeks before the war started in Europe and got the news that my parents' British visa had finally been granted. At school was a letter from them asking me what I thought they should do. Asking me? Yes, asking me! This was the first time I experienced the detachment that comes to me when important decisions must be made.

Decades later, I found a copy of the letter I sent to them in Sweden. There are these sentences: "Don't leave a neutral country because you hope that there won't be war. I think we will be at war within weeks. If you come to England, then we will all be stuck here. If you stay in neutral Sweden you will have a chance to get your visa to go to the United States on a Swedish ship and Helmut and I will join you there later. Stay where you are until you can go to America."

Three days after I wrote that letter, on September 3, 1939, England was at war with Germany. That Sunday morning we watched squadron after squadron of RAF planes flying low over Kent, headed for France. We were issued gas masks and even a few helmets for air raid wardens. I was designated to be one. Itching to do something for the English war effort, I suggested that we build air raid shelters. That project was a wonderful outlet for youthful energy, although it was quite ridiculous, because there was nothing within miles of our school that should ever have attracted a German bomb. And so far as I know, none ever fell anywhere near that grassy field where we dug madly to provide shelters for most of the school. To roof over our dugouts, we felled trees and cut them into logs. The roofs were then covered with several inches of sod, which made our shelters invisible from the air. Alas, the first rain filled our bunkers with water, and we realized that death by drowning would be no better than death by bombing.

The war touched us immediately. Several schoolmates never

returned from visits to their families in Nazi areas, and God only knows what fate befell them. Among those who disappeared was Fritz Feuerman, my travel companion, and a Polish boy, Gunnar, whose best girlfriends at school grieved together over him. These students disappeared as though the earth had swallowed them.

During those early days of the war, we never gave thought to how it was to be won. That France and England were finally standing up to Hitler was good news, even after Poland fell within days. Beyond that, there was only the confidence that England had never lost a war, except the one with America, and everyone instinctively looked to that great democracy on the other side of the Atlantic as a friend.

After those first exciting days in September, life at school continued much as before, but with one change. We were forbidden to ring the big bell by which the school was run, because bells were to be the alarm for invasion or the dropping of parachutists. To replace our big school bell, I now offered to install electric bells that would use existing wiring in an unconventional way. This system worked just fine, and I installed in my cubicle the button that rang the bells.

In 1939, I was a senior, a fifth-former, studying for the Cambridge Higher School Certificate, a British national test that, if passed, qualified students for college admission. For the English literature section, we prepared set books like Hardy's *Return of the Native*, Butler's *Erewhon*, and Emily Brontë's *Wuthering Heights*, and the test required us to write short essays or answer questions related to these books. From Shakespeare's *Julius Caesar* we had to be able to identify any two-line passage by speaker, act, and scene, and we were expected to write from memory key passages like "I come to bury Caesar, not to praise him. . . ."

Languages were easy for me because I knew German and my French was passable. I was still working on English. History meant memorizing dates, names, places, and events, and I had a good memory. Advanced science and math came to me naturally.

I was confident I would pass the national test, and then what? I realize now that I had not even thought about that. In those uncertain days I did not plan for the future.

In November of 1939, my parents got their visa in Sweden to go to the United States. Transportation from Nazi Europe across the Atlantic was now blockaded by the British navy, but suddenly American immigration quota numbers had become available for the very few Jews who could still find a way to travel to the United States on neutral ships. My advice to my parents in August to wait for their visas in Sweden, a neutral country, had been right. Now, Father and Mother crossed the U-boat-infested Atlantic on a Swedish passenger liner, which as a neutral ship was exempted from the British blockade, and they landed in New York that same November of 1939. There they planned to obtain American licenses to practice medicine once again, hoping to get their family back together. That reunion, however, proved impossible. Helmut and I could not get any transportation from England, because of the U-boat war.

While we boys no longer needed to be concerned about the physical safety of our parents in Nazi Germany, our parents were now worried about the safety of their children in England, a country at war.

At Bunce Court I was now one of the "old boys," expected to set an example to our juniors, even though we transgressed a little here and there. We were not to leave the school grounds without permission, but Peter Morley and I regularly sneaked away to Warren Street, a small general store about a mile away run by a Mr. Smith. There we bought Milky Ways, Bovril, cheddar cheese, and fuel called paraffin (kerosene) for our Primus stove, another forbidden possession, on which we prepared midnight snacks. To get to Warren Street, we had to walk on a narrow lane with dense hedgerows on each side, so it was impossible to hide if the school car came down the road. We established a warning system. Mr. Courtney, the chauffeur for the headmistress, drove an ancient sedan. When we saw Court warm up the car, we knew he was going to leave in about twenty minutes, and then was unlikely to come back for a couple of hours or so. A more reliable warning system was Court's love life. A buxom redhead, Stella, who worked in the kitchen, had an arrangement with Court. If he did not have to drive, she would walk to his room at about two in the afternoon. When we spotted her on her way to her tryst, we knew that Court would be occupied long enough for us to get to Warren Street and back. Our intelligence system worked flawlessly.

Twenty years after I had left Bunce Court, on a visit to England in 1960 I found Mr. Smith and his wife behind their counter in Warren Street, as though time had stood still. He greeted me, "Just down from town, eh?" "Town," of course, was London, and since I did not want to review all that had happened to me since I saw him last, I just said, "Yes," and bought a couple of Milky Ways, for old times' sake.

At Bunce Court, one of my most memorable courses was Old Testament History. That course deepened my devotion to Judaic principles and also my aversion to Jewish ritual, in fact, to any ritual. I learned why the dietary laws made eminent sense in biblical times and how the ancients made a virtue of personal hygiene and isolation of persons with virulent disease. I hoped then, as I do now, that the diagnostics described in the Bible for leprosy and other plagues are not relied on today by even the most ardent religionists. I was fascinated by the prophets and social reformers and turned off by the Old Testament kings, the knaves, and the clerics. I became more and more convinced that Jesus was rejected because he had threatened the supremacy of what looked to me like the rabbis' union. I have often thought about what would have happened if the Jews of the first century had embraced Jesus as one of their own. What if there had never been Catholics, Protestants, and Moslems, in addition to militant Jews? Religions have encouraged fanatics to engage in untold bloodshed and cruelty in the name of commandments that ordain love, forgiveness, and neighborliness.

Lest you think that I became anti-Semitic or a militant athe-ist, let me assure you that I feel free to love and admire that which is good and to abhor that which is bad in the history of my people and in the history of other peoples. But just as I refused to let Hitler make me into an observant Jew, I refuse to let Jews or anybody make me feel that I must pretend to be something I am not in order to be regarded as respectable. My study of Old Tes-tament history confirmed my views. In an irreverent moment I observed that the Jews had invented God, who then revealed to them that He had chosen them. But I must confess that on occa-sion I regret not deriving any solace from rites that seem to com-fort those who practice them.

And meanwhile there was a war, then called the *sitzkrieg* (the sitting war) because neither side moved. The stalemate ended shockingly when the Germans took Denmark and Norway in one day, a coup that gave their U-boats and battleships access to the open sea and protected their imports of ores and steel from Sweden.

Once a week at Bunce Court, a senior would address the student assembly on a subject he or she chose. When my turn came in March of 1940, I chose as my subject "The War." I pre-dicted that Germans would march into Holland and Belgium, outflank the Maginot Line, and make it to the Channel. I re-member a spellbound and horrified audience. Unfortunately, I was uncannily prescient.

Finally Winston Churchill became prime minister. When I heard him speak for the first time, my enthusiasm was unbounded, and my relief at seeing Chamberlain gone was immense. I thought of Chamberlain as that dour and limp shill for Hitler with a stiff collar around a scrawny neck, that feeble old man who sought shelter under his umbrella even when it was not raining. I re-member our horror at the rapid collapse of Holland and Bel-gium, the rout of the French army that forgot to fight, and finally the miracle of Dunkirk, where the British evacuated their men but not their weapons.

The threat of invasion was now all too real. We listened to the news several times a day, and the Germans appeared to be unstoppable. The stories about quislings in Norway were retold and amplified with stories about fifth columnists in England. The myth of Nazis as supermen thrived while the world was crumbling before Hitler, and we all felt a numbing fear that German parachutists or fifth columnists could conquer England in a blink. Having come from Germany, with its jackbooted hordes of brown- and black-shirted troopers and its steel-helmeted robotlike soldiers, I began to fear for myself and for England. It now seemed so puny compared to Germany, which had conquered most of Europe in three short months. From Kent, the Germans were now only twenty miles across the Channel. Just weeks earlier, I had imagined I would be secure forever in England. Now the Nazis were at my doorstep and fears I thought I had safely left back in Germany returned. But Churchill rallied England to the fight, and I was spellbound every time I heard him over the radio.

One Sunday morning in early May of 1940, Mr. Horowitz, my history master, roused me at six o'clock in the morning. He told me to get up, dress, and pack necessities, because I was going to camp. I said, "I did not ask to go to camp." He said, "I know, but you are going to internment camp." In the coastal area where my school was located, all males over sixteen years of age with a German passport were now being interned and sent to prison camps for enemy aliens. Presumably that was to protect England against Nazi sympathizers and saboteurs who could aid German landings by sea or by air.

After grabbing some clothes, toilet articles, my passport, my treasured Parker fountain pen, a gift from Miriam Leale, and some math and physics books, I joined several other students and two teachers on a police bus. I thought how ironic it was that my saviors and protectors, the British, were now imprisoning me, when the Nazis had put my father into a concentration camp just eighteen months earlier.

I had no opportunity to say goodbye to my brother who was still fast asleep. He was just twelve then and too young to be caught in this dragnet. At that moment, as I was bused away as a prisoner, a so-called internee, I had mixed emotions. One part of me applauded the British for finally taking action and the other part of me complained, "How stupid of them to put me behind barbed wire when I can help them defeat Hitler!"

And so I went off, under armed guard, into the great unknown as a prisoner of my beloved English!

VII

Internment

I WONDERED WHETHER I HAD BEEN INTERNED by the English because my German passport had a swastika stamp on my picture and lacked the big red J stamp that identified German Jews who were issued passports after I left Germany.

My faith in British fairness was supreme, and I was sure that when they found out who I really was, His Majesty's government would set me free to fight our common enemy, the Nazis. I wrote His Majesty the King and Prime Minister Churchill about the grave error they had committed by interning me, a Jew, who was eager to fight the Germans. I commended them for interning people who could aid the German cause. But why me? I was the sworn enemy of the Nazis. I do not know whether anyone ever received and read my letters; I never got an answer.

Our first stop was a makeshift camp in Maidstone, not far from our school. That first Sunday morning we were fed a hearty English breakfast of fried eggs and bacon, army style in tin mess kits. We were kept in a barn, where we were issued sacks and straw to make palliasses, army-style mattresses. An enormous, middle-aged, ruddy-faced major of the Territorials, a sort of British National Guard, seemed as bewildered as we were when I asked — in English — when I was to be released. He had no idea who we were. He was so ponderous that I hoped I would not have to rely on him to defend me against the Germans.

We did latrine duty, served as mess orderlies, and appeared for roll call. To respond to the parade-ground bellow of a cockney sergeant major, we stood in what passed for a line. Some of the older internees were potbellied and a few were lame or stoop-shouldered; there were a few eager lads like myself. Mispronouncing every name in his cockney accent, the sergeant soon gave up trying to instill martial bearing in us bloody civilians. During roll call, there were endless interruptions when stragglers broke into the line, anxious to have their presence noted long after their names had been called. They managed to be late even when they had nothing to do.

Maidstone, in the invasion zone, was a poor place to keep suspected German sympathizers. Within a week we were loaded aboard a train, which moved in fits and starts throughout the night. Through a crack in the blackout paint on the windows, I discerned a signal tower at Reading as we moved west. The next morning we got out in Liverpool and were then trucked to Huyton, a suburb, where an unfinished public-housing development had been converted into a prison camp for thousands of internees collected from all over the British Isles.

My fluent English and youthful aplomb got me appointed majordomo for the mess of the officers who commanded the troops guarding us. I waited on tables, washed dishes, swept the floor, ate amply, and got all the cigarettes I wanted and a few drinks of beer and whiskey as well. Between chores, we orderlies enjoyed great games of bridge, darts, and chess. We became Very Important Persons because we doled out cigarettes, chocolate bars, and yesterday's newspapers to our fellow internees.

When the Blitz hit England, I could hear distant thunder from bombs falling on Liverpool. Still, there was no invasion. The Germans were apparently trying to win the air war before they would let their barges brave the Royal Navy.

Among the inmates at Huyton were university professors, international financiers, authors, and actors. Many of them offered impromptu lectures on history, finance, and the arts. The barbed wire created an egalitarian society, and I listened to and questioned authorities who in normal circumstances would not have admitted me to their classes.

While the Battle of Britain raged, the government decided that it was too dangerous to keep internees and German POWs (who had been taken in Norway, France, and even at Dunkirk) on their small island. Captured Nazi soldiers had no choice, but we civilian internees were allowed to volunteer to be sent to Canada. I volunteered, because it meant getting farther away from the Nazis. I also hoped that I might be able to escape from Canada to the United States to join my parents, who were now living in the Baltimore area. To prepare for my escape, I listened to American shortwave radio programs in the officers' mess and began to practice an American accent. When one is sixteen, everything seems possible.

After volunteering for deportation, the first contingent of internees destined for Canada left Huyton. They were torpedoed a day later on the ill-fated *Andorra Star*, a liner converted into a prison ship. Many of the German-Jewish internees aboard drowned, and survivors that rejoined us told horrible tales of their ordeal. My enthusiasm for going to Canada now evaporated, but it was too late; my name was on the list. Soon the survivors from the *Andorra Star* and we were trucked to Liverpool's docks and herded onto the gangplank of a waiting troopship, HMT *Dunera*. My few possessions — textbooks, notepaper, my treasured Parker pen, my toilet articles and scant extra clothing, even my boots — were ripped from me. I had nothing left but the clothes on my back. Then soldiers with bayonets mounted on their rifles chased us down companionways to a hold far below the water line. It all happened so quickly that only when I sat on the bare deck did shock set in, soon to be replaced by fear bordering on panic. What were we in for now? Why were we being treated like this? What would we do to get off this ship if it were to be torpedoed?

Years later, when I read the report of a British parliamentary inquiry, I understood what had happened. Some of our guards were soldiers of the line who had recently escaped from Dunkirk, while others were jailbirds who had been pardoned to enlist. Among the prisoners herded onto the *Dunera* were Nazi soldiers captured in Norway and at Dunkirk. The commander of the guards encouraged the sadistic treatment of prisoners. He was later reprimanded by Parliament.

Of course, we knew none of this as we were herded to our hold below the water line. The space was bare except for long benches and tables and sleeping hammocks strung from the ceiling. Sixteen holes in boards, with seawater flowing beneath them in an open gutter, were the "head," or toilet facilities, for our contingent of 980 internees up forward. The shallow gutter often flooded from accumulations of human waste, which spilled onto the floor and then floated back and forth with the rolling of the boat. The queues to the head were never-ending and accidents happened.

Soon after leaving Liverpool, the ship began to toss and pitch in the Irish Sea, and most of my shipmates became seasick. Their symptoms ranged from total indifference to what was happening to repeated vomiting, followed by stupor. The rough sea made the heads overflow into our living quarters, there to mix with the smell of vomit, the stench of sweat and unwashed bodies, and the aroma of fried bacon and eggs. The only thing normal on the *Dunera* was the food, which apparently was the regular British army ration. Immune to seasickness and with nothing else to do, I ate all I wanted.

On the third evening out, in the storm-tossed Bay of Biscay, we heard a loud clang and a dull thud, followed by a big explosion that shook the boat. All the lights went out. After a seeming eternity, they came back on. We later learned that a German submarine had launched two torpedoes. One was a dud and the other had glanced off the stern and then exploded away from the boat. I never found out why the lights went out. Years later I learned that German radio, not knowing Nazi POWs and interned German Jews were on board, announced that the British troopship *Dunera* had been sunk.

Down in that lowest hold, we had no life vests. No abandon-ship drill was ever conducted, and all passages to the upper decks were blocked with barbed-wire barricades. There was one port-hole up in the head, barely above the water line, through which I hoped I might be able to squeeze in an emergency.

Everything seemed to have conspired against me. After escaping from the Nazis, I was now incarcerated by my erstwhile saviors in a floating coffin and was destined to die if a torpedo struck again. I had no life vest to sustain me in the water even if I managed to get out. At first, because there was nothing to do during the day and especially at night, I worried about all of the things that might happen. I feared being drowned like a rat or being crushed in a stampede by prisoners as the ship sank or turned over. I could invent no sure way to save myself. I feared what might happen, I feared the unknown. There was no end to the disasters I imagined and no way I could see myself surviving if they struck. But, paradoxically, within days, after I had worn myself out with fear and anxiety, I experienced an incredible feeling that I would live to do important things.

Never taught or trained to counter peril, I wondered whether this new sensation of calm was a self-protective denial of dangerous reality or perhaps a hidden, primal resource to cope with mortal danger. I had a lot of angst for things that never happened, yet I coped well when they did happen. As my fears receded, miraculously my confidence grew.

Many of my shipmates slept all the time. The barbed wire and the shared misery leveled all distinctions of age and status.

I learned to interpret the steering engine's groaning noises, caused by the endless zigs and zags in our course that were meant to fool U-boats. After a few days, by counting off more and more seconds between those noises, I realized we were steering a straighter course. I figured that Canada could not be more than ten days away, and that king and country would surely realize the terrible mistake they had made in my case. But soon I realized that something was wrong with my assumptions. By comparing ship's time, indicated by the sound of bells, to the times of sunset and sunrise, which I observed from that porthole in the head, I realized we were heading south, not east. Where were we going?

With my rudimentary knowledge of spherical geometry (the basis of navigation), acquired under the tutelage of my wonderful teacher Benson Herbert, and with a borrowed pencil, I scribbled formulae on a wad of toilet paper. I deduced that we were going to South Africa. As it got warmer and the seas grew calmer, I became an oracle to my fellow prisoners. With a wristwatch secretly saved by one of my fellow prisoners and my pencil and paper, I calculated, then announced that we would soon be crossing the equator. Sure enough, a day later we put into Freetown on the west coast of Africa. The grapevine was — yes, even in the lowest hold of a prison ship there was a grapevine — that we were taking on water, fuel, and food for the journey to Australia around the Cape of Good Hope.

My plan to escape to the United States from Canada was obviously shot.

After leaving U-boat-infested waters, prisoners were herded up on deck twice a week for ten minutes of fresh air. We had to run around the deck, barefoot, under the guard of soldiers with machine guns at the ready. They sometimes amused themselves by throwing broken beer bottles in our path. We developed eagle eyes and quick motions to avoid cutting our feet. One day an internee jumped overboard. No attempt was made to rescue him.

Days and nights followed each other monotonously on the *Dunera*. Some of my younger shipmates relived their preinternment sex lives by telling us about them until we all knew the private habits of their girlfriends, while others just stared ahead dully. One tall, bearded man constantly took off his money belt, which he had been able to keep with him undetected by the guards, and counted his money over and over. Unbeknownst to him, several of us counted his thousands of pounds silently with him. That ritual seemed to calm him, but never for long.

At night a hundred hammocks swayed in ghostly synchronism as the ship rolled in the undulating seas. Some slept quietly; others mumbled in their sleep. Several times each night someone, evidently caught up in some frightening nightmare, yelled for help. Strange how many called out for their mothers and none for their fathers. During the day, which differed from night mainly in that the guards made us get out of the sack, seasickness and the fear of U-boats were now mostly replaced by a dull indifference. There was nothing to do, nothing to plan, only cleaning duty to be shirked. There were the usual rumors that we were being tranquilized with saltpeter to disable our sex drive. Day and night blended into one another in our hold, with its dim electric lights supplemented only by faint illumination coming from the gangway to the deck above.

Once a week we stowed our meager possessions in the hammocks to swab and squeegee the teak deck. Everybody was herded first into a corner, which was swabbed and squeegeed last. Seeing that gleaming, golden teak deck so clean was always a pleasure to me. Otherwise, I had a feeling of being in some kind of nether world without beginning or end. I remember men crying and praying, and occasional screaming outbursts. But we survived.

Fear wears thin when nothing happens, this voyage had to come to an end sometime. With every turn of the propeller, I was getting farther away from the Nazis, whom, even then, I still feared more than the British.

Off the southwest coast of Africa, I developed a debilitating case of dysentery with a high fever and yellowing of the skin. We had elected a deck leader, and he insisted that I be moved from that overcrowded hold. Being in the ship's infirmary, lying in a real bed, despite my illness, was an unbelievable luxury. When the Irish doctor heard my story, he kept me in his overcrowded sick bay for extra days. I must have slept most of the time. I rose only to make it to the toilet — a real toilet on the *Dunera*! After I was discharged as an inpatient, the kindly doctor arranged for me to spend extra time in his clean surroundings by making me wait for hours for my daily spoonful of medicine and quinine pills.

We were separated from the Nazis on board by a passage with barbed wire on each side. They would stand at the wire and wait for someone to appear, so they could taunt him. One day I got tired of their jazz and told them that when we got to Australia, they would be circumcised and that the officers would have a Star of David tattooed on their arms. I urged them to pray that Hitler would be gone when they got back to Germany, otherwise they would be put in concentration camps. And then I pulled my pants down and farted in their faces. They rattled the wire and called me a dirty Jew, and I called them stupid bastards. In fact, Hitler *was* gone when they got back to Germany after 1945, something they and we could not imagine in 1940.

The *Dunera* stopped again at Takoradi, still on the west coast of Africa, to refuel and then headed south for Cape Town. There, through a porthole in the infirmary, I saw Table Mountain and the city. My sense of adventure was still intact. Here I was, a kid from dull landlocked Gardelegen, now in Africa, or at least a few hundred yards off Africa, about to round the Cape of Good Hope and cross the Indian Ocean to Australia. I was seeing the world, even if it was through a porthole of a prison ship!

With my rudimentary system of navigation, I predicted our landfall on Australia's western coast within a day of its actual occurrence, an error of about two hundred miles. We stopped in Perth-Freemantle. There, Australian officers boarded the *Dunera* and were horrified at what they heard and saw. Their reports of conditions aboard led to inquiries in the Australian and British parliaments, where all I have told here, and more, was documented. Books have been written about the *Dunera*.

The *Dunera* stopped in Melbourne to offload the Nazis, who were to have a great life for five years as POWs, escaping the cataclysm of defeat that befell their fighting comrades. The only thing they had to worry about was my warning of impending circumcision and Star of David tattoos and a premature return to Nazi land.

We internees left the *Dunera* in Sydney. Johnny, the most feared and sadistic of the guards, was at the gangplank to see us off. A long-faced, slightly cross-eyed sergeant major with CIC (counterintelligence) emblems on his uniform, Johnny had slunk around, stirring up miserable heaps of our remaining possessions with his NCO stick and talking in a barely audible, rasping voice. Every few days he would grab an internee to put in the "hole," a solitary confinement cell in the brig normally reserved for deserters and mutineers. Johnny was a natural sadist. There he stood now at the head of the gangway. He looked sad, I was sure about losing his power over defenseless prisoners. As I passed him, I told him I hoped he would drown on the way back to England.

I felt faint when we emerged into the sunlight after weeks in the dark hold of the ship. Our Australian guards were flabbergasted when they discovered we were Jewish refugees from Nazi Germany. We were put aboard a string of ancient railroad cars that made up a train to the Australian outback. We rattled down crooked tracks, mile after mile, hour after hour, becoming grimier from the soot of the engine and the sand stirred up by the train. As we snaked into the Australian bush, wallabies leapt next to the track. We were heading for the never-heard-of town of Hay. The guards began to doze, and one lost his grip on his rifle. I picked it up and noticed it was not loaded.

Hay is a dot on the map by the Hay River, which was dry when we arrived. From there we were trucked to our camp. The first thing I noticed was hardly any barbed wire around. The commanding officer explained it to us: "We are not guarding you very much, because the nearest water is over eighty miles away. We guard the water tanks, and you will only be allowed to have one canteen of water at a time. If you want to jump camp and die of thirst, go ahead."

Every evening at sunset there was a gale of dust so fine it got into every pore and opening of our bodies, into the toilet kits we had been issued, into everything. While the days were hot, the nights were cool and the stars were unbelievably bright. I marveled at seeing the Southern Cross. The food was good, and soon we were busy adjusting to our new routine, as the *Dunera* and its perils receded in our minds. And of course, we were now safely away from the Nazis. It was as though we were suspended in time. It was now the middle of August 1940.

On the fifth day in Hay, I asked to speak to the commandant. He reminded me of the beefy major in Maidstone. But he listened. I explained to him how stupid the British (he called them Limeys) were to send me to Hay when all I wanted was to fight the Germans. I told him I would gladly join the Australian Army. When I finished, the commandant said, "Laddie, I can't enlist you in the army and I cannot get you out of here, but you are my orderly from now on."

"What does that mean?" I asked.

He said, "You come back here at seven tomorrow morning and you'll find out."

Next morning he said, "Climb into that truck; we're going hunting." Ten minutes later he said, "You carry my gun; I need a gun boy to go hunting." And so we went hunting for wallabies and killed a few snakes and birds with his shotgun. Back by eleven before the heat would kill us.

I had been in Hay only ten days when the loudspeaker announced that I was to report to the camp office, where I was told to pack my scant belongings immediately. I was to be shipped back to England, to be released from internment on arrival there.

I asked, "Why not now?"

"Orders," they said.

I was stunned. I never found out why the British government decided to free me, and five others, out of thousands in our group. Now I was to go back to England, while most of my fellow internees were to remain imprisoned in Australia. Glad as I was to head back for freedom, I also realized I would once again have to brave U-boat-infested seas.

Departure for Melbourne immediately, I was told. I was issued new Australian army fatigues and soft black kangaroo-leather boots, which I loved. We rode in a better compartment in a better train than the one that had brought us to Hay, but it still took twenty-three hours. Though we were under guard, the Australian guards regarded us as some sort of VIPs.

To my consternation, we were taken to the city prison in Melbourne, because we had to be kept "safe." When we were placed in a wing with hardened criminals, I complained. To the great mirth of our keepers, we were then moved to the prostitute wing, where we were promised good entertainment. It was definitely that. Those ladies of the streets loved male company and put on the granddaddy of all strip shows for us. It left nothing to my imagination! They were witty, talented, uninhibited, and lewd. My knowledge of the female anatomy increased immeasurably. The ladies offered us for free through the bars what they had been selling on the streets, sales that had made them guests of the state. Had it not been for my fear of syphilis, drilled into me by my parents, this could have been a high point in my young life. Alas, the bliss of their company lasted only two days.

Since leaving England, I had not been able to mail a letter to anyone. My jailer promised to bring me paper, pen, and postage, but before he did, we six "returnees" were suddenly loaded into a truck that took us — incredibly — back aboard HMT *Dunera*.

What a shock!

Johnny and the other guards were all there. Though we were prisoners no more, they knew we would regain our freedom only upon reaching England. We were still under the authority of the ship's commanding officer, fortunately not the same sadist we had on the way out. We had the run of the boat, but we were made to clean everything: pots, pans, dishes, decks, tables, and benches. As in all military services, when something is clean, one cleans it again, because idleness is assumed to be injurious to morale and character. I became a superb cleaner and "swabbie" six hours a day, even when a second and a third cleaning accomplished nothing useful.

Every day I wondered why we had lifeboat and abandon-ship drills. Was this not overdoing it a little? The *Dunera* rounded Australia and headed into the Indian Ocean. Then one day the alarms went off. It was not a drill. The *Dunera's* four-inch stern gun let go with a loud bang. I happened to see Johnny near one of the lifeboats, and I could see he was scared. He looked at me and I thumbed my nose at him. He could not even grimace. After that he never came near me again.

A few shells exploded in the water near us. Later I was told that the *Dunera* was being used as a decoy to lure German and Italian raiders — fast, converted ocean liners that had been armed to attack merchant vessels. Soon a British cruiser appeared. I never found out what had been the source of the shelling.

Now, mysteriously, we were diverted to Bombay. There, our small group of internees-to-be-freed-in-England was dumped onto the pier and placed in the care of an Indian police inspector. Soon after, there appeared a welcoming committee of the Bombay Jewish Relief Association, led by a corpulent Jewish man from southern Germany in khaki shorts and a pith helmet. He spoke English with a heavy accent, but told us that he was a British citizen. After hearing our story, he vouched for us with the police inspector.

We were fingerprinted and issued identification papers. Admonished by the police to own no weapons, cameras, binoculars, or radio transmitters (very funny, I thought when I didn't even have a second pair of underpants), we were then taken by our champion to Habib Chambers, an apartment house operated by the relief association in the native quarter of Bombay. He said good-bye and turned us over to the matron who ran that establishment.

Next day, I stepped out on the street. I had not taken ten steps when I ran into Mr. and Mrs. Helms, German Jews from a town near Gardelegen. Their attempts to conceive a child had been fruitless before my mother helped them. Their baby daughter, now in a pram on Byculla Road, had been born in the birthing suite in our house. I had always felt uncomfortable in their presence — there was something sugary false about them — but here they were, and I exclaimed, "Why, Mr. and Mrs. Helms, what are you doing here?" They had some money, and had escaped to Bombay from Nazi Germany.

I borrowed (and later repaid) enough from them to send a telegram to my parents, who were now in the United States and who had heard nothing from me since June, when I had left England. They believed I was dead. It was September now and I was in India. I found the telegram I sent from Bombay in my father's desk after he died. It said, "Released Bombay, send money c/o Cooks." I assumed of course that they knew I meant the Cooks travel and forwarding agency.

The relief organization fed and housed me. The heat was intolerable, and in the middle of the first night I moved out onto the porch. I soon noticed huge birds circling and diving at me. They retreated every time I moved. I went back into the sweltering bedroom. Next day I learned that these birds were vultures that normally circled the nearby Tower of Silence, where they were in the habit of picking the flesh from the bones of Parsi dead until the skeletons were clean; later, the bones were incinerated. An inert body on a porch at night was a potential meal for those vultures.

Back in the bedroom, I heard noises like soldiers marching in the distance. When I turned on the light, an army of huge cockroaches began scrambling posthaste over the stone floor into any dark crack they could find. I was taught to shake my boots before putting them on to make sure there were no scorpions in them. Boots were preferred to shoes, in case we stepped on a cobra. I never did.

My parents, happily relieved that I was alive and totally mystified about how I had landed in Bombay, somehow scraped up fifty dollars to send me — they were earning twenty dollars a month between them. But it was enough in Bombay in 1940 to buy underwear, have a khaki cotton suit made, buy cigarettes, and, most important, get myself a sun helmet, a topi, which was de rigueur for any white man. I still had my beloved Australian kangaroo leather boots.

There were a number of Jewish refugee families in Bombay. One of these families had a daughter, and either she or they took a fancy to me. At any rate, I was invited to their house more frequently than I could tolerate. Teenagers have strong likes and strong aversions, and this girl was not for me. She eventually married another man from Habib Chambers.

In the meantime, I was corresponding with my parents. Through friends, they put me in touch with several American Quakers who were in India on missions of mercy. They, in turn, introduced me to a Swiss couple who were most hospitable to me. He was a banker and his wife was a lovely young Jewish woman who had escaped from Nazi Germany. I spent many congenial hours with them in their apartment and at the beach, where monkeys tossed coconuts at us from palm trees.

I soon met Parsis, Hindus, and members of Nehru's Congress Party. I learned a little Urdu to talk to *dhobi wallas* (laundry men) and *ghari wallas* (taxi men) and to ask, *"Kidna badja hai"* (What time is it?) and more. From these service people I was amazed to receive the deferential respect that natives inevitably paid to their imperial masters.

In the native quarters, one was lucky to avoid bright red spurts of betel juice, which people spat through open windows onto the splotched sidewalks. Homeless people by the hundreds slept on the streets. I saw people with noses eaten away by syphilis or leprosy. Cows, with extra tails incredibly grafted onto their flanks, ambled along busy streets. No one stopped these sacred bovines from eating vegetables from open stalls at the central market, while humans were starving. At monsoon time, I saw sewers clogged with rats drowned in the torrents that came with the heavy rains.

Habib Chambers was on Byculla Road, a main artery with streetcars and buses. I walked around freely, never witnessed any violence, and never feared for my safety. Not far from us was a huge red-light district, where buxom Indian beauties sat in open windows and freely displayed their wares. If our morals didn't stop us, the fear of Asian syphilis, a debilitating and mutilating disease rarely treated among the natives, certainly discouraged us from physical contact. Looking, conversing, and observing the pleasure with which the women greeted customers was enough.

There were tea and hashish shops everywhere, and their smell pervaded the air in the evenings. In these shops, I joined many a conversation about colonialism, conducted with insistent fervor in that distinctive Indian-accented English. I also learned for the first time that persecuted people feel that their suffering bestows on them some kind of sainthood and makes them morally superior. Like my companions, I was led to believe that the end of colonialism would cure the poverty and other ills of this exotic land.

I also began to understand some of the fundamental differences between the culture of the East and my own. As I grew up, I had been taught to perfect my practice of moral values, and tried to become proficient at everything I did. I saw Western culture, even the abhorrent morals of the Nazis, as a culture of activism where one lived to do but did to live. By contrast, I discovered the culture of Hinduism, or at least what I thought was Hinduism, as a culture of being. If one was a good coolie in this life, he might be a taxi owner in the next.

India, in my day, had a caste of banyas, moneylenders, who extended credit to the poorest of the poor. Debts were hereditary, and sons had to assume payment, with interest, of the loans their fathers had taken out to finance the traditional weddings of their daughters. It was said that no Hindu ever escaped the moneylenders by moving or changing his name. Gandhi raged about the banyas. I met one who had an Oxford education, and I asked him how he justified, given the Western values he espoused, exploiting the poorest of the poor. He answered, "Providence has put the poor into this world to suffer poverty, and Providence selected me to be a good moneylender. I am not to interfere with a world order, but I am here to serve it." He was sincere and slept well at night.

Just as my banya friend had a superficial Western appearance, so did Bombay as a city, except for the signs on shops and the clothing of the people. Buses, streetcars, and automobiles predominated over carts. But meandering sacred cows lent a truly distinctive flavor.

In Bombay I met a few Parsis, a people apart, who were invariably rich, contemplative, and devoted to their ancient Zoroastrian creed. A young woman named Usha and I shared a philosophical harmony that was most unusual between a German of Jewish descent with an affinity for the English and a descendant of the old Persians. We were young and of the same spirit. We believed in the brotherhood of man, we detested prejudice, we loved the prophets but hated organized religion, and we abhorred colonialism. We were as one intellectually and were emotionally close, though never physically intimate. A sexual relationship before marriage would have ruined Usha for life.

Around this time I got an especially nice, long letter from brother Helmut, who told me that the school had moved out of the invasion zone to Wem in Shropshire and how relieved all were to know that I was alive. He also mentioned a girlfriend pining to hear from me. I never wrote her. Ah, how cruel we can be when teenage infatuations pass! And I had a lovely letter from Betty, whom I did want to remember, although we were now oceans apart and, I thought, might be thus forever.

I decided to find a job. But I, as a member of the white man's race, the Raj, was barred from menial jobs, and I was not qualified for the typical white man's work. What to do?

In England, I had studied *The Admiralty Handbook of Wireless*

Telegraphy, an official training manual for British navy radio officers. I now found a copy in the library in Bombay. I reread it until I knew it practically word for word. I wanted to get a job in
radio.

By this time I had become friendly with a quartet of
German-Jewish bachelors who shared a large apartment, where
they were well tended by a butler, a cook, and cleaners. When I
told them that I planned to go to work, they were incredulous,
but one of them introduced me to a Hindu gentleman who ran a
shop that made simple radios, a good business because imports
were no longer available. He had me work on unpaid probation
for a month, but I was soon supervising a dozen Hindus who assembled simple two-tube radios. I was becoming adept at assuming roles assigned me by fate: I was now carrying the White
Man's Burden in Bombay and getting paid quite nicely for doing
it. I knew that this latest incarnation would also be temporary.
What next? I wondered.

I was a seventeen-year-old boy with no parental or other supervision, with adult friends, with a job and living in an interesting city, far removed from Nazis and British jailers. I was free to
come, go, and do as I wanted. That wonderful freedom and my
ability to manage for myself compensated for the uncertainties
of my future and my lack of family contact. I did miss having a
steady girlfriend and male friends my age.

One day I went to the American consulate. As I entered the
building, I noticed how pleasantly cool it was. There was a sign,
"Air Conditioning by Carrier." I had never been in an air-
conditioned building before. In the heat of Bombay I got my first
taste of America, and it was wonderful and cool. That's for me, I
thought.

The vice-consul, Mr. Wallace La Rue, was tall and slim and
had a trim haircut. He was wearing an immaculate tan suit of a
kind I had never seen before — later I learned to recognize it as
Palm Beach. He asked what I wanted, and I told him, "I want to
go to America." He asked for my papers. I had only my certificate

of identity, issued by the police commissioner of Bombay, but Mr. La Rue needed proof of birth so that he could assign me to the German quota. He then asked me why I wanted to go to America, and I told him that my parents were living in Baltimore.

"Do you know anyone in Baltimore?" he asked. I only knew of a Mr. Lansbury, who had signed the guarantee for my parents' visa. Mr. La Rue was startled. "Did you say Lansbury? Are you trying to put me on?" I was baffled. I did not understand what he meant. He told me he knew Mr. Lansbury and added, "We will contact you."

Within a week I heard that Mr. La Rue had confirmed my original visa application, made in Berlin in 1937, and had verified the rest of my story. He had a visa for me, he said. But I didn't have a passport. "No problem," he said. He would issue identity papers for me. But I needed to show him a ticket for passage to the United States before he could issue the visa.

Nobody could believe this turn of events. I was America bound! My brother was still at school in besieged England, and the U-boat war had stopped transatlantic passenger traffic from there and from Nazi Europe. None of my fellow ex-internees in Bombay, now loyal enemy-aliens of the British government of India, had any place to go. All the hundreds of other internees with whom I had sailed to Australia were still in the bush. How was it that only I was to get an American visa?

One way to reach the United States from Bombay was to sail via Ceylon and Indonesia to Yokohama, Japan, and from there to the West Coast of the United States. It appealed to my sense of adventure to nearly circle the globe before arriving in New York, but I feared that Japan could soon be at war with the United States. The possibility of winding up in a Japanese stockade was not appealing.

The other route was via South Africa to South America and the Caribbean. The American President Line plied this route but offered only expensive first-class passage. Their SS *President Wilson* was due to sail from Bombay about March 21, 1941, with an estimated arrival in New York of April 26. First-class passage cost $660, an enormous sum to me at that time.

My parents were able to raise a portion of the fare. I had saved several hundred dollars from my wages and borrowed the final twenty dollars from those helpful bachelors. With my last rupees I bought a third shirt and a few inexpensive souvenirs. My friends gave me a farewell banquet. On the morning of my departure, I hired a taxi and went aboard the *President Wilson* with a black metal box as my baggage. I was dressed in a gray linen suit, freshly laundered and pressed, and I wore a khaki pith helmet. I was now a first-class passenger. My roommate was a Turk who never spoke to me. Aboard were also several attractive American girls going home to get away from the threat of war in Asia and the Near East.

With America still neutral, "United States" was spelled out in bright lights along the side of our ship to warn off U-boats. That was as safe as ocean travel could get in 1941.

A few days out at sea, I impressed the radio operator with my knowledge of wireless communications. He made a deal with me that was to be totally secret. For several hours every day, I would monitor radios in the shack while he took a snooze, remaining instantly available if something happened. He paid me quite handsomely, but I managed to spend that money on whiskey and cigarettes, and on more clothing and other articles at our ports of call. I played a lot of bridge with a British baronet and his wife. It was a most pleasant five-week journey, and what a contrast with my previous crossing!

By the end of the trip, I had enough money to repay my debts, and still had three dollars to take care of myself in the United States. There were a few missionaries on the boat, and my lifestyle did not earn their approbation. But I got along famously with others who had no ambition to convert me. I remember having good food and a very nice social life in secluded corners of the boat deck with Sally Simms, who was very adept at apportioning her time between me and a handsome young steward. I learned more about radio, as electronics was then called, and the laws of the sea. Barbed wire, the *Dunera*, and the hustle and bustle of Bombay were now receding fast. There were American movies shown in the salon, and I watched some of those movies several times. Sally, who had a cute Texas accent, made me practice Hollywood English and then assured me that I spoke like a real Yankee.

After stops in Cape Town, Trinidad, and Havana, New York drew nearer, and I thought about how I was now reaching the goal I had set when I volunteered to be deported from England. It seemed incredible that less than a year had passed since that morning when I left Bunce Court to be interned.

Why was I so lucky when others on the *Andorra Star* had drowned just days before the *Dunera* sailed? Why was I one of only six among three thousand to be released from internment in Australia? And why was I the only one in Bombay to be granted an American visa and obtain transportation? My brother Helmut and thousands of others were stuck in England and elsewhere. Wasn't it odd that I, who had left England under such inauspicious circumstances, should now reach the United States? It seemed to me that the future could only pale in comparison to my past.

Now I thought about losing my freedom if normal family life were once more to resume. That did not appeal to me. Just before the sun rose, that last morning at sea, one thing became certain: I would not go back to being my parents' schoolboy. I was not going to give up my independence. When I got to America I would be on my own!

VIII

America

O<small>N THE MORNING OF APRIL 26, 1941</small>, it was dawn when I walked up to the boat deck. The sun, still below the horizon behind us, already bathed the tops of the New York skyline in pink, an unforgettable sight. The skyscrapers got bigger, and soon I saw land on both sides. We steamed past Sandy Hook, sighted the Statue of Liberty, and docked in Hoboken, across from Manhattan. There an immigration inspector came aboard and barely glanced at my papers before admitting me to the United States.

I looked for Sally Simms to kiss her good-bye. From the deck I saw my parents and my Uncle Hans, who had also been able to get out of Germany. Apparently they had noticed me before I saw them. They looked so little in a knot of people at the foot of the gangway.

As I waved to my family, reporters and photographers looking for stories of war, deprivation, and adventure found me and surrounded me. They had no great events to report at this moment. The RAF had won the Battle of Britain and was bombing Germany at night. The Germans had not yet invaded the Soviet Union. The United States was organizing its own armed forces while continuing deadlocked negotiations with Japan.

And here was I, a seventeen-year-old boy completely on my

own, hounded out of Germany, first welcomed in England, then put on a British prison ship that was torpedoed but did not sink. A roaming refugee who, after imprisonment in Australia, work in India, and another crossing of the U-boat-infested oceans, was now free in America. That was the stuff that tabloid readers ate up. There seemed to be no end to the questions and the popping of flash bulbs.

Meanwhile, my parents were waiting and waiting to greet me. Finally I reached them and said, "Hello, how are you?" — in English. That was my way of telling them that I was no longer the boy to whom they had said good-bye less than three years earlier.

I noticed immediately that my mother was unnecessarily diffident when she addressed porters and taxi drivers. I was annoyed even more when she insisted right away that I follow her cue. Not then, but later, I came to understand how Nazi persecution had sapped the self-respect of its victims. Many of them, like my parents, regained their poise only after passing exams to practice their professions once more. And this often took time. Meanwhile, they did not speak the language well, a handicap that further reduced their status and self-esteem.

By now I had twitted Nazis, who were as scared as I was of dying in a floating coffin; I had coped with British captors; and I had run a small factory in Bombay where, as a white man, I had been respected though perhaps not loved. I had traveled as a first-class passenger with Americans with whom I had effortlessly socialized. And I was seventeen! I did not think I needed lessons on how to behave. I asked the taxi driver, who had a heavy accent, how long he had been in America. "Five years, and I'll soon be a citizen," he said. We went through the Holland Tunnel to Washington Heights, our destination, where I said, "Thanks, cabby."

Uncle Hans, Aunt Lottie, and Cousin Walter lived in a small walk-up apartment in a virtual German-Jewish ghetto, amid relatives and friends from Berlin. They all spoke German to each other. Their English was heavily accented, and the syntax was transliterated German. My parents spoke better English. Though living in poor circumstances while Mother worked at a sanitarium, at least they were with people who spoke no German. Uncle Hans, the original family black sheep who had become a millionaire and *Grosser Macher* (big shot), had blithely assumed that, upon his arrival in New York, people would be knocking at his door to make deals with him. But nobody knocked. Hans was reduced to selling newspapers in a subway kiosk, polishing boots at a shoeshine stand, and moping at home, while Aunt Lottie worked variously in chocolate and brassiere factories "downtown." She was very timid, to the point of refusing a promotion to forewoman, being terrified of dealing with coworkers who were citizens.

One friend of my father's, Hans Hesse, was studying for his state board examinations in medicine while his wife, Loscha, worked to support the family. They lived in a crowded apartment, but she had a bubbly personality and was less cowed than the rest of them. As an East European who had married into a German-Jewish family, she had less emotional baggage than her in-laws. Of all of them, she alone remained her old self. The children, in their early teens and younger, went to New York schools where they learned English, still speaking German at home. While I was glad to see them all, I also knew this was not where I wanted to live. My family foresaw their future only as a comedown from their past. I treasured my school days in England and had fully gained my freedom at age seventeen. To me, my past was just a prelude to my future.

My parents and I stayed in New York for a few days. Strangers who had read about me in the newspapers stopped me in the street. My relatives and their friends were wide-eyed. Nobody had noticed *their* arrival in the States. But I soon tired of being paraded around.

A highlight of my first experiences in New York was eating at a Schrafft's restaurant. To me, its marble stairs, brass railings, mirrors, and chandeliers were the height of elegance, so much more impressive than the décor of the automats, which I had admired in Berlin. Everything in midtown Manhattan seemed so modern, so big, the elevators, the escalators, the polished marble floors in Rockefeller Center, even the movie houses, where you could see the same film three times for seventeen cents and buy a candy bar for a nickel. This was as wondrous as Berlin had been to me as a three-year-old! I loved vanilla milk shakes. And I got used to everyone asking, "How do you like America?" Well, it seemed like a fabulous country to me.

On the train from New York to Baltimore, I marveled at the electric locomotive and the luxurious coaches. The train was much quieter than anything I had ever been on. Everything in the United States seemed much bigger than it had anywhere else.

In Baltimore, a diminutive black man from the sanitarium met us with a Ford station wagon. I had never seen a car with wooden side panels, and it was so big and quiet with an eight-cylinder engine. We were driven out to Harlem Lodge in suburban Catonsville. This was a private institution for mentally disturbed patients, a few of them "in restraint" but most of them ambulatory with supervision. My mother had a job as assistant to the medical director, with room and board for herself and Father. A common practice in those days was electric shock treatment, and every day I remember hearing horrible accounts of this procedure. My father was not employed and was studying to regain his license to practice medicine.

A Mr. Grundy owned Harlem Lodge, and he graciously allowed me to live with my parents. He had two daughters. The younger one, Marly, fat and nasty, mocked my ignorance about things American, but her elder sister, Cissy, was very nice. Getting to know American girls was interesting. They acted so cool and remote while they waited for me to break the ice, but they necked enthusiastically after the movies, even before we had established an intellectual affinity or a real emotional harmony.

My girlfriends in England and I always talked about history, philosophy, and ethics before kissing. But kissing first was fine with me.

Not far from Harlem Lodge there lived a German family who had emigrated to the States before Hitler rose to power. Friendly with my parents, they extended their hospitality to me, too. The husband was a metalworker, and he taught me how to get a Social Security number and how to apply for a job.

My parents assumed that I would live with them, finish high school, and then go on to college and university and earn a doctor's degree. In their German-Jewish culture, children regressed to a lower status than that of their parents if they didn't earn the obligatory degree of "Herr Doktor." My parents assumed that their child, sheltered by parental love, would gratefully follow the trodden path.

My mother took me to meet Mrs. Julia Strauss, the head of the Baltimore Jewish Refugee Relief Committee, a lovely and regal lady who in 1937 had helped obtain that all-important affidavit for our family, as she had for many others. She had also secured my parents' meager existence. When we arrived, several people were waiting to see that august lady and were discussing how to get help from her. Mrs. Strauss mentioned how much my parents had suffered in not hearing from me for so many months. "What were my plans?" she asked. "Go to work," I said. She asked, "As what?" and I said, "As an electrician." Unbeknownst to my parents, I had already obtained a Social Security card and had registered at the Maryland State Employment Office as "foreman, electrical." Nobody commented that I was only seventeen.

Mrs. Strauss was shocked that I wanted nothing from her and was even more shocked when I said that I was never going to be a "refujew." After I landed a job she became a great fan of mine. She held me up as example to those who asked for support instead of seeking opportunity.

I found a job with the Simpson Electric Company in Annapolis, about thirty miles from where my parents lived; it paid seventy cents an hour, twenty-eight dollars a week. My parents, together, were then earning thirty dollars a month plus room and board! America was still emerging from the Depression, and although the country was arming for war, the economy had not yet produced much traction. In those days, at a White Tower restaurant, I could buy a hamburger or a cherry pie for a dime, and coffee, all I could drink, cost five cents. In Annapolis I found room and board for nine dollars a week that included a hot breakfast at six in the morning, a packed lunch, and dinner at the home of my landlady.

I noticed for the first time that rooms and closets in her house were not locked and that during the day even the front door of her house was unlocked. I was impressed by how much Americans trusted each other. In Germany, everything lockable was locked all the time, and the fear of thieves and pickpockets was ever present.

Jesse Simpson, my boss, decided to call me Dick when he saw that one of my middle names was Richard. That name stuck, and I have been Dick ever since. Nobody ever called me *Wölfchen* (little Wolfgang) again!

To see my parents on weekends, I needed a car. I found a 1937 Ford, a dog of an automobile if ever there was one. It had a sixty-horsepower V-8 engine with sixty thousand miles on it; at any rate, that is what the odometer showed. It had anemic mechanical brakes, a dent in its trunk lid, and pockmarked fenders. It was otherwise serviceable. I paid "seventy down and twenty-one a month" for a year. I borrowed sixty dollars from my landlady and bought the car. Six weeks after coming to America I had a job, earned a living wage, had a driver's license, and owned a car!

My parents asked me to move back in with them. I felt bad that they had been deprived of seeing their children grow up — my brother was still stuck in England with no prospect of transportation across the U-boat-infested Atlantic. I did try living with them for a few weeks, but it was very tough on us all.

I managed a few dates on weekends. One of those was arranged by the family of Dr. Leo Kanner, a former classmate of my father in Berlin, a noted professor of child psychiatry at Johns Hopkins University. The Kanners had a daughter, Anita, two years older than I, and they invited me to stay at their house on weekends "because I had no friends." I soon realized that their daughter was socializing with a young man who was leaning far, far left. Though they must have realized that Anita and I would never be an item, they may have hoped that I might be able to wean her away from a flaming Red with a college education. I liked Anita but had no romantic interest in her.

Through Leo Kanner I met other Johns Hopkins psychiatrists with whom I became very friendly. I must have been great material for their studies of adolescent development!.

As far as I was concerned, psychiatrists with a love for humanity were as helpful as priests or grandparents who helped distraught youngsters or oldsters by listening to them and giving them confidence in their ability to master their problems. I loved their company because they made me feel that I was living a useful life as a craftsman who regarded his past not as an unjust fate but as a prelude.

I had little in common with girls and boys my own age to whom I was introduced. They were sheltered in secure families; they knew nothing of the world at war; they were not working as I was. Many came from observant Jewish families, and my rejection of organized religion was as abhorrent to them as their religious practices were to me.

My parents held on to that "high holiday Judaism" that they had developed in Nazi Germany, but I refused to attend services and was not interested in social activities sponsored by synagogues. Fortunately, I met a Professor Feise, the chairman of the German language department at Johns Hopkins University. His wife invited me to socials at their house, where I met young faculty members who did not hold my lack of formal education against me. None of these academics had traveled to Australia, India, or South Africa or been on a prison ship at sea with U-boats shooting off torpedoes, nor had the Melbourne ladies of the streets entertained them — an event that was always good for an introduction. The dangers of war were far removed from my life then — yet deep down I knew Hitler would never be beaten without America subduing him. And I suspected that I would become involved again.

Three months after Jesse Simpson had hired me as an electrician helper, he took me down to Indian Head, not far from Washington. There the navy was building a large prefabricated residential development, and an electrician was needed to connect the wires of the different apartment sections, which arrived separately. The local crews were stymied because there were no blueprints. Jesse Simpson knew I could connect wires correctly when nobody else could. At Indian Head, Mr. Oscar Bryce, the local construction manager, asked me to hook up one of the prefabs. I did, and soon everything was working. Mr. Bryce hired me on the spot as the lead electrician and named me the foreman. I had to join the United Construction Workers of the CIO and received union scale wages, $1.35 an hour plus a living allowance of $10 a week. With overtime I was suddenly earning more than a hundred dollars a week, then a huge amount.

At Indian Head, south of La Plata, Maryland, I roomed with farmers for whom boarders were big money. There I shared a room with the carpenter Jerry, of English stock, and the plumber Paddy, with an Irish brogue, both easily twice or three times my age, those two in a double bed and I on a makeshift cot. During the day I worked in the unventilated attics of those prefabs, with temperatures close to 120 degrees Fahrenheit. I remember tasting my first iced tea, so incredibly cooling. My helpers were traveling roustabouts, and I never tired of hearing their stories.

Jerry had a truck, and after work the three of us squeezed together on the front seat "to have a few" in the local bar, where there were also pinball machines and dispensers with Mounds candy bars, which I consumed regularly before dinner. One evening, as we were leaving our favorite bar in Marlborough, a man appeared out of the shadows. "Stick 'em up, boys, and hand it over," he said. I was reaching for my wallet when I heard drunk Paddy say, "Hey, big boy, that is my racket and I'm from New York." Incredibly, the man shrank back into the shadows whence he had come. Being from New York apparently was quite a threat in southern Maryland.

The Indian Head project came to an end. After two short stints with contractors who hired and fired electricians as they booked and finished projects, I landed a job with the Charles Electric Company of Baltimore. Its owner was Arther (yes, that is how he spelled his name!) Raffel, an industrial electrical contractor, a relative of Gertrude Stein who looked somewhat like her. Arther took a fatherly interest in me.

The arming of America was now accelerating, and Raffel served businesses gearing up for the national defense, among them the shipyards at Sparrows Point and the Maryland Dry Dock Company. He recognized my talent as electrician and asked me to study for the state board examination for master electrician. If I passed it, I would be entitled to work without supervision; I would get paid more, and Raffel could charge more for my work. I passed with high marks and was told I was the youngest master electrician in the state of Maryland.

While working for Charles Electric, I discovered new aspects of American life. I recall putting alarm circuits into Baltimore's best-known strip joint, the Oasis, to warn the performers of police raids. The entertainers lavished lots of suggestions on me, and the madam always had a drink for me. I also worked in the big houses of Roland Avenue, which Baltimore high society considered a restricted area — not for Jews or blacks! I rewired kitchens of greasy spoons and made new installations in premier restaurants, in department stores, in a factory that made maraschino cherries, in a mattress factory, and at a famous dairy outside Baltimore called Dunloggin. There, along with all the other available men, I was once enlisted to restrain a prize bull that was enticed to mount a heifer, while an adroit breeder caught the bull's sperm in a canvas sock. The sperm would then

169

be sold to service a multitude of cows. Another day at Dunlog-gin, I saw a kitten catching drops of fresh warm milk from a cow's udder, just when the cow let go a big heap of green excrement. If you need a definition of misery, just picture a kitten completely covered by cow dung.

On big jobs, I sometimes teamed with Paul Ingraham, a black man about twice my size. In Baltimore in 1941 it was virtu-ally unheard of for blacks to work with whites, or for blacks to be electrician journeymen. Once, a customer objected to having Paul on his job, and I grabbed my tools and supplies to walk off. The customer called us back. I invited him to touch Paul to make sure that "it did not come off." We were a pair, all right, the refugee Jew from Germany and the American black who was considered "uppity" just because he was trying to do a good job as a craftsman. Paul was not married, but had a large sexual ap-petite, which he satisfied with frequent stops during lunch hour or between jobs. I met some of his many women friends as they were waving good-bye to him.

Paul had a good instinct for people and a colorful vocabu-lary. Of someone stingy he would say, "This guy wouldn't give you the sleeves from his vest." If something was really rare, it was "scarcer than hen's teeth." From Paul, I learned what it meant to pull up my socks, to get my finger out of my ass (it wasn't there!), and not to be too big for my breeches. I heard him warn people not to get tangled in their underwear and not to get their tit in the wringer. He informed me that the early bird always gets the worm, that stuck-up people believe that their shit does not smell, and that when something is easy, it is like taking candy from a baby or like shooting fish in a barrel, or it is a lead-pipe cinch. Something close was within a gnat's eyelash. A happy person was as "happy as a pig in shit," while an angry one was as "mad as a wet hen." When something was useless, it was "as useful as tits on a boar." From Paul I also learned the meanings of "Uncle Tom," "whitey," "kikes," and "bagels." Paul was not only a lin-guist of great range but also street smart, and he knew how to get what he wanted. He contributed greatly to my education in spoken English and American folklore, knowledge that came in handy when I later served in the infantry of the United States Army, where I wanted to sound and act like an American.

One night we were rewiring a steam laundry with Smitty, another master electrician who was also a master craftsman. While Smitty was at the switchboard, I was sorting through a big bundle of cables. Somehow I touched two live wires at the same time. I could not let go and I could not speak. I was paralyzed. Then my vision blurred and everything went dark. My mind was not yet gone, and my entire life flashed before me. The last thing I remember was an enormous regret that my unfulfilled life was now ending so abruptly. When I woke up, Smitty was pumping my chest to revive me. He had seen what was happening and, by throwing the master switch, had saved my life.

That experience left me with several impressions I have never forgotten. The first was how painless it was to die by electrocution. The second was how my mind could still function when all else was gone. Another memorable effect was an indescribable clarity of the mind afterwards, approaching a state of pleasurable serenity, even euphoria. As a physical memento of this incident, I had electrical burns on four fingers all the way down to the bone. The burns turned gangrenous before they healed, several months later. Those burns are now but the faintest of scars in my fingerprints.

In June of 1941 Hitler invaded Russia. The Germans advanced deeper and deeper, slicing up the Red Army like liverwurst. Rommel, the Desert Fox, was also on the move in North Africa again. Japan had invaded China, and all of the Allies were on the defensive. America was still neutral. Many believed that Hitler had a master plan and was making good on it.

On Sunday, December 7, 1941, I was listening to the radio at noon when I heard the first news of Pearl Harbor. It was a terrible shock, of course, and "a day to live in infamy," as Franklin Roosevelt said. Things happened fast after that. America declared

171

war on Japan, and Hitler declared war on the United States. Momentarily, I was jubilant. Having seen the developing might of the United States in just one city, Baltimore, I was convinced that Hitler could not win, though I of course had no idea how he could be defeated. Japan moved into the Philippines, Indonesia, and Singapore, nearly to the edge of India. The Russians kept falling back. Would the Japanese and the Germans meet in the Middle East? Was it possible they might conquer all but the Western Hemisphere?

After the United States declared war, I saw the Liberty and Victory ships slide into the water and saw them leave with tanks, trucks, ammunition, and soldiers. I tried to enlist but was not accepted, because of my German birth. Once again, I was technically an enemy alien! However, this time, because the authorities were intelligent enough to recognize that I was an anti-Nazi refugee, I was allowed to work and live with virtually no restrictions.

When I heard about the West Coast internment of Japanese, even those with U.S. citizenship, I was reminded of my own internment by the British. I am now chagrined to remember that I regarded that indefensible panic action as a prudent security measure, as I later regretted that Japanese were not promptly released when found loyal. Let it forever be a warning to all of us that even the most democratic of leaders can gain support from courts for unconstitutional actions when panic among their citizens is fanned by the media, which in turn thrive on such events.

Though still lacking their licenses to practice medicine, my parents became the beneficiaries of America at war. As more and more physicians entered the armed forces, doctors with foreign credentials were permitted to work under the supervision of licensed physicians. My mother obtained a position at Sheppard Pratt, a private hospital in Towson, Maryland, for the affluent mentally ill. This was a huge establishment in a beautiful country setting, with hospital-like wards but also the most elaborate leisure-time facilities. Mother's remuneration included a beautifully furnished apartment, all meals, and decent pay. My father became a staff physician at Springfield State Hospital in Sykesville, Maryland, a huge and sprawling colony for the not-so-affluent mentally ill. Within months, my father also obtained a position at Sheppard Pratt. I remember my first visit there. Located in a huge wooded estate with gardens, it was a world unto itself. I soon learned to tell staff from patients, because only the doctors, nurses, and attendants wore white uniforms and carried prominent key rings.

I lived in a rooming house in downtown Baltimore and often visited Sheppard Pratt, where I was allowed to eat in the staff dining room. There, with about a dozen therapists of various schools around the big table, I listened to what psychiatrists talked about. Freudians, then a minority still struggling to be accepted into the psychiatric fraternity, analyzed their colleagues for me, and I am sure typecast me, too.

The psychiatric staff at Sheppard, however, were not devoid of ordinary human characteristics. One habitually spoke first so that others could respond. Another always proposed a better way of doing everything. I soon learned who was compulsive, obsessive, assertive, passive-aggressive, repressed, hypochondriac, or neurotic. In the Sheppard staff dining room, I thought I recognized personalities like those that had swung in hammocks as our prison ship rocked from England to Australia.

My parents were included in this circle, of course. A young Freudian once provoked Mother into declaring that she was never ever wrong. The sound of her own statement stunned her into silence. What an education for a teenager to see his parents through the prism of psychiatric theory!

I was the electrician journeyman without a high school diploma among psychiatrists with six years and more of university education, but I had a car and a gasoline permit when nobody else did, because I worked in "defense." By nursing my car carefully for minimum gas consumption, I managed to save a little for nondefense activities. That had a way of making me popular with the younger doctors who needed transportation to meet their dates. They often included me in their social activities, one of which was skinny-dipping in an abandoned quarry.

In the staff dining room at Sheppard Pratt, I met G. Wilson Shaffer, a clinical psychologist. He was also dean of McCoy College, the evening division of Johns Hopkins University. I will never know whether my parents put him up to it, or whether what followed was his idea. All efforts to push me to go back to high school had failed. One day Wilson told me that if I passed his special entrance test to enroll in McCoy College, and got grades of B or better in all of my subjects for the first two terms, my lack of a high school diploma would be forgiven. The promise of not having to return to high school, and of still preserving my independence, made me jump at the offer.

I passed Dean Shaffer's test and suddenly, now nineteen, I was enrolled in college. I got better than B in all my courses, even the one in mechanical drawing, although I was forever spilling black ink on those drawings after hours of work on them. I passed the course thanks to Waldemar Ziegler, my chemistry professor, who concocted a solution to remove ink without damaging the paper.

I remember getting up at 5 A.M., being at work before seven, quitting at four in the afternoon, dashing home for a shower and a change of clothes, and arriving at Hopkins at 6:30 for courses until 10 P.M., three times a week. I was always tired, and on weekends I had to do homework. At work I was the only one who went to college, and at college I was the only one with a master electrician's license. These contrasts appealed to my sense of being different and opened up many social contacts. In addition to the friendly psychiatrists at Sheppard Pratt and my rough-hewn buddies at work, I met fellow students at Hopkins, among them a few bright women, not admitted to daytime courses at Hopkins in those days, and even friendly professors with whom I discussed technical ideas.

But this first American phase of my life was about to end. The United States Army, having won Africa, was slogging through Italy. With its invasion of Europe imminent, the army needed cannon fodder, and I was ordered to report to an induction center. The war had finally caught up with me again.

IX

U.S. Army

Since I was not an American citizen, I was not allowed to enlist in a military service of my choice, as I wanted to do early in 1942, but had to wait until I was called up. I was also told that, because I was an alien, the government would choose my branch of service.

In November 1943, I was told to report to the Seventh Regiment Armory in Baltimore and passed my physical with flying colors, except for my flat feet, which I assumed would keep me out of the infantry. Days later I was shipped off to nearby Camp Meade, the induction center. My friends were sure that I would end up with the Engineers, the Signal Corps, or Army Intelligence, or even the Army Air Force, as it was then called. After scoring well on the standard induction tests, I expressed interest in an assignment where my experience and knowledge of Germany and German and my qualifications as an electrician and radio technician would be valuable.

And so, the next day, I found myself on a train with an ancient steam locomotive, belching black smoke and chugging its way to Camp Blanding in north Florida, where I was to receive infantry basic training. The army now needed cannon fodder more than specialists. I made up my mind to try to get rid of any last trace of an accent. I wanted to make sure not to be mistaken for a German by American troops.

After three weeks of basic training at Camp Blanding, I was trucked with others to the U.S. District Court in Jacksonville. Up to the instant when I stood up to swear allegiance, I had no idea why I was there. Suddenly I was an American citizen. No ceremony, just raise your right hand and say, "I do." And "Do you want to change your name?" I did, from Heinz Wolfgang Richard Sonnenfeldt, to Richard W. (Wolfgang) Sonnenfeldt.

To become an American citizen had been my fondest dream. Suddenly, unceremoniously, the dream had turned into reality. I was stunned.

And so I, the latest arrival, was the first in my family and among our friends to become an American citizen. My citizenship was helpful to my parents, who were now related to a citizen-soldier. I was overjoyed to be a full and equal citizen of the greatest country in the world. I was aglow and breathed more deeply what was now my air as much as it was that of any other American. Never again would I be a refugee.

At Camp Blanding, I learned how to fold my blanket, polish my boots, pack my footlocker and duffel bag, carry a rifle, and attack potato sacks with a bayonet. I scored so well as a marksman that I received special training in the use of the Springfield rifle with a telescopic sight for sniping. Going through training in street and house-to-house fighting, all doubt was removed that we were being trained for war in Europe. Among other skills, we were taught that if a hand grenade landed in our midst and could not be tossed back, someone had to cover it with his body to save his comrades. Several days later, the lieutenant in charge of our training company demonstrated how to toss live grenades. He activated one by pulling the pin; the fuse started smoking and, as he fumbled, the grenade fell at his feet. We had five seconds before it would explode. A fellow trainee, a tall and handsome young man, fell upon it while the rest of us took cover as best we could. Of course, it was a fake, a grenade without a charge in it.

The handsome young soldier wound up in Officer Candidate School because he had "sacrificed" himself. Or did he? He always was a pet of Sergeant Vittacco, who was in charge of our section. One of Vittacco's more memorable pronouncements was, "Soldier, when you sit on the hopper and you hear me yell, 'Fall in for roll call,' you just snap her off and come a-runnin."

An important part of our training was to watch horror movies showing chancres and other ravages of venereal disease. With our rifles, backpacks, and helmets we would be herded into a huge auditorium, which went pitch black as the VD movie came on to show us festering penises as large as blimps. We were always tired and had learned how to put the rifle between our legs while hanging the helmet on top of the barrel and using it as a chin rest to catch a few winks. When these makeshift rests collapsed, there was a great clatter. The auditorium lights came on instantly to catch the offender. We had to be fast indeed to avoid being punished with onerous make-work chores. Our military maxim was never to get caught, and I used my belt to prevent the rifle from falling when I nodded off. My system was discovered, but I got off with just a monumental chewing out because this was not an offense listed in the book.

In my army questionnaire, I had indicated that in civilian life, as an electrician, I drove a truck. When the time came for us to go on bivouac, I was picked to drive an army truck, a "six-by-six." Briefly trained to handle this monster, which had six-wheel drive and eight gears, I managed it very well. The bivouac exercise included a forced march of twenty-five miles with a heavy pack on one's back and a rifle slung over the shoulder. Driving that truck saved me from the forced march, but not from the rigors of bivouac. In the dark of night, after digging a foxhole whose bottom soon started filling with water, I felt something slither up my leg and realized it was a snake. As I jumped out of the foxhole, the drill sergeant yelled at me to get back in. When told that I had a snake on my leg, he did the forbidden: he turned on his flashlight just long enough to see a live snake slither away. He hollered, "Sonnenfeldt, where in hell did you find that snake?" I was forever obliged to him for not gigging me for leaving that foxhole.

Guided by a compass and crude maps, we patrolled the Florida swamps, encountering alligators, rattlesnakes, and wild pigs. We fired away at them with blanks, though we were supposed to hide ourselves from the enemy. But the "enemy," too, was firing away at his rattlesnakes and alligators.

We climbed vertical walls and crawled on our bellies through muddy fields to keep below the tracer bullets of live machine-gun bursts. We stabbed fake Germans with our bayonets, booby-trapped imaginary foes and were booby-trapped by invisible enemies, and learned how to fire mortars and bazookas. We also learned how to survive on K rations. I got my sharpshooter medal. I was now certified cannon fodder.

We were given a week's leave, and then back to the army. Shortly after arriving at the embarkation area in Norfolk, I came down with a very high fever from a bad strep throat. These were the days before sophisticated antibiotics, and strep throat was serious. I remained in sick bay for two weeks with huge doses of sulfa drugs. Then I was ordered to a depot in North Africa to replace casualties in Italy. On June 4, 1944, as I was waiting to embark for North Africa, Rome fell, and two days later the invasion of Normandy began. Those were exciting days indeed. I was as much afraid that I might miss the end of the war as I was relieved that I might not have to fight as an infantry soldier. I was no longer as enthusiastic about hand-to-hand combat as I had been three years earlier in England. But I was prepared to do my duty.

We embarked on a large and brand-new troopship, the *General M.K. Meigs*. It was a far cry from the below-water hold of the overcrowded *Dunera*. We had lifeboat drills before we departed, and everyone was issued a life vest. I saw for the first time rotating radar antennas at the top of a mast. The *General Meigs* carried racks of depth charges and a decent naval gun on the fantail.

After a day or two of destroyer escorts, we were on our own in the Atlantic Ocean. Our boat was said to be fast enough to outrun any U-boat, and we did not even zigzag. Several times a day we saw the contrails of high-altitude patrol planes, Liberators, long-range four-engine bombers. We were told they were watching over us.

One day, as the sailors did gunnery and depth charge exercises, a rivet next to my bunk popped out. A stream of water as thick as my thumb poured in. I quickly twirled one of my underpants into a stopgap plug, which I forced into the hole. After I reported the leak, a sailor arrived with a bung, a corklike tapered wooden plug, and banged it into the hole. I could not believe that this was the fix, but realized that wood would swell and make a watertight seal.

Within sight of the coast of Africa, off Tunisia, the ship suddenly veered violently and soldiers were sent tumbling across the deck. They were fortunately saved from falling overboard by stanchions and lifelines. The ship continued circling, and we expected an enemy attack. Then the engines stopped. Only a failure of the steering engine, we were told. The rest of our crossing went uneventfully.

Instead of going to Tunisia, where we were originally headed, we went to the Bay of Naples, where we were unloaded into LST landing craft. We had to climb down cargo nets with combat gear, which included packs and rifles, on our backs. On the way down, a soldier above me stepped on the fingers of my left hand. While I was trying to get him to move his foot, he then stepped on my other hand with his other foot. What a way to arrive in a combat zone!

We were trucked to a "repple-depple" — colloquialism for "replacement depot" — north of Naples, where we waited till we were needed at the front. In the sizzling hot Italian summer, we marched five miles to the beach every day for a swim and lunch before returning in the late afternoon. We bathed and swam in the nude — swimming trunks were not included in GI clothing.

Italian children and not quite so young Italian maidens came around to watch us, commenting on our physiques, also selling oranges, grapes, olives, and, when they could, peasant wine. We always invited them to join the party, but our officers kept us apart. One day, while hundreds of us naked soldiers were on the beach, two German fighter planes suddenly appeared and started strafing. Why does one feel so much more vulnerable when naked? Even when one knows that shirts, underwear, and pants stop no bullets? The instinctive and immediate reaction by all was to get into the water and stay under, except for an occasional breath. Miraculously, no one was hit.

To break the monotony, I volunteered to drive supply trucks. I was soon hauling not only supplies but also ammunition, again in the ubiquitous six-by-six all-purpose army truck. The roads were winding and narrow, often barely wide enough for one vehicle. A few of the switchbacks were exposed to German artillery fire. Once, being fired upon and leaving my truck to take cover, I felt those killer projectiles from the famous German 88-mm guns whoosh by me, within inches, I thought. My heart stood still as they hit an embankment only a few feet from me. A close one! The experienced drivers knew that the Germans would now move their guns, to prevent our planes from destroying them. So we heaved a sigh of relief and got back behind the wheel.

On our route, passing a U.S. Army Air Force base, we usually stopped to get Cokes and doughnuts in the well-stocked PX. Boeing Flying Fortresses, of the B-17 class, flew from that base to drop supplies to Tito's partisans in Yugoslavia, a trip that was considered a milk run. They also flew sorties to bomb Romania's oil fields at Ploesti, or Vienna, or even southern Germany, missions that were far from being milk runs. Several of my fellow drivers had finagled rides in the tail gunner bubble of the B-17s on the milk runs, and I was eager to try it, too, but had to return to my repple-depple before my turn came up. At the air base, I remember seeing a *Time* magazine advertisement by Boeing, the builder of the Flying Fortress bomber, with the caption "Who's afraid of a Messerschmidt now?" The Messerschmidt was the most feared German fighter plane. Every pilot on that base had signed his name on the ad, which was prominently displayed.

At noon one day, we were told to pack and be ready to move out in two hours. We were trucked to the port of Naples, where we climbed the cargo nets onto another troopship. Via the ever-present grapevine we found out we were heading for southern France, which had been invaded two days earlier. We were issued combat rations and ammunition and given lectures about what we were to do "on the beach." Also, we were paid. On the boat deck, floating crap games started up, while poker and blackjack were played on army blankets. Thousands of dollars changed hands.

Off Sardinia the sea got rough. We had on board a contingent of Spahis, bearded French North African soldiers, who had brought their goats and women. They had been housed in a deck between mine and the boat deck. The stench of food, goats, excrement, and vomit emanating from those quarters reminded me of the worst days on the *Dunera*. I stayed up on the boat deck, where gambling continued until France came into view at dawn. The beaches were deserted and not a shot was fired. Once again it was down the cargo nets and into LSTs, which were driven right up on the beach. We came ashore near St. Raphael on the fabled French Riviera. Soon there appeared French women, hugging and kissing us. In my rudimentary French, I found out that the Germans had left days before. Personnel carriers were unloaded from the ships, and we were trucked about five miles inland, where we set up camp.

Not long thereafter a Frenchwoman made a great commotion at the captain's tent. Because he had seen me converse with the natives, he sent for me. Little did he know the limitations of my French, especially when it came to dealing with a very excited woman who was speaking very fast and with an accent that baffled me. However, after a while I understood that she was here to complain that her daughter's honor had been violated. I did not know the French word for rape, but "violated" had an ominous ring because under the Articles of War, as I remembered, rape was punishable by death.

The captain asked me to go with this woman and investigate the details. Off we went to her house, a mere hovel. There I met her daughter, whose breasts were oozing out of a scanty dress. And so I began my investigation. "*Mais oui, ce soldat américain est entré dans ma chambre*" . . . something like that. And then what? "*Ah, Monsieur le Capitaine,*" she said, "he looked at me and then he pulled down his pants — *les pantalons.*" And now what? Did he violate her? "*Oh non, Monsieur le Capitaine,* he made love to me." And then what? He pulled up his pants, took his rifle, put on his helmet, and left.

I got it. Yes, I got it. I reached in my pocket, found my wallet, and watched her face as one by one I pulled out one-hundred-franc notes, which we had just been issued, nice and crisp. I saw her face light up before I got to the third note, and knew that two would restore her honor, settle the case, and protect one of my buddies from a terrible fate. When I handed her the money, I detected an invitation, but explained I had to leave now to fight a war.

Back at camp, my company commander wanted to know what happened. The woman had signed a release that I had written. It said in English that it had all been a terrible misunderstanding. Thus was friendship and honor restored among allies. And I became the company interpreter.

We were soon following our advance troops and the retreating Germans day after day. Eventually we wound up in Dijon, many hundred kilometers north from where we had landed. On the way, we passed through beautiful Grenoble, where I was able to drive up the gorgeous Val d'Isère toward Mont Blanc. I was now chauffeuring a jeep for the captain, who was using me as his interpreter and dealmaker. We bought some French brie cheese, which I put into the pocket of my combat jacket. Weeks later the forgotten cheese had completely bonded with the material, and, to save myself from the pervading odor, I had to cut out the pocket in which the cheese had festered.

By November, the advance of the Allies had stalled all along the line in France. I volunteered to be transferred to the 121st Cavalry Reconnaissance Squadron, a unit of the 106th Reconnaissance Group, which had been in the van of Patton's famed Third Army, through France and into Germany. The group was now U.S. Seventh Army Reconnaissance. If I had to be killed or wounded, it would at least be in the comfort of riding a tank or jeep, not while walking, digging, freezing, and grubbing as a dogface. My new unit was quartered near Sarreguemines, soon to become the southern shoulder of the Battle of the Bulge.

I spent my first night on the front line with six troopers in a farmhouse, where we fired up a cast-iron stove and cooked ourselves a meal. Artillery shells thumped continually, and it took me a while to believe my new buddies, who assured me the shells were too far away to worry about. My fellow soldiers were all veterans of Normandy, the Falaise Gap, and the battle of Lunéville, where the squadron had suffered very heavy casualties leading Patton's Third Army. Naturally, I ate up their stories of past battles, their experiences with the Germans, and their glory as the best of the best of Patton's Third Army. There I heard for the first time that SS troopers had cut off the testicles of American prisoners and stuffed them into their mouths.

On the strength of my marksmanship, I became a rifle-carrying scout, riding in the lead jeep. I had no armored-car or tank training and no training as a gunner or radio operator. The life expectancy of riders in the lead reconnaissance jeep was said to be no better than that of aircraft tail gunners when Messerschmidts were still a menace. I was excited and scared about my new role in the war to defeat Hitler.

Our troop had three squads, each with two jeeps and an M8 armored car. The M8 was a six-wheeled, armor-clad vehicle with a 37-mm gun on a rotating turret and two machine guns. It was fairly efficient in moderately rough terrain, useless in woods, but fast on paved roads, and it had a shortwave radio with a respectable range. Once I raised a radio ham in Harrisburg, Pennsylvania, and sent strictly forbidden greetings to my family. The M8 also had a short-range FM transceiver for vehicle-to-vehicle communications.

In combat, our jeeps were driven with the windshield down, a machine gun on a post or on the hood, everything imaginable hanging from rails on the side, and three men per vehicle. When out of the front line, the jeeps had covers, and some even had plastic side curtains, great in the cold of December and January.

The squadron also had light tanks, which were downright ridiculous. They had high silhouettes and a 37-mm gun, no good for anything except shooting at soldiers and unarmored trucks and buildings. Their shells just bounced off German armor. We were well aware that the Russian T-34 was the best tank in the world, followed by the German Tigers and Panthers. British Cromwells and American M4s were way down on the list. Our own M5s, called General Stuarts, with their anemic 37-mm guns, were the worst of the lot. It was only after the war that America caught up in tank design and eventually became a leader.

In 1944, what U.S. armor lacked in firepower and low silhouettes was made up in numbers, mobility, and the turning ability of gun turrets. We also had tank destroyers, very lightly armored vehicles attached to us that were fast, very mobile, and armed with deadly effective 90-mm guns. If they got their hits in first, they were great. Otherwise it was "Good-bye, Charlie."

The backs of our armored cars and other vehicles were loaded with pots and pans, chairs, radios, mattresses, and other amenities that had been picked up on the way. Our squadron also had a repair truck for field maintenance, and command and Red Cross half-tracks with wheels in front and caterpillar treads in the back.

Our three medics included a big bear of a doctor with a long black beard, huge hands, grizzled hair, and a Russian accent. Assisting him were two enlisted first-aid technicians, with red-cross armbands. I could never figure out how the medics managed to keep a goat in their half-track and usually one or two women. From time to time, they all emerged and the doctor would make an occasional "short arm inspection." We would line up with our flies open and hands at the ready to "milk" our penises so the taciturn doctor could see whether there was any sign of gonorrhea. We all looked around to see who had the biggest tool. The only one who ever got the clap was one of the medics.

As I was learning about armored reconnaissance, Germans continued to enlarge "the Bulge," targeting Antwerp as their ultimate goal. We were on the southern shoulder, away from the main thrust. Nevertheless, we were ordered out of the houses in which we had camped and told to dig in our armored cars and tanks, with only the gun turrets above ground level and a sloping rear-entry into each revetment.

Digging these shelters with shovels was a huge job, and we realized that one of the diesel bulldozers used by troops in our rear would save our backs. To the west of us was a quartermaster unit that had those machines. One evening, two of our tanks roamed the quartermaster compound with guns firing and ordered everyone to take cover because Germans were coming. While this was happening, two dozers were appropriated by two of our tankers, who drove them to where we were digging. After we used them, the bulldozers were returned with a note of thanks attached to each.

Meanwhile we lived and slept under the large vehicles whose engines provided heat and whose radios provided entertainment and news. We slowly realized that we were dug in against Germans who would never come. Each day, we heard that deep, melodic drone filling the sky as hundreds of heavy bombers, with propellers all at the same speed, often too high to be visible but marked by their white contrails, headed east toward Germany. By timing their going and returning, we could figure out how far east they had been. One day, in a clear sky, they turned around practically overhead, and we could hear the thunder and rumble of bombs. Instead of cities, they were targeting German ammunition dumps, and we knew the end of the Battle of the Bulge could not be far off.

Sure enough, a week or two later we were moved farther south to become Second Corps Reconnaissance, and joined famous divisions that had fought and won in Sicily, at Monte Cassino, and at Salerno. We were positioned on the northern edge of an enclave of Wehrmacht holdouts, north of the corner where France, Germany, and Switzerland meet. It was called the Colmar pocket.

As the Germans started to crumble, I had my first combat experience. We were reconnoitering with two jeeps and an armored car, and found ourselves confused as to where we were. I noticed signs pointing to a German army headquarters. On impulse, I turned the signs around. We soon found a nearby farmhouse and ate a still warm meal of chicken, carrots, and potatoes and realized that the Germans had recently been there. We holed up in a barn and camouflaged ourselves with straw.

Soon our lookout reported a car coming down the road. Using binoculars, I realized that it was a German army command car. When it was about a hundred yards away, we fired our 37-mm gun. Five Germans jumped out of the car into ditches on both sides of the road. One of them had the red-striped trousers of a German general. We then shot up their command car and ran out of our armored car. I yelled at them, "Hände hoch" (Raise your hands), the command to come out and surrender. They did, the general last. We took their weapons, searched them, and put them under guard in our hideaway.

Meanwhile, the German general was complaining that some idiot had pointed the signs to his headquarters the wrong way. When I told him that I had done it, he demanded to be freed immediately, because this was not fair. I told him to shut up or we would gag him. I noticed that his staff did not seem upset to be prisoners.

We still did not know where we were, relative to our own troops, until we heard American voices on the short-range FM radio the next morning and saw some U.S. infantry. We realized that, inadvertently, we had driven far ahead of our own troops. When U.S. trucks, following the infantry, reached us, we arranged for our prisoners to be taken to a stockade. Our German general objected to being stood up in the back of an army truck together with ordinary German prisoners, so I arranged for him to walk in front of the truck, which followed him at a very fast walking speed.

A few other German prisoners were not so lucky. An American soldier was delegated to march several of them to the rear. He returned alone. What had happened to his prisoners? The American had a terrible attack of diarrhea. When he could no longer hold it in, he squatted. One of the German prisoners saw him and then caused the others to turn and rush him. In desperation the American shot all of them with his burp gun. Yes, "don't ask, don't tell" is not just today's invention. While Waffen SS soldiers defiled, mutilated, and tortured American soldiers that they captured, I never witnessed any mistreatment of German POWs or civilians by American soldiers. But who knows?

Whenever we reported to our troop commander, our radio transmission would always start with "Charlie Oboe, come in, Charlie Oboe, come in." Those were the radio phonetics for CO, commanding officer. Once, when we listened to German radio chatter, I heard the Germans ask each other, *"Wer ist der Charlie Oboe, wer ist der Charlie Oboe?"* (Who is that Charlie Oboe), and I interrupted, *"Halt dein Maul, du Dummkopf, der Charlie Oboe schreibt jetzt deinen Namen in sein Buch."* (Shut up, you idiot, Charlie Oboe is now writing your name in his book). I also called them *Dummkopf Nazis* (stupid Nazis.)

Days later, near the Rhine River, we saw remnants of the Siegfrid Line. There, among blackened and busted bunkers, lay dead horses with their legs up in the air and dead German soldiers whose faces had an eerie waxen look. The stench of their bodies and of the dead horses, mixed with the smell of gunpowder and gasoline, was overwhelming. That is how battlefields

smell. Groups of dazed German soldiers and civilians were walking west, out of the war. The sun was warming this stink as well
as a layer of fine dust, which I began to recognize as characteris-
tic of cannon fire. Aerial bombs make deep craters and collapse
structures; shells pulverize concrete, brick, mortar, and everything else into dust.

After crossing the Rhine on a pontoon bridge, we reassumed
our mandated mission, reconnaissance. Getting our vehicles up
on an elevated railroad track with a commanding view of the sur-
rounding low meadows and fens, we spotted groups of retreating
Nazis. I yelled that we were the American SS. That got their instant attention, and most surrendered. Over the following days,
my martial German improved as my buddies egged me on to get
Germans to give up. Shots were fired and we lost a few of our men.

For the most part, Wehrmacht vehicles were sitting ducks,
out of fuel and many without ammunition. We shot them up to
prevent further use. One night, after being on reconnaissance for
thirty hours straight, we set up bivouac, circling our vehicles
with guns pointing out, and went to sleep without guards. We
woke up the next morning to about two hundred German soldiers wandering nearby, with a big white flag, looking for someone to surrender to! We told them to keep walking west until
somebody captured them. Stacking their rifles and mortars next
to a heap of potato-masher hand grenades, they left.

And so it went until we came to Freudenstadt in the Black
Forest, a town that blocked our path east to southern Germany.
Barely inside the town, we were fired upon, so we withdrew as
fast as we could. Soon a group of German civilians and army men
came out with a white flag. They wanted to surrender the town
but could not, because an SS unit was holed up there. I told them
to have the SS surrender or leave. They said they could not control the SS. We commanded, "Get them out by three o'clock, or
we will shoot up your town." We brought up heavy tanks and
artillery. At three o'clock, the artillery cleared a path for our
advance through the town by turning it to dust. As we went

through, we still heard occasional shooting, but we left the mop-
ping up to the infantry.

A comic incident occurred in the next village. All excited,
two of our troopers captured a German in a dark blue uniform.
He was wearing a splendid cap with braid and a visor, an Iron
Cross upon his chest, and gold stripes on his sleeves. They were
sure they had an admiral, until I explained that this was the local
postmaster, who was wearing his World War I medals.

Moving east, we ran into pockets of snipers and, occasionally, hard-core Waffen SS. None of us wanted to get killed in the
last days of this war, but we went on. Sometimes we drove for
more than twenty-four hours. I remember falling asleep while
sitting up and slumping over the steering wheel of my jeep. In
one village, a replacement soldier fresh from the States, who had
joined us only hours before, was killed by a sniper's bullet. Seeing that it had come from a gap in the roof tiles of the village
church, I fired my own sniper's rifle at it and the body of a German soldier fell into the church in front of the altar. We rooted
out and killed a dozen snipers there.

In another town, we came upon a state-maintained mater-
nity home. Women had agreed to be impregnated by SS men,
who, with the mission of improving the race, had been tem-
porarily detached for this essential service. I was delegated to investigate. Here were about forty women, some nursing newly
delivered babies, others waiting for the stork, others already in
labor. There was not a German nurse, midwife, or doctor in
sight. I called in our medics, none of whom had ever delivered a
baby. With instruction from the more experienced women, who
themselves were expecting, they delivered two babies. We named
them Moses and Aaron.

By this time I had served my tour in the lead jeep and was
assigned to an armored car. I learned how to drive it, to load,
aim, and fire the gun, to rotate the turret, and operate the radios.

As we rolled into one German town, its mayor rushed out
with a formal surrender, which he had written out on parchment.

He was crushed when I told him that we had no time for him, and that he would have to wait for the next American unit. Still, we had time for a little fun. Some roads were too narrow to turn an armored car around when it was fired upon. I invented a maneuver unique in armored warfare. We rigged a rearview mirror so we could back into the enemy with our 37-mm cannon rotated from its regular forward position. At the first shot from the enemy, the driver rammed the gear into forward and it was go, man, go! I was then known as "Rear View Sunny." All of this was consistent with our mission to draw fire, so others with bigger guns could demolish the opposition while we moved on for the next day's fight.

My other nickname was Leroy. I don't know how I got it. It was a derivation from Kilroy, that GI who appeared everywhere. Once in a while, even today, I am startled when somebody walks up to me and greets me: "Leroy, how the hell are you?" A far cry from Heinz Wolfgang Richard Sonnenfeldt.

When President Roosevelt died, I was listening to the BBC on the shortwave radio. It was strange how the death of this great leader had such minimal impact on us soldiers. We knew we had won the war, except for the formalities. But not the Germans. I picked up a broadcast in which the infamous Dr. Goebbels interpreted Roosevelt's death as the long-awaited turning point that would lead to German victory!

Our war went on in skirmishes with die-hard German soldiers, whom we mostly took prisoner by the thousands as they headed west to get away from the Russians. We were then sent for R&R to Heidelberg, which was unharmed by the war except for the old Roman bridge over the Neckar, which had been dynamited. Good work! The Americans were already on both sides of the river.

In Heidelberg we were quartered in a lovely hotel, slept in beds with real linens, and were served meals by German waiters who were happy to eat American food and save cigarette butts to make into hand-rolled cigarettes. Their "homemade" cigarettes made for a terrific business. This was the time of "nonfraternization," when American soldiers were forbidden to socialize with German women. I met a lovely Dutch woman and we had good times together. U.S. army MPs always thought they were onto something when I dated her, until they saw her Dutch passport.

In Heidelberg, just before the war ended, we finally got new tanks to replace those useless M5s. The new ones, M24s, were much bigger, had lower silhouettes, and had a 75-mm gun — still nothing like the dreaded German 88s, but a lot better than those anemic 37-mm peashooters.

The Germans were retreating so fast that we, the reconnaissance troops, now followed the infantry and armored divisions, and only when the advance stalled did we move out front again. We still had our share of firefights before the Germans retreated again. Every now and then we had to root out snipers. Once I saw one relieving himself under a tree, and on impulse I aimed low. Luckily for him — and, I suppose, ultimately for my conscience — the bullet went in and out one cheek and then in and out the other and missed all else.

One day when we were parked in an open field, I heard an eerie noise, a mixture of "swoosh" and "roar" moving at great speed in the sky. It was a low-flying brand-new German twin-jet fighter. We realized instantly how much faster it was than our prop-driven Mustangs and Thunderbolts. Although we were approaching the end of the war, somebody said, "Boys, it ain't over till it's over."

The German army disintegrated before our eyes, and the citizenry, contrary to Hitler's last mad exhortations, did not turn into werewolves. Only the most fanatical SS and Waffen SS units fought on doggedly. There were too few German jet planes; German tanks and trucks were out of fuel and their horses were dying. Nevertheless, there were still firefights in towns like Würzburg and Nuremberg, and American soldiers were still being wounded and killed.

We entered Munich, and I was able to finagle a side trip to Dachau after telling my commanding officer that I had heard on the armored car radio that Germans, disguised as prisoners, were hiding inside the Dachau concentration camp. Having seen pictures in the army newspaper *Stars and Stripes* of newly liberated concentration camps farther west, both of us should have known that well-fed Nazis with Gestapo tattoos on their arms would have stood out like sore thumbs among sick and emaciated ex-prisoners. I had assumed that the newspaper pictures I had seen had prepared me for what awaited me. But no picture could prepare one for what I was to experience. The half hour I spent in Dachau was to be the most heartrending of my life.

Dachau was no single entity but a main camp with — hard to believe — 123 subcamps and slave labor factories clustered about the town named Dachau. The American 42nd and 45th Divisions had already entered several of these units.

We drove our jeep through an open gate where no GIs had yet been, and the wretches inside the camp, in their striped suits with shorn heads and emaciated faces, stood as though frozen. Only when we shouted "Amerikaner" did they surge forward. From their shouts and speech I realized immediately that this group was neither Jewish nor German like most other inmates of Dachau. The barbed wire fences were still up, but someone had smashed the electric feeds that had made them lethal barriers until minutes ago. The guard towers were empty, and machine guns poking through their sides were now unmanned. Three inmates were clubbing a huge German Shepherd dog to death — apparently one of those man-killers had been used by the SS guards to hound prisoners. It was midafternoon on Sunday, April 29, 1945.

Many inmates had not yet shed their look of fright. Two American army medics who drove in behind us in an ambulance warned us to avoid physical contact with these wretched humans, because of fears that disease might spread. Reception centers had not yet opened to register and care for these pitiable humans. Some were so weak that they died before our eyes. The joy of liberation was too much for their weakened bodies.

Various Holocaust centers have recorded the horror of Nazi concentration camps, so I will only write about my own twenty minutes at Dachau. The stacks of silent, rotting, unburied corpses with open eyes did not shock me as much as did the survivors I saw. Faces were tilted in an angle of permanent appeal.

How could they grasp, after years of indescribable suffering, anticipating only more torture and death, that life and freedom were now to be theirs? All they saw was two American soldiers and two medics. How did they know that their guards had really left and would not return? That this was not a trap? How could they believe that they had outlived thousands (and, as we now know, millions) of others? Did they yet grasp that the letters "SS" stood no longer for an all-powerful, malevolent, murdering authority but for depravity, dishonor, and defeat?

Not being able to comprehend fully that they had miraculously been saved, they had not yet started on that long road to emotional and physical rehabilitation. What I remember most are the eyes of the unbelieving liberated — eyes that had an indescribable mixture of wonder, suffering, and helplessness.

Though there are reports from American soldiers who entered other parts of the Dachau complex that inmates danced and shouted when they saw massed American troops and tanks, the wretches we faced were too stunned, too weak to give immediate expression to joy. The warning not to touch these survivors or let them kiss us was well founded. More than a thousand Dachau inmates, despite intensive efforts to save them, died of vicious disease soon after their liberation!

And here was I, a soldier of the liberating army. Except for the resourcefulness of my mother and the generosity of an English school principal, I would assuredly have been dead or one of the human wrecks that I now looked at. I thought of my days as a British prisoner on the *Dunera*, but realized that even my worst days bore no comparison to what these people and their dead comrades had suffered.

It was just four years and three days since I had set foot on

American soil, not yet knowing I was to become a member of a conquering army.

We tried to talk. They understood a little German. I could only utter: "It's over, it's over. You are alive and others are coming to help you. We must go, the Nazis are still fighting." The ex-prisoners tried to cling to us, symbols of their freedom. Again the question haunted me: Why was I spared? Was it accident or was there a purpose?

If for them the war was finally over, for me it was back to combat. We had to finish the job. I felt wave after wave of anger well up in me. The only Nazis still resisting were the SS, the Gestapo, and other remnants of Himmler's evil killers. Until I saw the corpses, the near dead, faced the dehumanized victims of concentration camp, I had almost looked on German soldiers who surrendered to us with pity. That was especially true for the young boys and the old men who I knew had been pressed into suicidal service by a depraved dictator. Dachau had not been run by drafted soldiers but by trained sadists. Those SS fanatics deserved to be killed, and for the first time I felt a lust to kill them. But unlike their victims who lay dead in mass graves and the muck of abandoned camps, unless they chose to fight, the killers had all but disappeared.

After I rejoined my unit in the rubble of east Munich, we saw the first civilian German vehicle: a huge beer wagon pulled by enormous horses! We drove down the autobahn to Salzburg in Austria without meeting resistance. There, in the city of Mozart, in its famous castle towering over the city and its river, the Salzach, was the last headquarters of Field Marshall Albert Kesselring, commander in chief of all German troops in Italy and Austria. The Fifth American Army and British troops were crossing Italy into northern Austria; the Russians had conquered eastern Austria and Vienna; and we were coming in from the west. We arrived in Salzburg as Kesselring, who had no organized forces left, surrendered to a sister reconnaissance troop, just minutes ahead of us. On the outskirts of Salzburg, I saw a huge chrome swastika atop a factory. I brought it down with one shot of our armored-car gun. When we were sniped at from inside a bank, I blasted the front door and the safe room with my armored-car cannon. This had been the German army paymaster's depository, and hundred-mark notes fluttered about like snowflakes. We picked them up by the thousands to use as toilet paper. I realized only too late that each mark was still worth about ten cents to the dollar.

From Salzburg we went ahead of all other American troops for one last time to St. Gilgen, which lies at the mouth of the Wolfgangsee, a beautiful lake in the Salzkammergut district of Austria. On May 7, two days before the war ended officially, my lieutenant told me to get into a jeep with him to reconnoiter the entire long and narrow lake. The two of us drove kilometer after kilometer over the deserted lakeside road into Ischl and Fuschl. We found the exiled King Leopold of the Belgians on the eastern lakeshore and radioed for others to pick him up. All along our route we saw Austrian villagers peeking from behind drawn curtains and doors barely ajar. We were the first Americans they had ever seen. On we went through an eerily deserted land.

No one was on the street when we parked in front of the mayor's office in Fuschl, a picturesque resort town, where we accepted his surrender. And then, having seen no German soldiers, we decided to turn back. As we neared the yellow road sign marking the village limits of Fuschl, we heard gunfire and the roar of cannon. I stepped on the accelerator and raced the twenty kilometers back to St. Gilgen. There we were told that a regiment of Waffen SS was holed up in Fuschl and was fighting regular German army troops, who had supported the mayor surrendering to us. It would have been child's play for the SS to kill or capture us or throw us in the lake. The firefight in Fuschl between the German army troops and the SS lasted two days, and the combatants disappeared into the woods. That trip to Fuschl was the last day of the war for me. It could also easily have been the last day of my life.

For the next two weeks, we went on patrol from our base in St. Gilgen to round up German stragglers. With two jeeps, one ahead and the other behind an armored car, we scoured the countryside. When roads were too narrow for the armored car, we just went ahead in the jeeps and kept in radio contact. Every day we collected dozens of German army stragglers. We had them march back on a patrolled road to a reception center. Most were hungry, tired, and disheveled, so the idea of becoming American prisoners of war was appealing to them. Some, however, we had to chase down with machine guns. As they surrendered, we made them lie flat on the hoods of our jeeps, where they had to hold on for dear life as we drove them to the stockade.

One day, as we reconnoitered a narrow road between the lake on our right and vertical cliffs on our left, we collided with a German car. As I registered that the car was full of black-uniformed SS officers, our jeep flipped into the lake. While under water, I expected to be shot when I came up for air, as eventually I would have to. Fortunately, the jeep behind us arrived at that moment. In the collision, the German car had been forced against the cliff, and its doors would not open.

After the Germans surrendered, we looked for our jeep. Only a portion of its steering wheel was visible. When I found my steel helmet in the water, it had a dent about three inches long and a half inch deep, where I had struck an underwater rock. I still have a photo of that helmet. We dragged the jeep out of the lake and, after cleaning critical engine parts, we managed to get started again. The steering column was bent, but we got back to base, once in a while having to lift the front wheels of the jeep to get around a particularly sharp bend.

Soon after our accident, I was given four days' R&R in Brussels. I piled into an army supply truck with other soldiers. We sat on a wooden bench for twenty hours as we roared west through captured Germany and then north and west through France and Belgium to Brussels. There I decided to inquire after a Jewish girl, Eva Lemberg, who had grown up in Gardelegen and who I heard had fled to Brussels after Helmut and I left for England. Inquiries at the city hall and at the central police registry were in vain. I saw the sign of a refugee organization on a side street, and there again my inquiries remained without result. But suddenly a woman approached me and asked, in German, "Did you say Eva Lemberg? Tell me who you are, and I will talk to her."

And so I went to meet Eva, whom I had last seen as a thirteen-year-old girl in Gardelegen in 1938. She had survived thanks to a Belgian family who had hidden her from the Germans from 1940 to 1944.

I asked her out for dinner. The only item on the menu in still war-ravaged Brussels was eel, which we consumed with a bottle of Chablis. Eva was younger than I, closer to my brother Helmut in age, and she had never attracted me. She did not then know that her parents had been exterminated, only that they were among the many whose fate was unknown. Naturally she and I compared notes about our very different fates since leaving Gardelegen, she as an Anne-Frank-like girl in four years of nerve-racking hiding, and I, after my circuitous journey to Baltimore, now a soldier of the victorious American army. Her hosts feted me as a hero! I noticed how they still spoke of the Nazis with fear in their voices, when to me Germany was a defeated nation.

I gave Eva's address to my parents, who sent her CARE packages. Later she married a Belgian widower, a distinguished engineer and professor, and she still lives in Brussels. Eva, unlike me, never again referred to her German origins.

From Brussels, I drove a supply truck back to Austria and rejoined my unit, which was soon ordered back to the States to be demobilized. Soldiers like me, with not enough combat service to be repatriated, were detached for additional service in Europe. I was transferred to Second Corps in Salzburg, and became a driver in the headquarters motor pool.

Considering the alternative — an assignment to the Pacific Theater of Operations — I was happy to stay in Salzburg. I drove a major of the Judge Advocate Corps who was investigating crimes and misdemeanors by American soldiers. He and I stretched our trips whenever possible to include stops at delightful roadhouses in the beautiful countryside around Salzburg.

The nonfraternization policy for American soldiers applied only in Germany and did not extend to the ladies of Salzburg. Strangely, the victors did not consider Austria a Nazi country, despite its unbridled enthusiasm for Hitler, so it was easy for Austrians to represent themselves as victims and not as perpetrators.

Austrian women were attracted by American soldiers, who showered them with cigarettes, soap, coffee, and sugar, available in the PX stores that soon sprang up wherever GIs were located. We were constantly warned that many of these women were carriers of VD, personified by that creation of U.S. Army public relations, the buxom, blond, infected German lass Veronica Dankeschoen, who beckoned sex-starved GIs seductively from huge posters. However, the company of comely Austrian women was most pleasant during the balmy evenings of early summer in Salzburg, which had then, much as it does now, a full quota of concerts, operas, and even marching bands.

Once more I was suspended in time. The European war was over, the war with Japan was unfinished, and my discharge date from the army was uncertain, but I was not marked for shipment to the Far East. Just as I was settling into the life of the Second Corps motor pool, I did not know that my life would soon take the most amazing turn of all. I did not know that I was soon to become the chief interpreter to the American prosecution at the Nuremberg trials, nor could I anticipate visiting Germany fifty years hence.

X

Visiting Gardelegen

*A*FTER LEAVING GERMANY IN 1938, I no longer gave Gardelegen any thought. I had nothing either memorably great or unforgettably horrible to remember about my youth there, and, after the war, no one I cared about lived in Gardelegen. No adult Jew of Gardelegen had survived Hitler's rule except my parents. Two women had committed suicide to avoid deportation, and one man was summarily shot when he asked a Gestapo thug a question. The remaining twenty-seven Gardelegen Jewish adults had been obliterated: deported and exterminated. Of the eight Jewish children, two were killed, one survived Auschwitz, one hid in Belgium, and the other four, including my brother and me, were able to emigrate in time.

During my work at Nuremberg in 1945 I did not visit Gardelegen. Over the next five decades, memories of Gardelegen became ever more remote. After Johns Hopkins, I became an engineer-inventor at RCA, where I helped to develop color television. I subsequently became a business executive and later a corporate director and consultant to businesses around the world. Ultimately, I became CEO of a company called NAPP. I had a happy married life, and as husband and the father of three children also briefly became the loving guardian of my parents in their last days. My wife, Shirley, died. Some time later, I was a husband once again to Barbara. Together we had fifteen grandchildren. As an adventurous sailor, I crossed the Atlantic Ocean three times in my own sailboat, the last trip to celebrate my seventy-fifth birthday and my retirement.

But before I retired, in 1977 I went to Germany on business, and my British Airways flight from Hanover to Berlin flew directly over Gardelegen, still in the communist eastern zone of Germany. From the mandated height of ten thousand feet on a clear day, through binoculars borrowed from the pilot, I could make out the churches, the city hall, my old school, the street on which I had lived, and even my house. From that height, at least, all seemed to be as I remembered it from almost forty years earlier. A few months later my brother Hal, who had retired from the State Department, visited Gardelegen on June 17, 1978 (the twenty-fifth anniversary of the East German worker uprising) with his wife, and they brought back photos. As I looked at old familiar scenes, I congratulated myself on the accuracy of my memory. And that was that.

Eleven years later, shortly after the Berlin Wall came down and Germany was reunified, I was driving on the newly opened autobahn from Berlin to Hanover on business. A sign pointing to Gardelegen appeared, and I decided to make a detour. The familiar streets, our house in the Sandstrasse, the schools I had attended, and the short central shopping street, though shabbier and smaller than I had remembered, seemed intact. The ruin of a church remained unrestored after an American bomb had landed on it forty-seven years before, as noted on a small sign. The communist government had left it that way. I saw no familiar faces in the streets, no familiar names on the stores or even in the local telephone book. After taking a few color slides, I got back into my car and left.

In March of 1993, three years after my impromptu detour, I received an envelope in the mail with German postage. It was a letter from the mayor of Gardelegen. He was writing suggesting

I visit "the places of your youth" and invited me to "bring your family and be guests of the town — if," he wrote, "you can set aside memories of past horrors and the injustices of fate." A Mrs. Bunge had given him my address.

I found out that my brother Hal had paid a surprise visit to this Gisela Bunge, who was researching the history of the Jews of Gardelegen in 1988, and Hal had arranged for her to come to Washington with German foreign minister Genscher shortly after reunification. I did not know her and had no desire to see Gardelegen again. I wrote back that fate had been kind to me — kinder, perhaps, than to the citizens of Gardelegen. "Thanks, Mr. Mayor, for the invitation," I wrote, "but no thank you."

Within weeks Mrs. Gisela Bunge wrote to me. The widow of a Lutheran minister, in her seventies, she had been collecting information about the Jewish families that had once lived in Gardelegen. She was preparing a booklet about the Jews of Gardelegen that would mention my parents.

Gisela had moved to Gardelegen as a minister's wife during the Soviet occupation of East Germany, and her interest had been piqued when she heard about ruined gravestones with Hebrew writing in a deserted yard. Little by little she reconstructed the history of those markers and the vanished Jews of Gardelegen and began talking to those who remembered what had happened. Gisela wrote that even now, sixty years later, former patients of my parents still ascribed medical miracles to them.

Gisela had seen to it that the desecrated gravestones were restored and then reset in a special area of the town's Christian cemetery. She had also obtained funds to erect a memorial for those vanished souls who had been exterminated in the Holocaust and who had received no burial anywhere. She invited me to visit her and help her write the history of the Jews of Gardelegen.

With no idea of what to expect, I decided finally to go and arranged to meet Gisela in Gardelegen. She had straight white hair and wore the nondescript dark clothing favored by German

widows and ministers' wives. She captured my attention immediately with her bright blue eyes, her upright demeanor, and her
cordial welcome in the house of her daughter, Eva Reuschl.

The next morning, Gisela took me to visit our family's old
house, now a multi-family dwelling. A faded area on its stucco
front marked where my father's doctor shingle had hung fifty
years ago, and on the door frame there was a little rectangular
spot where his lighted night bell had been. In those days a bell
with a light was something to talk about! The entrance hall still
had the smooth, red-painted, polished concrete floor of which
my mother had been so proud. In my old room I found the keyhole through which my brother and I had peeked at our naked
maids taking their baths. Afterwards, visiting the Christian cemetery, I saw the marker for a Jewish neighbor. I remembered walking all through town for his funeral behind the horse-drawn hearse
when I was ten.

At the cemetery, I thought of my father's memoirs, written in
America in 1943. The local police had arrested him on November 10, 1938 — the morning after Kristallnacht. As they carted
him off to the Buchenwald concentration camp, his captors, all
former patients of his, whispered in his ear that their orders gave
them no choice. For my law-abiding German-Jewish father, too,
it was unthinkable to resist the representatives of the state. Jailers and victims alike were loyal servants of a government that
practiced arbitrary arrest and worse. Father kissed my mother
and went silently. She yelled for the policemen to take her, too.

Father reported in his notes that any resistance or challenge
to the authorities in the concentration camp meant torture or
death. He described how most prisoners bore their lot stoically,
while a few sought to curry favor by ratting on fellow prisoners.
The guards used the rats and then discarded them like so much
used toilet paper. No one thought of resisting this perversion of
state power, because Hitler had made anti-Semitism a law that
had to be complied with. The culture of German Jews was based

on being model citizens; given their lifelong training, resistance meant insurrection against the state. They could not conceive of bucking authority!

My father, a recipient of the Iron Cross for valor under enemy fire in World War I, was released after one week in the concentration camp, thanks to Hermann Göring's momentary spasm of sentimentality over old German war heroes. As a condition of his release, Father agreed to leave Germany and cede all of his possessions to the state. That was in November 1938, and it was the last time that Jewish concentration camp inmates were released by government order.

In my mind's eye, there at the cemetery, I could see the Jews of Gardelegen, many of them old, all feeble and frightened after unending abuse, being herded like lambs to the slaughter. How would I have reacted had I been there? I asked myself.

Gisela waited silently while I was lost in thought and remembrance. As I stared at the stones, the enormity of the fate that befell generations of Jews of Gardelegen overwhelmed me. Not even the dust of their bodies remained here. These transplanted stones were markers for Jews who had died before Hitler, but the coffins with their bodies had vanished. The bodies of their sons and daughters, the Holocaust generation, had disappeared into the hellfire of extermination. Nothing marked their earthly life except this Holocaust monument in the Christian cemetery and the memories of them held by the townspeople of Gardelegen and a handful of people like Hal and me. It struck me as richly ironic and symbolic that because the Nazis had destroyed the Jewish cemetery, the markers of the Gardelegen Jews had now joined those of their Christian neighbors in a single place.

Gisela took me to a memorial site outside Gardelegen where the SS had locked more than one thousand slave laborers in a barn and then burned them alive. The senseless slaughter had occurred only hours before the advancing U.S. 102nd Infantry Division could have liberated the inmates. I had heard of this revolting act of depraved malevolence when I was a GI in 1945. The American commanding general, seeing the still smoldering bodies, had ordered that Gardelegen be razed. The town was spared only when the Lutheran minister, Pastor Franz, a man who had often visited our home, fell to his knees and begged that the town be spared after convincing the Americans that SS guards, not the townspeople, had committed this terrible crime.

The men of Gardelegen, led by their mayor, were then ordered to build coffins and give the victims a decent burial. All the inhabitants were marched out to attend a funeral service conducted jointly by the Americans and Pastor Franz. The general ordered the town to erect a memorial to the victims and hold an annual service of repentance forever. For nearly sixty years now, the citizens of Gardelegen have participated in an annual candle-light procession, walking the two miles from the town church to the memorial to mark this horrible event.

"Are any of my classmates alive?" I asked Gisela. She told me that several had been killed as German soldiers in Russia and another had died from natural causes. She knew of Eva Lemberg, whom I had discovered in Brussels after the war. Two of my Jewish contemporaries, boys from the Behrens family, were alive and living in London. Gisela was also in contact with Lottie Behrens, who had been made a slave laborer at age fourteen and had survived Auschwitz and the infamous Dr. Mengele under the most gruesome conditions.

Gisela was better informed than I about the fates of the Jews, dead and alive, of Gardelegen. To us both they were martyrs, but for her it was more a matter of statistics than for me who had known them personally.

In 1996, a new mayor of Gardelegen invited me to bring my family to participate in the festivities for the eight-hundredth anniversary of the founding of Gardelegen. By then, three of my grandchildren had interviewed me for school assignments as an American immigrant. From those interviews my family had heard all the details about my youth in Germany, my school days in England. My wife, Barbara, my younger son, Michael, and his wife, Katja, expressed an interest in seeing where I grew up.

On this visit, I noticed that the town, preening for its eight-hundredth anniversary, looked spiffier than when I had seen it last. Since the collapse of the Soviet bloc it had been the recipient of enormous subsidies and grants from West Germany, and it looked so much better than I had remembered. We had reservations at a country inn about a mile from town at Lindenthal, a place where my parents had often taken Helmut and me for Sunday afternoon cake and coffee. The inn was virtually unchanged.

Later that afternoon, we met Joe Behrens and his cousin Fritz, both Jewish boyhood friends who had survived by fleeing to South Africa and who now lived in London. Despite the fifty-five-year span, I recognized Joe instantly. I reminded him of the great times we used to have at his house playing cards with his father and being served Milchkaffee — weak coffee with lots of milk in it — by his mother. Theirs had been a genial family indeed. Sadly, his parents had been killed in Auschwitz. I recalled how his father had let me help him in his motorcycle shop. Joe recalled how my father had made a house call every day for weeks to comfort his dying grandfather and to make sure he had enough morphine to relieve his pain.

Gisela Bunge had arranged a dinner for us with a group of townspeople. All of us acted as though we were walking on eggs. I do not remember anything that was said.

The next morning, after the obligatory tour of the town, Joe, Fritz, and I met with a class of high school students. These youngsters, educated until recently under Soviet control, had been taught to listen but not to question. Most spoke no English. The girls were shy and the boys seemed bored. No one was curious about our experiences under the Nazis. Gisela, who accompanied us, had us explain why we had left Gardelegen. Even the bare geography of our life histories confounded many students. When I asked how many had been abroad, only a few hands showed: Poland, Czechoslovakia, Austria, and one in England. I asked, "Would you like to see what is going on in the rest of the world?" Many hands came up. Where? The United States, England, and Scandinavia.

Later we met with the school principal and several teachers. Like their students they reflected decades of totalitarian indoctrination. My son Michael asked, "What has been the biggest change since the communists left?" They answered that teachers could now decide what to teach and parents now had a voice in deciding where their children would go after graduation. But almost three years after the communists had left, they had not yet updated the history curriculum! The teachers had not been retrained, and the ministry of their state, Sachsen-Anhalt, had not yet issued new textbooks. We asked, "What are you teaching these kids about the Nazis, the war, and the postwar period under the Soviets?" No recent history was being taught, he said.

The communist government had run Gardelegen for forty-five years, two generations. I pondered, how do you undo six decades of stultification under Hitler, Stalin, and the Soviets?

That evening the Lutheran minister, Pastor Dietmann, sponsored a town meeting for us in his church community center. When we arrived, the auditorium was packed, with people listening outside. We visitors were seated behind a long table, facing the Gardelegen burghers. Joe Behrens had previously donated a menorah to the minister's church, and its use was reserved for festive occasions. The minister stood up and said, "A man once asked a rabbi to tell him where God lives. And the rabbi said, 'Wherever he is welcome.'" He then lit the candles of the menorah, turned to us, and said, "Welcome."

After Gisela Bunge introduced us there was silence, just silence. After a long while I got up and said, "When I lived here, the people of Gardelegen were not shy. You had plenty to say then. Most of it was not nice. We are your old Jewish neighbors who left to stay alive and now we have come back to see you."

An elderly woman stood up and cried out: "How could God

allow this to happen? People who loved me and took care of me were tortured and killed. How could God allow this?" I realized that she was mourning a Jewish family who had treated her as their own child. When they were about to be arrested, her adopted mother had committed suicide. The rest of the family was exterminated. I finally walked over to her and put my arm around her to console her. I was tempted to say that God had not paid attention, but decided not to.

Then another woman stood up. I recognized her as one of the family who had owned the town's bookshop. We knew them as hypocrites who changed their political affiliation repeatedly, depending on who was winning the latest election. This woman lamented that "those who kept silent" also deserved credit. She was trying to cover up her family's complicity with the Nazis once they came to power, and she was treated to stony silence. She looked just like her mother, who had dropped my parents and their friendship like hot potatoes when Hitler appeared on the scene.

Then a man stood up and said, "You don't know me; my name is Horn." I replied, "If you are Wolfgang Horn, then I know that you are the son of my first-grade teacher." He nodded and I said, "I remember your father well because he once caned me for *schwatzen*" (talking to my neighbor when I was supposed to be doing my work). That brought down the house. Teacher Horn or his successor had probably caned some of them, and perhaps their parents, too.

There was a rush to the front of the hall. A man said, "You don't know me; my name is Fritz Schultze." I answered, "If you are from Jerchel" — a nearby hamlet — "then I know exactly who you are. You are the son of Fritz and Lieschen Schultze. You look just like your father!" He was the son of the poor peasants with whom I had worked as a youngster. The Schultzes had risked all to bring my parents food during their last desperate days in Germany. Fritz, the son, said, "Your mother gave me a toy steam engine that belonged to your brother, Helmut. It still works. Would you like to have it back?" "No," I said, "if you have kept it all these years, it means more to you than to us." We embraced each other.

And so it went. There were two long-forgotten schoolmates, my father's chauffeur, a babysitter, the baker, and others. Someone brought me a picture of my first-grade class, and I noticed a youngster with ears that stood out from his head. My mother had always wanted me to wear a cap and tuck my ears in. I asked after my grade school playmates, who had been friends before the Nazis severed all friendships for me. Two, including Willy Grueder with whom I had built the backyard cannon, were known to have died in Russia; others had moved from Gardelegen. Those who knew my parents were in their late seventies and eighties.

What had happened to Pannwitz, my sadistic high school tormentor, I asked. Vanished without a trace, they said. Our baker's daughter, a woman my age, then recalled how Pannwitz had asked her father repeatedly to put up that infamous sign "Jews Not Welcome Here" in his bakery shop window. After her father refused, then an act of great courage, Pannwitz always begged for a few free sugar cookies. What an obituary!

Where had I been on March 17, 1945, someone now asked. That was the day when my American army unit had pulverized a German town after SS diehards had refused to surrender. "For what? Why was that town destroyed? What was the SS fighting for? What did Hitler leave you besides defeat and shame?" There was a great shaking of the heads and rolling of the eyes.

When the meeting ended, I felt that there had been a renewal of acquaintance, though perhaps no complete clearing of the air. Not only had the Jews vanished from Gardelegen almost without a trace, so had the Nazis!

After the meeting, Gisela asked me whether I understood the significance of the question about March 17, 1945. I did not. This, she told me, was the day when the Gardelegen church had been bombed and more than a dozen people killed. For decades, rumor had it that it had been me who had dropped those bombs.

Perhaps one of our planes had dropped bombs just to shed

the load before returning to base, or perhaps the plane had been damaged by antiaircraft fire. Gardelegen was not worth the cost of those bombs! It was ridiculous to think that I would have bombed them had I been able to. I had not hated ordinary Germans in 1945, nor did I desire revenge on them.

The celebrations of the eight-hundredth anniversary of Gardelegen were to start the next morning. The reason for our visit had been for my wife and children to see where I had grown up. That was done. We wanted to leave. Meeting some good people who had helped my parents was a bonus, as was facing that Gardelegen crowd as free American citizens. We were surprised to see ourselves featured on the front pages of the local newspapers, bought a few copies, and left.

From Gardelegen we drove to Berlin, where we stayed at the Hotel Kempinski, across the street from the synagogue where my grandfather had occasionally attended services. The hotel was also near where my uncles Hans and Fritz had lived; to our surprise, their apartment building was still standing. Miraculously, the little candy shop under the viaduct for the S-bahn, the Berlin el, where my grandmother bought sprinkles for me, had also survived the destruction of Berlin. I went to Klopstock Strasse, where my grandparents' apartment house had been replaced by a new one.

After we returned home, I received many letters postmarked Gardelegen from people expressing regret and remorse that they had not been able to do more for my parents in their time of need. Gisela also told me that after the meeting at the church community center, old people started to talk about Nazi times. "Your visit uncorked their bottle of memories," she said.

On the trip back, and later on in the United States, I couldn't get Gisela Bunge out of my mind. She was doing what her conscience commanded her to do. I persuaded my son Michael and my brother, Hal, to join me in providing funds for her to print her history of the town's Jewish families, with copies to be given to each future eleventh-grade class to study and discuss.

After our trip to Gardelegen, my son Michael, a benefactor of Ben Gurion University in Israel, endowed a seat in Gisela's honor in a university auditorium that bears his daughter's name. Honoring Gisela in our midst was very appealing to me. Knowing that she had refused to accept a high decoration from the German government for her work, I requested the Ben Gurion University to fashion a plaque and a citation honoring Gisela. She is now venerated as a Righteous German in Israel, in the midst of Sonnenfeldts and their in-laws, the Goldmans. This distinction Gisela accepted with joy.

I next returned to Gardelegen two years later, on November 9, 1998. This time I was a guest of honor for a commemoration of the sixtieth anniversary of Kristallnacht. My daughter, Ann, and my nephew, Walter Sonnenfeldt, came along to see where their fathers had grown up.

We were greeted by Lottie Behrens, whom I had last seen when I was fifteen and she was twelve, sixty years earlier. I was amazed to see a woman upright in bearing, young for her years, with startling bright blue eyes and a smile that reminded me at once of her mother and of Lottie herself as a young girl. As a slave laborer, Lottie had lost her toes in the concentration camp, but with her specially fitted shoes, one could not notice it. We embraced and wept.

Lottie had come from Australia and we had come from America to help dedicate an exhibit that featured photographs and histories of the Sonnenfeldt and Behrens families.

"I am glad to be here among friends and family," I said. "I invite everyone to remember the victims of Nazism and to make an irrevocable commitment never to tolerate religious prejudice, racial discrimination, or authoritarianism. To me the brotherhood of man is a greater society than any religious, ethnic, political, or national grouping. Please join me in belonging to it."

Someone said "Amen." Lottie did not speak. She did not want to open the lockbox in which she kept her terrible memories. Her presence exemplified the spirit of reconciliation, which rejects the perpetuation of hate but is not the same as forgiveness for what cannot be forgiven. There we stood in the midst of the people of Gardelegen, from where her parents and every other adult Jew, except for my parents, had been hounded to their deaths.

On this trip, the Schulzes of Jerchel invited us for a festive meal at their home. I remembered their thatched roof, a little flower garden in front, and the primitive stalls for their ox, cow, and pig, all under one roof with the family. Sixty years later, things had evolved. Fritz, the son, had a car, the cottage was freshly painted, with gleaming windows and lace curtains, the roof was a red-tiled beauty, and the pig, rabbits, and chickens had separate quarters. There was a modern kitchen and bathroom, a television set, and central heating. All of this, they told me, had been acquired after reunification ended the forty-five-year communist regime. Life had improved in eastern Germany with the arrival of genuine democracy. Elizabeth, the wife, had prepared a marvelous Altmark feast, local to this area, and we sat down to eat and reminisce. This was a heart-warming reunion with a family whose older generation had risked so much to help my parents.

My trips back to Germany were becoming more frequent. On November 8, 1999, just a year later, I joined an American delegation in Berlin to commemorate the tenth anniversary of the fall of the Berlin Wall. A memorial dinner was held at a villa on Schwanenwerder, an island on the Wannsee, that popular resort lake outside Berlin where I had gone as a teenager with my girlfriend Fritzie during the summer of 1938. I was asked to address the assembled guests. I sensed that day that a new generation of Germans seemed determined to join the rest of the free world by sharing, rather than attacking, its values.

I then went back to Gardelegen. This time I went to meet with an eleventh-grade class. How different it was from my first conversation with Gardelegen high school students just three years earlier. This meeting was held after school hours, and there was standing room only in the town library. These students looked like an American high school class. Blue jeans, ponytails, ear and nose rings, tattoos, girls with and without bras, boys with Mohawks. Teachers wore casual attire, unthinkable in my day. After Gisela Bunge introduced me, I asked, "Who speaks English here?" and all hands went up. Wow! Then I asked, "Who has been abroad?" and again all hands went up! Paris, London, Madrid, Italy, and even America were on the list.

A girl asked, "How did you feel as an American soldier when you killed German soldiers, your compatriots?"

"Remember," I said, "Nazi Germany had spat me out as a Jew. I had committed no crime, but my citizenship was taken from me, even though my family had been German for centuries, like yours. The Nazis, not I, had decided I was an enemy. Your grandparents were told that Jews like me were subhuman and did not deserve to live. As an American soldier, I fought for democracy and human rights for all people, including yours. That's what I risked my life for, and I felt good about it. Do you know what your grandfathers fought for, or were made to fight for? For what did they risk their lives?" There was no answer. "I killed German soldiers not because I hated them but because in the war as a soldier, I had to."

There was silence. I continued, "Hitler's goals were those of conquest, hatred, and extermination, whereas we fought for human rights for all. I still have these values, and hope you do, too. If you had to make a choice, what would you fight for? Good or evil? Let's hope that in the future we can fight with our votes and never again with our guns."

"Tell us how the Nazis took over Germany. You were there. Explain it to us." They really wanted to know.

I responded, "That sounds like a simple question but the answer is not simple. Are you sure that you want to hear it?"

Several said, "Our grandparents won't tell us. We want to hear it from you."

"Hitler merely uncorked virulent hatreds and fears of Jews, gypsies, Russians, and others, poisonous feelings that had been slumbering in the German people. Another explanation is that this evil Führer first seduced, then enslaved, and finally grievously hurt the German people with promises of world domination.

"When I grew up in Gardelegen, I too believed Hitler's lies. He claimed that, to maintain law and order, he had to put his opponents in concentration camps. He got rid of judges so that nobody could appeal what his storm troopers did. But he also put the unemployed to work. When the Wehrmacht reoccupied the Rhineland, there was jubilation and Germans felt their honor had been restored. After that triumph, even German generals, who had opposed his march into the Rhineland, could no longer oppose him. He got rid of them. Then he went about claiming he hated war while taking over Austria and Czechoslovakia, and he lied declaring Poland had attacked Germany. He had to be obeyed as supreme commander, and it was too late to stop him. Germans believed his promises and his lies. England and France did not stop him when they could have done it. In the end, only the combined military might of his enemies brought him down. He then ordered Germany and Germans to die with him, and only then did people realize he had never cared about them, only about himself. Did you ever ask your grandparents how it felt to believe and fight for a liar and a criminal?

Someone — no, several — asked: "Can it happen again?"

"I hope not, but you can help make sure it will never happen again. You must guard your freedom and the freedom of the courts, the press, radio, and television. You must support free speech and never support politicians who want judges and teachers to do their bidding. When you see a demagogue or a hatemonger throwing dirty snowballs, stop him before there is an avalanche no one can stop. Don't let evil men deceive you; don't support politicians who blame scapegoats for problems. If you do all that, it won't happen again. You will be proud of your humanity and you will not become accessories to evil deeds." That was a lot for them to think about.

"Is there anti-Semitism in America?" they asked.

"Yes," I said, "there is anti-Semitism, and there is also hostility to African-Americans, Latinos, Poles, Italians, Greeks and Asians, Catholics and atheists. And most minorities don't like WASPs too much! But in the United States, the laws and the Constitution guarantee freedom and equal opportunity to every citizen, majority or minority. Under Hitler, anti-Semitism became a national duty for all Aryan citizens — your grandparents. When prejudice and hatred turn into murder, you get a holocaust. But when the power of the state protects the rights of all minorities, then you have a diversified society, as we have in the United States and as you do now in Germany. Treasure your freedom and the power of your constitution!"

Some of these youngsters were concerned they carried a hidden ethnic or racial gene for bigotry, and were looking for a prescription to counteract such an inherited flaw. "Was human nature in the United States basically different from human nature in Germany?"

"I am no authority on that," I said, "but I do not think so. Humans react and interact with the environment in which they live. A healthy and open society brings out the best in people, while a repressive and authoritarian political regime brings out the worst. You can make yourselves immune to bigotry and hatred by understanding what happened in Nazi Germany and not allowing it to happen again."

These young Germans have more in common with my American grandchildren than they have with the boy I once was in Gardelegen. I was raised in a society that glorified the wars Germany had won. We adored uniforms, and we marched with sticklike rifles over our shoulders. The "treasonous stab in the back" myth of Germany's defeat in World War I poisoned us, and we were steeped in obedience to authority. Taught to resent and hate the outside world, we were further isolated because Hitler deluded us into believing that Germany could achieve economic self-sufficiency. When I was growing up I never knew anyone, adult or child, who had traveled abroad. Today's young Germans have been to other countries; they have seen American television programs, good and bad, and of course now they are connected globally via the World Wide Web. These youngsters live in a country as economically interdependent with its neighbors as American states are with each other. They know that Germany was defeated in war and they know that Hitler, not some traitorous clique, was to blame for that. Today, knowledgeable young Germans understand that giving Hitler absolute power in Germany was the prelude to the destruction of almost fifty million people, including ten million Germans.

They continue to wonder, could they ever fall for another Führer?

I found myself contemplating a question they had not asked me, however, which my wife, Barbara, had articulated after our first visit to Gardelegen. Barbara had felt very uncomfortable sitting in the church community center in front of more than a hundred Germans, some of whom had been Nazis and many of whom were children of Nazis. But that same day, she also met those who had risked all to help my parents. "How many of my friends here in the United States would have stood up for me, if standing up meant risking their livelihood, the careers of their children, and perhaps worse?" Barbara asked. That very question goes right to the essence of dictatorships, when the power of the state punishes citizens with decent impulses. If another Führer came along, who would have the moral courage to resist?

I have heard Americans say, "If I had been in Nazi Germany, I would have stood by my friends; I would not have allowed them to be hurt!"

Really?

You would have protected your friends in a society where the government controlled the courts and the media, where only Nazis could publish newspapers, and where people were jailed or even executed for listening to foreign radio broadcasts? Where your livelihood and safety were in jeopardy if you failed to hate and debase those designated as enemies of the state? Where the government could incarcerate or incinerate you for not practicing anti-Semitism and xenophobia, or for merely asking what was happening to your neighbors?

Where would you have gone for support? To a political party? There weren't any, except the Nazi party. To a court of law? There were only Nazi judges and lawyers. To a church? The churches were silent. Supporters of the oppressed or mere questioners of the regime were like the oppressed themselves: naked humans facing an army of armored spear-carriers.

I do not mean to imply that moral courage was impossible. Under the Nazis, a relative handful of people did take real risks in making small attempts just to be *anständig,* the word Manfred Rommel used to describe ordinary decency. Over ten thousand Germans did risk their property, the careers of their children, and their very lives by trying to help Hitler's victims. The extensive documentation of Nazi crimes at the Nuremberg trials includes their tales of heroism.

But what of the millions of Germans in between those extremes of the evil Nazi leadership and the rare practitioners of moral goodness? Evil should never be defended, but it must be understood that evil can be imposed on a populace that has lost all means to resist. Where despotism rules, decency dies. The vast majority of Germans went along with Hitler after he acquired unlimited power, provided work for the unemployed, and promised to be Germany's savior. Germany looked invincible and they cheered him on. They embarked on Hitler's ship, believing they were going on a victory cruise when in reality their adored Führer was piloting their ship to inevitable, unimaginable disaster. When they recognized him for what he was, it was too late, and they were powerless to remove him.

In Gardelegen, as elsewhere in Germany, many wore the blue shirts of labor before Hitler came along. Some put on the brown and black shirts of the SA and SS when he came to power, and later they wore the field gray of the Wehrmacht to serve as proud soldiers. After the war, those in East Germany put on red shirts when the Soviets came along, and finally they put on white shirts and tees, like their West German brothers, when reunification brought them new prosperity and relaxation. Did they ever change underneath? What shirt will they wear next? Are they so different from the silent, oft compliant, majority elsewhere in the world?

After my last visit to Gardelegen and my conversation with those bright and questioning teenagers, I asked myself the question that they did not ask. Had Hitler not been an anti-Semite or had I not been a Jew, how would I have behaved in the Gardelegen of the Nazis? As a young teenager I was envious that I could not participate in the Hitler Youth. My former friends marched to band music and sang rousing Nazi songs, they camped and they hiked — they were building their bodies and molding their minds for the glory of Germany. Could I have been seduced to join the Hitler Youth? Would I have believed Hitler, when he proclaimed that Poland had attacked Germany, that France and England had declared war on Germany, and that he had invaded the Soviet Union only to forestall its attack on Germany? Would I have understood that "Deutschland über Alles," the song which rallied Germans to the flag, really meant "Down with Everybody Else?"

I might not have known better. It is too easy to claim that one would have refused to bite into the poisoned apple. Had I been an Aryan boy in Gardelegen, I might have followed Hitler and would probably lie dead in the steppes of Russia. Or, had I survived the war, as an Aryan adult I would have lived to rue having been one of Hitler's helpers.

The irony of my life is that Hitler spared me those temptations and those fates. Thanks largely to my mother's resourcefulness, I also avoided being a victim of Hitler's murder of German Jews. Instead, when I left Germany in 1938, Hitler and his Nazis had opened for me a world of opportunity and adventure that I seized and thrived in. I got an education in human values I embraced all my life.

Now, in my retirement, I have had a totally unexpected chance to share what I have learned about despotism, hatred, and prejudice, about the blessings of freedom in a democracy protected by a wisely written constitution, and about the brotherhood of humankind. Today, I have friends around the world, even in Gardelegen. My life has been immensely positive compared to anything that might have been if Hitler had never happened.

The official internet site of Gardelegen lists my brother, Hal, and me as two of its five distinguished sons of the past two centuries. One was overlooked. Under the leadership of Gisela Bunge, the citizens of Gardelegen have been able to learn about their past and build a better future. I regard her as the town's most distinguished citizen.

EPILOGUE

Nuremberg Fifty Years Later

*T*HE AMERICAN JEWISH COMMITTEE and the Academy of the Evangelical Church (the largest German Christian denomination) sponsored me to speak in 2002 at a principal cathedral in Berlin. To my astonishment, the German national press and broadcast media reported prominently my youth in Nazi Germany, my adventures as a teen all over the world, my personal conversations with Nazi defendants and witnesses at the Nuremberg trials, my life in America, my sailing adventures, and my visits to Gardelegen. In December of that year, I was invited to return to Nuremberg. A new museum and educational center, the Dokumentationszentrum, tracing the rise and fall of Hitler's Germany, had just been dedicated by Germany's president, Johannes Rau. I was honored to be its first speaker.

To refresh my memory I had asked to visit the courtroom before my speech. It was 5 P.M., April 24, 2002, in Nuremberg, sixty-one years less two days after I had arrived in America.

My escort opened the massive wooden door, shoved his hand under my elbow, and pushed me gently forward into Saal 600, the scene of the Nuremberg trials.

"Why is it so dark in here?" I asked.

I heard muffled voices but saw no faces. Suddenly camera

flashes and video lights blinded me. Someone opened the curtains, and I saw reporters with pencils poised over notebooks, audio engineers with microphones on booms marching toward me.

Surprise!

Instead of the quiet visit to the courtroom of Nuremberg that I had requested, unbeknownst to me, my hosts had arranged a press conference!

"You were the chief interpreter of the American prosecution at the trials here of major Nazis in 1945?" someone shouted.

"Yes," I said.

"Show us where the Nazis were sitting? Where were the judges, the prosecutors? Where were you?" The questions tumbled over each other.

Every detail of the 1945 courtroom was etched in my memory, but now the room's layout was different. There, at the left side of the room, the defendants had sat in two rows, and standing behind and around the defendants had been young American military police in gleaming white helmets, with white gloves and belts, trying to look alert and immobile at the same time.

I pointed to the spot where Justice Jackson, the chief American prosecutor, had stood as he said, "We must also be prepared that this court may find some of the defendants 'not guilty.' Otherwise we might just as well hang them all now!"

Gone was the glass cage up there by the back wall where the court interpreters had strained to catch every word. I explained,

"I was the chief interpreter and an interrogator for the American prosecution, and I spent hundreds of hours with defendants and witnesses in secluded interrogation rooms. But I was not a court interpreter, who had to listen to the defendants for months right over there but never had the opportunity to talk to them, face to face, one to one, as I did."

"And what was your job later, in the courtroom?"

"To verify that witnesses and defendants made the same statements in court as those they made in pretrial examinations."

Someone asked, "What did the trials accomplish?"

221

"For crimes they committed in the name of hate, race, and rabid nationalism, eleven of the most senior Nazi leaders were sentenced to hang by the neck. Seven others went to prison, and three were exonerated. But something even more important than punishment of the guilty was accomplished. The Nazis' trickery in assuming total government power, their killing and torturing of Germans who opposed them, the killing of Jews, and the ruination and enslavement of the nations they attacked were all documented with their own papers, signed by their own hands, and the testimony of their subordinates. SS killers testified how they had murdered tens of thousands, a few at a time, before the ovens of Auschwitz made such retail killings obsolete. The world would never have known the full and terrible extent of the Holocaust without the record of these trials, or have seen proof of the incredible duplicity and unbounded egotism of the Führer for whom millions of Germans died. The history of the Thousand Year Reich, which lasted just twelve years, was written in the Nuremberg trials, making it impossible forever to deny or explain away this dreadful chapter of the German past."

"The most dramatic scene in the courtroom, Herr Sonnenfeldt?" someone shouted.

"When captured films of horrifying concentration camp atrocities were shown, several defendants and their lawyers wept as they saw the endless lines of pitiable human beings herded to their deaths and the heaps of dead and dying bodies, some still writhing in agony. But Göring whispered, with a wink, that this was only a propaganda film, 'like Goebbels could have fabricated.' As though the Holocaust were a figment of the imagination! Well, the film was real, all right. It had the stamp of Himmler's SS on it!"

Next the reporters wanted to know, "How did you get to be chief interpreter for the American prosecution?"

"It will all be in my book," I responded.

"Were you sorry to leave Germany?"

"No," I said.

"Why are you here now?" they asked.

"It is a great honor for me to be the inaugural speaker at the Nuremberg Dokumentationszentrum, which was once Hitler's coliseum for Nazi party meetings. Tomorrow I will talk about my life as a German Jew and about my later adventures and my conversations with the Nuremberg defendants, Hitler's generals and concentration camp commandants. About a great life in the United States of America after the war and up to the present day that would have never happened without Hitler!"

"Why did the defendants at the Nuremberg trials talk? Were they forced to?" a reporter asked.

"No," I said. "We never used force or torture. I was puzzled to hear them talking until I realized that they tried to save their necks by blaming their deeds on Hitler, Himmler, Goebbels, and Bormann, all of whom were dead."

"Is it true that you served the indictments on the defendants in the jail here?" I was asked.

"Yes, that was on the afternoon of October 20, 1945. I still have an original copy of the oath that was administered to me and of the indictment itself," I answered.

"That's it, ladies and gentlemen," I said, trying to conclude the interview, but several reporters barred my way to the door.

"Just a few more questions, please — is it true that you invented color television?"

"Of course not!" I said. "But I was one of two dozen engineers and inventors who developed color TV in the United States in 1950, and I earned thirty-five patents doing it."

"What were the exciting things you worked on besides color TV?"

"Back in the 1960s, I worked on computers, medical electronics, factory automation, nuclear power plants, equipment for the NASA Man on the Moon program, video disks — communications satellites, whatever was new. In the 1980s I was a business executive, and after that I became a consultant."

Once more I started to push my way to the door, but another

reporter stood in my way. "Is it true that you sailed your own forty-four-foot boat across the Atlantic from America to Europe?"

"Yes, I crossed the Atlantic three times with a fine crew, but I don't sail any longer," I said. "I quit sailing after I celebrated my seventy-fifth birthday in midocean in a gale. Someone suggested that I was maybe the oldest man to have crossed the Atlantic three times in an open-cockpit boat. I decided then to tempt fate no more."

I had reached the door, but somebody tugged at my sleeve.

"Just one last question please! Did you hate the defendants in 1945 and do you hate Germans now?"

"At Nuremberg in 1945 I wanted to see the guilty punished for their crimes, but I never wanted to hate blindly like a Nazi, neither then or now. I don't want innocent people persecuted. Would I come to Germany if I hated Germans who are trying to make sure that there will never be a repetition of the Holocaust?"

Now, almost out in the hall, I said, "Thank you. Thank you very much, see you all tomorrow."

Out in the street, I remembered leaving that same courthouse fifty-six years earlier. For me then, the most adventurous chapters of my life had ended. Without Hitler, as a Jewish doctor's son in Germany I would probably have been pushed to get the obligatory Doktor's degree and lead a dull life ever after. Or, had I not been Jewish, I would most probably have become one of Hitler's dead soldiers. Yes, life had been good to me.

Before my talk, I watched once more the original newsreels of goose-stepping Nazi storm troopers saluting their Führer, German women swooning over him, and adorable little pigtailed girls on their tiptoes presenting bouquets to him. Again I watched the parades of steel-helmeted, square-jawed soldiers brandishing the blitzkrieg weapons of the Wehrmacht that had crushed Western Europe and devastated the Soviet Union. I listened once more to Hitler's lies about Jewish treachery, his veneration of Blood and Iron, and his claims to invincible Nazi might. I remembered how I had trembled when I saw those newsreels the first time.

Now, more than a half century after he had been defeated and dishonored, Hitler appeared on the screen as a histrionic ham actor who spouted discredited nonsense. Was it possible, I wondered, that such delusions and hatred could ever again convulse a civilized world and snuff out the lives of millions?

As I walked toward the speaker's podium that evening, I pictured again the monumental stage nearby where Hitler had pranced under an enormous swastika. There he had made Germans believe he was invincible and that they were the master race, destined to subjugate and rule millions of Untermenschen, subhumans like me.

I stood in front of a huge German audience, most too young to have been Nazis. I traced how Hitler had seized power by using and perverting the mindset of Germans in his day: their obedience to the state, their disenchantment with democracy (which was associated for them with economic deprivation), their hatred of neighboring countries, and their love of flag waving. This witches' brew of attitudes had been perfect for allowing a despot to cast himself as their national savior. I pointed out the flaws in the German prewar constitution that had enabled Hitler to cloak his power grab in legitimacy. I reminded them that France and England had fed his megalomania by tolerating his adventures. I explained why so many Jews had stayed in Germany until they had no place to go except to the slaughterhouse, and how I had managed to survive.

Then I turned to the Nuremberg trials, which had taken place almost within sight of my podium. My audience, like most Germans, knew very little about the top Nazis who had once ruled their land. I let Hitler's henchmen speak for themselves, quoting the infamous Dr. Goebbels, Hitler's mouthpiece, who had written:

> We had no intention to use power legally once we had it. Our domestic foes never saw that our path of legality was just a trick. That's exactly how it was in foreign policy, too.

In 1933, a French prime minister ought to have said (and if I had been that French premier, I would have said it): "The new Reich Chancellor is the man who wrote *Mein Kampf.* This man cannot be tolerated. Either he disappears or we march." But they left us alone. And when we were done and armed better than they, they declared war on us.

There was Göring, who proclaimed he had the power to decide who was a Jew. He was the jolly fat man who ordered the Final Solution of the Jewish Question and then claimed he had no idea that Himmler and his SS implemented his order by exterminating millions. Göring the braggart, who impressed his half-brother by releasing innocents from concentration camps but then claimed he had no power to send them there to be killed. Göring the bomber of Rotterdam, the looter of art, the drug addict, who chuckled about his satanic initiatives, the man with a brain without a conscience. Hitler's number-two man with the ambition to be number one.

I quoted Hoess, the robotic commandant of Auschwitz, the champion exterminator, who wanted it noted that of three and one-half million dead at Auschwitz, only two and one-half million had been gassed while the rest died of other causes — like starvation and disease. Hoess who had regarded not mass murder but only the stealing of victims' gold by his SS guards as a crime.

And I cited Hans Frank, the top Nazi jurist, who had proclaimed that the only law in Hitler's Third Reich was what the Führer wanted done.

"Listen now," I said, "to the few who later repented. That same Hans Frank, before he went to the gallows, wept: 'Now I know that [Hitler's] path became more and more that of a frightful adventurer without conscience or honesty.' And listen to Albert Speer, Hitler's minister of armaments, who said, 'I saw that the Führer principle [Hitler's power of absolute dictatorship] led to tremendous mistakes. The combination of this system and Hitler brought about terrible catastrophes.' And understand Field

Marshal Wilhelm Keitel's answer when asked how he would act if he were in the same position again. 'I would rather choose death than again allow myself to be drawn into the net of such criminal methods,' he moaned."

Finally, I exhorted them to remember Hitler himself, the megalomaniac, the ultimate egotist, who blamed the German people and wanted their land — "your land," I said to my audience — destroyed. He wanted Germany to go down in flames with him because he thought that his loyal followers, their forebears, who died for him by the millions, had been too weak to win a war for which he alone was to blame.

That night at Nuremberg, with my son Larry and my granddaughter Sara in the audience, I fielded questions for an hour after my speech. I, that Jewish teen of long ago who had fled Germany to escape extermination, was now here as a witness to tell Germans too young to have experienced them about the cruelties and inhuman perversions of Nazi Germany.

This audience, like others, wanted me to explain how all of this had happened in their Germany. "Tell us! You were there, and we were not," they were asking over and over.

Finally calling a halt to questions, I offered my hand to all who would be members of a human family with equal rights for everyone in a society, a nation, and a world that excludes only those who want to exclude themselves. The ovation that followed marked for me that I had been able to live my faith, in myself and in my fellow man.

After that appearance in Nuremberg, a German publisher had my memoirs, which I had written in English, translated into German in time for the September 2003 Frankfurt Book Fair, the world's largest. *Mehr als ein Leben* (More Than One Life) was the only book by an American author to be selected for a reading to a large audience in the Frankfurt city hall. This in turn was followed by a dozen more appearances on German TV, including the most popular talk shows.

My youth under Hitler was meant to end in extermination.

Instead, my life has been a terrific adventure, a twist on the ancient Chinese curse, "May it be your fate to live in interesting times." None of us knows what fate holds for us, even when we are eighty.

I certainly did not know what an interesting life awaited me when I heard the shout, "Sonnenfeldt! Private Sonnenfeldt! The generals need an interpreter!"

Acknowledgments

This book would never have been written if my grandchildren had not asked me to tell them where I grew up and what happened to me. They had to write school essays on immigrants. My family knew me as an American business executive and an ocean sailor, and by 1990 my youth in Hitler's Germany had receded far into the past. I rarely thought about my life then more than fifty years ago, and we never talked about it. But now, when my children, their spouses, and my second wife saw what the grandchildren wrote, they urged me to write my life story for the family.

As I started to write, in 1993, I received an invitation, on the occasion of the eight-hundredth anniversary of its founding, to visit Gardelegen in Germany, where I was raised. My son Michael, his wife, Katja, and my wife, Barbara, wanted me to take them along, to see where I had come from. Michael then made a video of our visit and my early life in Gardelegen.

Soon after, Leslie Gelb, then president of the Council on Foreign Relations, invited me to speak to that organization, and he and Henry Grunwald, former editor of *Time* magazine and American ambassador to Austria, urged me to write about my life. It would not have happened without their encouragement. I thank them.

While I was trying to shape up one of many drafts, the secretary general of the American Jewish Committee (AJC), David Harris, asked me whether I would speak in Germany, and he then arranged for the Evangelical Church of Germany to be a cosponsor with AJC. My presentations at a premier Berlin cathedral and as the inaugural speaker, following Germany's president, at the Nürnberg Dokumentationszentrum, were prominently reported by the German press and also led to numerous TV appearances. Now a Frankfurt house offered to publish my book in German, sight unseen. It took a year to convert my English draft into the German best seller *Mehr als ein Leben.*

The book was introduced by the German authority on the trial of the Nazis, Nuremberg chief judge Klaus Kastner, in the same courtroom where I had worked. Afterward I returned to complete the draft of the present book.

First I want to thank Barbara, my wife, who allowed me to use the carpet of my office as a filing cabinet, while I worked without a secretary. Far more important, she has been an invaluable constructive critic, and her insights have been most helpful. My daughter, Ann, a public relations professional, has made sure that my appearances were properly announced, and her editorial comments were highly important to me in the development of the manuscript. While I thank her and all of my children and grandchildren, many of whom accompanied me to Germany, I must single out my son Michael and my granddaughter Sara, who watched over me on my last trip, after illness forced me to travel in a wheelchair.

Special thanks are also due Lloyd G. Schermer, on whose board I served for eighteen years, who encouraged me, and Lewis Smoler, my dentist, and his wife Carol, who read and critiqued several drafts with the same attention he lavishes on my root canals.

Many other friends have been very helpful and patient with me, a first-time author. I thank you.

Thanks are also due to Bill Hanna, my agent, and Jeannette Seaver, my editor, without whose efforts this book would not have been published.